BEST-EVER
PASTA COOKBOOK

BEST-EVER

PASTA COOKBOOK

THE COMPLETE GUIDE TO CHOOSING, COOKING AND MAKING PASTA: 150 INSPIRING RECIPES SHOWN IN 350 STUNNING PHOTOGRAPHS

JENI WRIGHT

HERMES HOUSE

This edition is published by Hermes House,
an imprint of Anness Publishing Ltd,
Hermes House,
88–89 Blackfriars Road,
London SE1 8HA
tel. 020 7401 2077; fax 020 7633 9499

www.hermeshouse.com; www.annesspublishing.com

If you like the images in this book and would like to investigate using them for publishing, promotions or advertising, please visit our website www.practicalpictures.com for more information.

Publisher: Joanna Lorenz
Editors: Brian Burns and Kate Eddison
Recipes: Jeni Wright
Photography: William Lingwood (recipes) and Janine Hosegood (techniques and cut-outs)
Food for photography: Lucy McKelvie and Kate Jay (recipes) and Annabel Ford (techniques)
Designer: Nigel Partridge
Production Controller: Don Campaniello
Editorial Reader: Lauren Farnsworth
Indexer: Diana LeCore

A CIP catalogue record for this book is available from the British Library.

ETHICAL TRADING POLICY

At Anness Publishing we believe that business should be conducted in an ethical and ecologically sustainable way, with respect for the environment and a proper regard to the replacement of the natural resources we employ.

As a publisher, we use a lot of wood pulp to make high-quality paper for printing, and that wood commonly comes from spruce trees. We are therefore currently growing more than 750,000 trees in three Scottish forest plantations: Berrymoss (130 hectares/320 acres), West Touxhill (125 hectares/305 acres) and Deveron Forest (75 hectares/185 acres). The forests we manage contain more than 3.5 times the number of trees employed each year in making paper for the books we manufacture.

Because of this ongoing ecological investment programme, you, as our customer, can have the pleasure and reassurance of knowing that a tree is being cultivated on your behalf to naturally replace the materials used to make the book you are holding.

Our forestry programme is run in accordance with the UK Woodland Assurance Scheme (UKWAS) and will be certified by the internationally recognized Forest Stewardship Council (FSC). The FSC is a non-government organization dedicated to promoting responsible management of the world's forests. Certification ensures forests are managed in an environmentally sustainable and socially responsible way. For further information about this scheme, go to www.annesspublishing.com/trees

Recipes in this book previously appeared in *The Pasta Bible*

PUBLISHER'S NOTE

Although the advice and information in this book are believed to be accurate and true at the time of going to press, neither the authors nor the publisher can accept any legal responsibility or liability for any errors or omissions that may be made.

NOTES

Bracketed terms are intended for American readers.

For all recipes, quantities are given in both metric and imperial measures and, where appropriate, in standard cups and spoons. Follow one set of measures, but not a mixture, because they are not interchangeable.

Standard spoon and cup measures are level.
1 tsp = 5ml, 1 tbsp = 15ml, 1 cup = 250ml/8fl oz.

Australian standard tablespoons are 20ml. Australian readers should use 3 tsp in place of 1 tbsp for measuring small quantities.

American pints are 16fl oz/2 cups. American readers should use 20fl oz/2.5 cups in place of 1 pint when measuring liquids.

Electric oven temperatures in this book are for conventional ovens. When using a fan oven, the temperature will probably need to be reduced by about 10–20°C/20–40°F. Since ovens vary, you should check with your manufacturer's instruction book for guidance.

The nutritional analysis given for each recipe is calculated per portion (i.e. serving or item), unless otherwise stated. If the recipe gives a range, such as Serves 4–6, then the nutritional analysis will be for the smaller portion size, i.e. 6 servings. Measurements for sodium do not include salt added to taste.

Medium (US large) eggs are used unless otherwise stated.

Front cover shows Spaghetti with Tomatoes and Pancetta – for recipe, see page 35.

Contents

Introduction

Pasta is one of the most popular foods in the world today. Available in an amazing range of shapes and flavours, it can be served in countless different ways. Simple or sophisticated, quick and easy to cook, it is the perfect choice for everyday and spur-of-the-moment meals.

Food historians debate whether the Chinese, Arabs or Italians invented pasta. Whoever it was, it does seem to have been the Sicilians who first boiled it in water, and the Calabrians who mastered the art of twisting pasta strips to make tubes very similar to modern-day macaroni. Meanwhile, the credit for inventing commercially produced dried pasta shapes must go to the Neapolitans.

The right kind of wheat

The fertile soil in the region around Naples was found to be ideal for growing durum wheat (Triticum durum), which Italians call *grano duro*. Durum wheat makes the best flour for commercial pasta, which, contrary to popular opinion, is in no way inferior to fresh homemade pasta. Italian cooks always keep a few packets of dried pasta in their store cupboards and use it daily – even in the north, where the tradition of making fresh pasta at home endured for longer than it did in the south.

The majority of durum wheat for the Italian pasta-making industry is grown in Italy or imported from North America. The flour from durum wheat, called semola in Italian, makes high-quality pasta that holds its shape well. Cooked properly until *al dente*, it should be just tender, with a pleasant nutty bite. For the best results, when buying pasta in packets or boxes, always check that it is made from 100 per cent durum wheat – *pasta di semola di grano duro*. Generally, the Italian makes, though expensive, are the best, and you will find that it pays to buy the best.

Nutritional value

Pasta is a completely natural complex carbohydrate food that contains no additives. Always check the label when buying coloured pasta, because some varieties include artificial colourings. Pasta with egg (pasta all'uovo) contains the most nutrients, while wholewheat pasta has the highest percentage of vitamins and fibre. Rich in protein, pasta provides as much energy as a pure protein like steak, but with little or no fat. As it contains six of the eight amino acids essential to make up a complete protein, it only needs a

LEFT: *Gorgonzola adds a welcome tang to this fresh and healthy chicken, farfalle and broccoli salad.*

ABOVE: *Conchiglie with roasted vegetables is a simple yet superb dish.*

ABOVE: *Delicious and zesty, spaghetti with lemon can be made in just a few minutes.*

ABOVE: *Orecchiette with rocket is a satisfying dish from south-east Italy.*

small quantity of cheese, meat, fish, pulses or egg to make it complete. If you are using pasta all'uovo, you need even less additional protein.

The key to healthy eating lies in eating pasta with only a small amount of extra ingredients. In Italy, it is traditional for pasta to be served as a first course, before the main course of fish or meat. Eaten with a little sauce and a light sprinkling of grated cheese, nothing could be more satisfying and delicious.

In Italian cooking also, ingredients such as extra virgin olive oil, fresh and canned tomatoes, garlic, onions, olives, red (bell) peppers and fresh parsley are used all the time, plus lots of fresh fish, vegetables and salad leaves, fruit, pulses and lemon juice. Most of these ingredients combine wonderfully well with pasta, and they are used over and over again in the recipes in this book. For ease of use, these are organized into broths and soups, dishes in tomato sauces and cream sauces, fish and shellfish, meat and poultry, vegetables and vegetarian dishes, baked pasta, stuffed pasta, light and easy meals, and fresh and tasty pasta salads.

An everyday meal

When you are serving pasta as a first course, the usual amount is 65–90g/2½–3½oz uncooked weight per person. Sauce is added sparingly; this is usually tossed with the freshly drained hot pasta in the kitchen, and the mixture is then brought to the table in one large, heated bowl.

If you prefer to serve pasta as a main course for lunch or dinner, simply increase the weight of uncooked pasta to 115–175g/4–6oz per person and make more of whichever sauce you are serving.

If you accompany your main course with a fresh leafy green salad and follow it with some fresh fruit, you will have a tasty, nutritious and supremely satisfying meal. Buon Appetito!

Broths and soups

Soups made with pasta range from clear broths with a sprinkling of pastina to filling and substantial minestre or zuppe, *with chunkier pieces of pasta, vegetables, fish or meat. Broth, called* brodo *in Italian, is generally served as a first course or* primo piatto, *especially for evening meals. It also makes a marvellous pick-me-up if you are tired or unwell.*

Pasta, bean and vegetable soup

***The name of this Calabrian speciality,* Millecosedde, *comes from* millecose, *meaning 'a thousand things'. Almost anything can go in this soup. In Calabria they include a bean called* cicerchia.**

SERVES 4–6

75g/3oz/scant 1/2 cup brown lentils
15g/1/2 oz dried mushrooms
60ml/4 tbsp olive oil
1 carrot, diced
1 celery stick, diced
1 onion, finely chopped
1 garlic clove, finely chopped
a little chopped fresh flat leaf parsley
a good pinch of crushed red chillies (optional)
1.5 litres/21/2 pints/61/4 cups vegetable stock
150g/5oz/1 cup each canned red kidney beans, cannellini beans and chickpeas, rinsed and drained
115g/4oz/1 cup dried small pasta shapes, e.g. rigatoni, penne or penne rigate
salt and ground black pepper
chopped flat leaf parsley, to garnish
freshly grated Pecorino cheese, to serve

1 Put the lentils in a medium pan, add 475ml/16fl oz/2 cups water and bring to the boil over a high heat. Lower the heat and simmer gently, stirring occasionally, for 15–20 minutes until the lentils are just tender. Meanwhile, soak the dried mushrooms in 175ml/6fl oz/3/4 cup warm water for 15–20 minutes.

2 Transfer the lentils into a sieve (strainer) to drain, then rinse under cold water. Drain the soaked mushrooms and reserve the soaking liquid. Finely chop the mushrooms and set aside.

3 Heat the oil in a large pan and add the carrot, celery, onion, garlic, parsley and chillies, if using. Cook over a low heat, stirring constantly, for 5–7 minutes.

4 Add the stock, then the mushrooms and their soaking liquid. Bring to the boil, then add the beans, chickpeas and lentils, with salt and pepper to taste. Cover, and simmer gently for 20 minutes.

5 Add the pasta and bring the soup back to the boil, stirring. Simmer, stirring frequently, until the pasta is *al dente*: 7–8 minutes or according to the instructions on the packet. Season, then serve hot in soup bowls, with grated Pecorino and chopped parsley.

Nutritional information per portion: Energy 669kcal/2831kJ; Protein 41.4g; Carbohydrate 100.8g, of which sugars 7.5g; Fat 14g, of which saturates 2g; Cholesterol 0mg; Calcium 178mg; Fibre 26.1g; Sodium 44mg.

Bean and **pasta soup**

***This hearty main meal soup sometimes goes by the simpler name of* Pasta e Fagioli, *while some Italians refer to it as* Minestrone di Pasta e Fagioli.**

SERVES 4–6

1 onion
1 carrot
1 celery stick
30ml/2 tbsp olive oil
115g/4oz pancetta or rindless smoked streaky (fatty) bacon, diced
1.75 litres/3 pints/7½ cups beef stock
1 cinnamon stick or a good pinch of ground cinnamon
90g/3½oz/scant 1 cup dried pasta shapes, e.g. conchiglie or corallini
400g/14oz can borlotti beans, rinsed and drained
1 thick slice cooked ham, about 225g/8oz, diced
salt and ground black pepper
coarsely shaved Parmesan cheese, to serve

1 Chop the vegetables. Heat the oil in a large pan, add the pancetta or bacon and cook, stirring, until lightly coloured. Add the chopped vegetable mixture to the pan and cook for about 10 minutes, stirring frequently, until lightly coloured.

2 Pour in the stock, add the cinnamon with salt and pepper to taste, and bring to the boil. Cover and simmer gently for 15–20 minutes.

3 Add the pasta and bring back to the boil, stirring all the time. Lower the heat and simmer, stirring frequently, for 5 minutes. Add the beans and ham and simmer until the pasta is *al dente*: 2–3 minutes or according to the instructions on the packet.

4 Taste the soup for seasoning. Serve hot in warmed bowls, sprinkled with shavings of Parmesan.

Nutritional information per portion: Energy 240kcal/1010kJ; Protein 16.7g; Carbohydrate 25.1g, of which sugars 4.8g; Fat 8.8g, of which saturates 2.2g; Cholesterol 32mg; Calcium 60mg; Fibre 5g; Sodium 1009mg.

Pasta and **chickpea soup**

A simple, country-style soup. Although you can use other shapes of pasta, the conchiglie and the beans complement one another beautifully.

SERVES 4–6

1 onion
2 carrots
2 celery sticks
60ml/4 tbsp olive oil
400g/14oz can chickpeas, rinsed and drained
200g/7oz can cannellini beans, rinsed and drained
150ml/¼ pint/⅔ cup passata (bottled strained tomatoes)
120ml/4fl oz/½ cup water
1.5 litres/2½ pints/6¼ cups vegetable or chicken stock
2 fresh or dried rosemary sprigs
200g/7oz/scant 2 cups dried conchiglie
salt and ground black pepper
freshly grated Parmesan cheese, to serve

1 Chop the onion, carrots and celery finely, either in a food processor or by hand.

2 Heat the oil in a large pan, add the chopped vegetable mixture and cook over a low heat, stirring frequently, for 5–7 minutes.

3 Add the chickpeas and cannellini beans, stir well to mix thoroughly, then cook for 5 minutes. Stir in the passata and water. Cook, stirring, for 2–3 minutes.

4 Add 475ml/16fl oz/2 cups of the stock, a sprig of rosemary and salt and pepper, to taste. Bring to the boil, cover, then simmer gently, stirring occasionally, for 1 hour.

5 Add the remaining stock and the pasta and bring to the boil, stirring. Lower the heat and simmer, stirring often, until the pasta is *al dente*: 7–8 minutes (though check the pack). Season, remove the rosemary and serve in warmed bowls, topped with grated Parmesan and rosemary leaves.

Nutritional information per portion: Energy 454kcal/1916kJ; Protein 17.3g; Carbohydrate 66.3g, of which sugars 7.7g; Fat 15.2g, of which saturates 2.1g; Cholesterol 0mg; Calcium 105mg; Fibre 9.7g; Sodium 510mg.

Lentil and **pasta soup**

This rustic vegetarian soup makes a warming meal for a cold winter's evening and goes especially well with some granary or crusty Italian bread.

SERVES 4–6

175g/6oz/¾ cup brown lentils
3 garlic cloves
1 litre/1¾ pints/4 cups water
45ml/3 tbsp olive oil
25g/1oz/2 tbsp butter
1 onion, finely chopped
2 celery sticks, finely chopped
30ml/2 tbsp sun-dried tomato paste
1.75 litres/3 pints/7½ cups vegetable stock
a few fresh marjoram leaves
a few fresh basil leaves
leaves from 1 fresh thyme sprig
50g/2oz/½ cup dried small pasta shapes, e.g. tubetti
salt and ground black pepper
tiny fresh herb leaves, to garnish

1 Put the lentils and 1 smashed, unpeeled garlic clove in a large pan. Add the water and bring to the boil. Lower the heat and simmer gently, stirring occasionally, for 20 minutes until the lentils are tender. Transfer into a sieve (strainer), remove the garlic and set aside. Rinse the lentils under cold water, then leave to drain.

2 Heat 30ml/2 tbsp of the oil with half of the butter in a large pan. Add the onion and celery and cook gently, stirring often, for 5–7 minutes until softened.

3 Crush the remaining garlic, then peel and mash the reserved garlic. Add to the vegetables with the remaining oil, the tomato paste and the lentils. Stir, then add the stock, the fresh herbs and salt and pepper to taste. Bring to the boil, stirring. Simmer for 30 minutes, stirring occasionally.

4 Add the pasta and bring the water back to the boil, stirring. Simmer, stirring frequently, until the pasta is *al dente*: 7–8 minutes or according to the packet instructions. Add the remaining butter and taste for seasoning. Serve hot in warmed bowls, sprinkled with the herb leaves.

Nutritional information per portion: Energy 206kcal/865kJ; Protein 8.1g; Carbohydrate 23.5g, of which sugars 1.7g; Fat 9.5g, of which saturates 3g; Cholesterol 9mg; Calcium 24mg; Fibre 1.9g; Sodium 42mg.

Farmhouse soup

Root vegetables form the base of this chunky, minestrone-style main meal soup. You can vary the vegetables according to what you have to hand.

SERVES 4

30ml/2 tbsp olive oil
1 onion, roughly chopped
3 carrots, cut into large chunks
175–200g/6–7oz turnips, in large chunks
about 175g/6oz swede (rutabaga), in large chunks
400g/14oz can chopped Italian tomatoes
15ml/1 tbsp tomato purée (paste)
5ml/1 tsp dried mixed herbs
5ml/1 tsp dried oregano
1.5 litres/2½ pints/6¼ cups vegetable stock or water
50g/2oz/½ cup dried small macaroni or conchiglie
400g/14oz can red kidney beans, rinsed
30ml/2 tbsp chopped fresh flat leaf parsley
salt and ground black pepper
freshly grated Parmesan cheese, to serve

1 Heat the oil in a large pan, add the onion and cook over a low heat for about 5 minutes until softened. Add the fresh vegetables, canned tomatoes, tomato purée and dried herbs. Stir in salt and pepper to taste. Pour in the stock or water and bring to the boil. Stir well, cover, lower the heat and simmer for 30 minutes, stirring occasionally.

2 Add the pasta and bring to the boil, stirring. Lower the heat and simmer, uncovered, until the pasta is only just *al dente*: about 5 minutes or according to the instructions on the packet. Stir frequently.

3 Stir in the beans. Heat through for 2–3 minutes, then remove from the heat and stir in the parsley. Taste the soup for seasoning. Serve hot in warmed soup bowls, with grated Parmesan handed around separately.

COOK'S TIP

Packets of dried Italian peppers are sold in many supermarkets and in delicatessens.

Nutritional information per portion: Energy 161kcal/678kJ; Protein 7.1g; Carbohydrate 28.2g, of which sugars 12.3g; Fat 3g, of which saturates 0.5g; Cholesterol 0mg; Calcium 100mg; Fibre 7.8g; Sodium 294mg.

Roasted tomato and pasta soup

When the only tomatoes you can buy do not have much flavour, make this soup. The oven-roasting compensates for any lack of flavour in the tomatoes, and the soup has a wonderful smoky taste.

SERVES 4

450g/1lb ripe Italian plum tomatoes, halved lengthways
1 large red (bell) pepper, quartered lengthways and seeded
1 large red onion, quartered lengthways
2 garlic cloves, unpeeled
15ml/1 tbsp olive oil
1.2 litres/2 pints/5 cups vegetable stock or water
good pinch of sugar
90g/3½oz/scant 1 cup dried small pasta shapes, e.g. tubetti or small macaroni
salt and ground black pepper
fresh basil leaves, to garnish

1 Preheat the oven to 190°C/375°F/Gas 5. Spread out the tomatoes, red pepper, onion and garlic in a roasting pan and drizzle with the olive oil. Roast for 30–40 minutes until the vegetables are soft and charred, stirring and turning them halfway.

2 Transfer the vegetables into a food processor, add about 250ml/8fl oz/ 1 cup of the stock or water and process until puréed. Scrape into a sieve (strainer) placed over a large pan and press the purée through into the pan.

3 Add the remaining stock or water, sugar, and salt and pepper to taste. Bring to the boil, stirring.

4 Add the pasta and simmer, stirring frequently, until *al dente*: 7–8 minutes or according to the instructions on the packet. Taste for seasoning. Serve hot in warmed bowls, garnished with the fresh basil.

Nutritional information per portion: Energy 128kcal/543kJ; Protein 4.5g; Carbohydrate 26.9g, of which sugars 9.7g; Fat 1g, of which saturates 0.2g; Cholesterol 0mg; Calcium 30mg; Fibre 3.2g; Sodium 14mg.

Clam and pasta soup

Subtly sweet and spicy, this soup is substantial enough to be served on its own for lunch or dinner. A crusty Italian loaf such as pugliese is the ideal accompaniment.

SERVES 4–6

30ml/2 tbsp olive oil
1 onion, finely chopped
leaves from 1 fresh or dried thyme sprig, chopped, plus extra to garnish
2 garlic cloves, crushed
5–6 fresh basil leaves, plus extra to garnish
1.5–2.5ml/$^{1}/_{4}$–$^{1}/_{2}$ tsp crushed red chillies, to taste
1 litre/1$^{3}/_{4}$ pints/4 cups fish stock
350ml/12fl oz/1$^{1}/_{2}$ cups passata (bottled strained tomatoes)
5ml/1 tsp sugar
90g/3$^{1}/_{2}$oz/scant 1 cup frozen peas
65g/2$^{1}/_{2}$oz/$^{2}/_{3}$ cup dried small pasta shapes, e.g. chifferini
225g/8oz frozen clams or bottled clams in their shells
salt and ground black pepper

1 Heat the oil in a large pan, add the onion and cook gently for about 5 minutes until softened, but not coloured. Add the thyme, then stir in the garlic, basil leaves and chillies.

2 Add the stock, passata and sugar to the pan, with salt and pepper to taste. Bring to the boil, then lower the heat and simmer gently, stirring occasionally, for 15 minutes. Add the peas and cook for a further 5 minutes.

3 Add the pasta to the stock mixture and bring to the boil, stirring. Lower the heat and simmer, stirring frequently, until the pasta is only just *al dente*: about 5 minutes or according to the packet instructions.

4 Turn the heat down to low, add the frozen or bottled clams and heat through for 2–3 minutes. Taste for seasoning. Serve hot in warmed bowls, garnished with basil and thyme.

Nutritional information per portion: Energy 196kcal/821kJ; Protein 9.3g; Carbohydrate 20.2g, of which sugars 8.9g; Fat 6.5g, of which saturates 1g; Cholesterol 25mg; Calcium 67mg; Fibre 2.6g; Sodium 466mg.

Broccoli, anchovy and pasta soup

This soup is a favourite from Puglia in the south of Italy, where anchovies and broccoli are often used together.

SERVES 4

30ml/2 tbsp olive oil
1 small onion, finely chopped
1 garlic clove, finely chopped
1/4–1/3 fresh red chilli, seeded and finely chopped
2 canned anchovies, drained
200ml/7fl oz/scant 1 cup passata (bottled strained tomatoes)
45ml/3 tbsp dry white wine
1.2 litres/2 pints/5 cups vegetable stock
300g/11oz/2 cups broccoli florets
200g/7oz/1 3/4 cups dried orecchiette
salt and ground black pepper
freshly grated Pecorino cheese, to serve

1 Heat the oil in a large pan. Add the onion, garlic, chilli and anchovies and cook over a low heat, stirring constantly, for 5–6 minutes.

2 Add the passata and wine, with salt and pepper to taste. Bring to the boil, cover the pan, then cook over a low heat, stirring occasionally, for 12–15 minutes.

3 Pour in the stock. Bring to the boil, then add the broccoli and simmer for about 5 minutes. Add the pasta and bring back to the boil, stirring. Simmer, stirring often, until the pasta is *al dente*: 7–8 minutes or according to the instructions on the packet. Taste for seasoning. Serve hot, in warmed bowls. Hand around grated Pecorino separately.

Nutritional information per portion: Energy 268kcal/1131kJ; Protein 10.3g; Carbohydrate 41.2g, of which sugars 5.2g; Fat 7.3g, of which saturates 1.1g; Cholesterol 1mg; Calcium 69mg; Fibre 3.9g; Sodium 182mg.

Pasta squares and peas in broth

This thick soup originated in Lazio, where it is traditionally made with fresh homemade pasta and peas.

SERVES 4–6

25g/1oz/2 tbsp butter
50g/2oz pancetta or rindless smoked streaky (fatty) bacon, chopped
1 small onion, finely chopped
1 celery stick, finely chopped
400g/14oz/3 1/2 cups frozen peas
5ml/1 tsp tomato purée (paste)
5–10ml/1–2 tsp finely chopped fresh flat leaf parsley
1 litre/1 3/4 pints/4 cups chicken stock
300g/11oz fresh lasagne sheets
about 50g/2oz prosciutto crudo, cut into cubes
salt and ground black pepper
freshly grated Parmesan cheese, to serve

1 Melt the butter in a large pan and add the pancetta or bacon, the onion and celery. Cook gently, stirring constantly, for 5 minutes.

2 Add the peas and cook, stirring, for 3–4 minutes. Stir in the tomato purée and parsley, then the chicken stock, with salt and pepper to taste. Bring to the boil. Cover, lower the heat and simmer for 10 minutes. Meanwhile, cut the lasagne sheets into 2cm/3/4in squares.

3 Taste for seasoning. Drop in the pasta, stir and bring to the boil. Simmer for 2–3 minutes until the pasta is *al dente*, then stir in the prosciutto. Serve hot in warmed bowls, with grated Parmesan handed around separately.

Nutritional information per portion: Energy 240kcal/1013kJ; Protein 9.2g; Carbohydrate 38.4g, of which sugars 2.7g; Fat 6.6g, of which saturates 3.1g; Cholesterol 19mg; Calcium 20mg; Fibre 1.7g; Sodium 241mg.

Little stuffed hats in broth

This soup is served in northern Italy on Santo Stefano (St Stephen's Day) and New Year's Day.

SERVES 4

1.2 litres/2 pints/5 cups chicken stock
90–115g/3½–4oz/1 cup fresh or dried cappelletti
30ml/2 tbsp dry white wine (optional)
about 15ml/1 tbsp finely chopped fresh flat leaf parsley (optional)
salt and ground black pepper
shredded flat leaf parsley, to garnish
about 30ml/2 tbsp freshly grated Parmesan cheese, to serve

1 Pour the chicken stock into a large pan and bring to the boil. Add a little salt and pepper to taste, then drop in the pasta.

2 Stir well and bring back to the boil. Lower the heat to a simmer and cook according to the instructions on the packet, until the pasta is *al dente*. Stir frequently during cooking to ensure the pasta cooks evenly.

3 Stir in the wine and parsley, if using, then taste for seasoning. Ladle into four warmed soup plates, then sprinkle with grated Parmesan and flat leaf parsley. Serve immediately.

COOK'S TIP

Cappelletti is just another name for tortellini, which come from Romagna. You can buy them or make your own.

Nutritional information per portion: Energy 77kcal/328kJ; Protein 2.9g; Carbohydrate 16.7g, of which sugars 0.8g; Fat 0.5g, of which saturates 0.1g; Cholesterol 0mg; Calcium 6mg; Fibre 0.7g; Sodium 183mg.

Tiny pasta in broth

In Italy this soup is often served with bread for a light evening meal.

SERVES 4

1.2 litres/2 pints/5 cups beef stock
75g/3oz/¾ cup dried tiny soup pasta, e.g. funghetti
2 pieces bottled roasted red pepper, about 50g/2oz
salt and ground black pepper
coarsely shaved Parmesan cheese, to serve

1 Bring the beef stock to the boil in a large pan. Add salt and pepper to taste, then drop in the dried soup pasta. Stir well and bring the stock back to the boil.

2 Lower the heat to a simmer and cook until the pasta is *al dente*: 7–8 minutes or according to the packet instructions. Stir frequently during cooking to prevent the pasta shapes from sticking together.

3 Drain the pieces of roasted pepper and dice them finely. Place them in the bottom of four warmed soup plates. Taste the soup for seasoning and ladle into the soup plates. Serve immediately, with shavings of Parmesan handed around separately.

COOK'S TIP

Stock (bouillon) cubes are not really suitable for a recipe like this, in which the flavour of the broth is so important. If you don't have time to make your own stock, use two 300g/11oz cans of condensed beef consommé, adding water as instructed on the labels.

Nutritional information per portion: Energy 104kcal/439kJ; Protein 5.6g; Carbohydrate 15.1g, of which sugars 1.8g; Fat 3g, of which saturates 1.7g; Cholesterol 8mg; Calcium 97mg; Fibre 0.9g; Sodium 265mg.

Puglia-style minestrone

This tasty soup for a Monday dinner can be made with the leftover carcass of Sunday's roast chicken. The sprinkling of salty ricotta salata at the finish is typical of Puglian cooking.

SERVES 4

1 roast chicken carcass, broken into pieces
1 onion, quartered lengthways
1 carrot, roughly chopped
1 celery stick, roughly chopped
a few black peppercorns
1 small handful mixed fresh herbs, such as parsley and thyme
1 chicken stock (bouillon) cube
50g/2oz/½ cup tubetti
salt and ground black pepper
50g/2oz ricotta salata, coarsely grated or crumbled and 30ml/2 tbsp fresh mint leaves, to serve

1 Place the carcass pieces in a large pan. Add the onion, carrot, celery, peppercorns and herbs, then the stock cube and a good pinch of salt. Cover with 1.5 litres/2½ pints/6¼ cups cold water and quickly bring to the boil.

2 Lower the heat, half cover the pan and simmer gently for 1 hour. Remove from the heat and leave to cool, then strain through a colander or sieve (strainer) into a clean large pan.

3 Remove any meat from the chicken bones, cut it into bitesize pieces and set aside. Discard the carcass and flavouring ingredients.

4 Bring the stock in the pan to the boil, add the pasta and simmer, stirring often, until only just *al dente*: 5–6 minutes (though check pack instructions).

5 Add the pieces of chicken and heat through for a few minutes, by which time the pasta will be ready. Taste for seasoning. Serve hot in warmed bowls, sprinkled with the ricotta salata and mint leaves.

Nutritional information per portion: Energy 78kcal/327kJ; Protein 3g; Carbohydrate 12.4g, of which sugars 3.1g; Fat 2.2g, of which saturates 1.2g; Cholesterol 5mg; Calcium 15mg; Fibre 1.1g; Sodium 10mg.

Pasta soup with **chicken livers**

A soup that can be served as either a first or main course. The fried fegatini are so delicious that even if you do not normally like chicken livers you will find yourself loving them in this soup.

SERVES 4–6

115g/4oz/$^2/_3$ cup chicken livers, thawed if frozen
3 sprigs each fresh parsley, marjoram and sage
leaves from 1 fresh thyme sprig
5–6 fresh basil leaves
15ml/1 tbsp olive oil
knob (pat) of butter
4 garlic cloves, crushed
15–30ml/1–2 tbsp dry white wine
2 x 300g/11oz cans condensed chicken consommé
225g/8oz/2 cups frozen peas
50g/2oz/$^1/_2$ cup dried pasta shapes, e.g. farfalle
2–3 spring onions (scallions), diagonally sliced
salt and ground black pepper

1 Cut the chicken livers into small pieces with scissors. Chop the herbs. Heat the oil and butter in a frying pan, add the garlic and herbs, with salt and pepper to taste, and fry gently for a few minutes. Add the livers, increase the heat to high and stir-fry for a few minutes until they change colour and become dry. Pour the wine over the livers, cook until the wine evaporates, then remove from the heat and taste for seasoning.

2 Pour both cans of chicken consommé into a large pan and add water as directed on the labels. Add an extra can of water, then stir in a little salt and pepper to taste and bring to the boil.

3 Add the frozen peas and simmer for 5 minutes. Add the small pasta shapes and bring back to the boil, stirring. Simmer, stirring often, until the pasta is only just *al dente*: about 5 minutes (though check pack instructions).

4 Add the fried chicken livers and spring onions and heat through for 2–3 minutes. Taste for seasoning. Serve hot, in warmed bowls.

Nutritional information per portion: Energy 88kcal/367kJ; Protein 6.4g; Carbohydrate 9.2g, of which sugars 1.3g; Fat 2.9g, of which saturates 0.5g; Cholesterol 61mg; Calcium 28mg; Fibre 2.1g; Sodium 355mg.

Rich minestrone

This special variation on a traditional minestrone sees the addition of chicken to the usual vegetable and pasta broth. Served with crusty Italian bread, it makes a filling meal.

SERVES 4–6

15ml/1 tbsp olive oil
2 chicken thighs
3 rindless streaky (fatty) bacon rashers (strips), chopped
1 onion, finely chopped
a few fresh basil leaves, shredded
a few fresh rosemary leaves, finely chopped
15ml/1 tbsp chopped fresh flat leaf parsley
2 potatoes, cut into 1cm/½in cubes
1 large carrot, cut into 1cm/½in cubes
2 small courgettes (zucchini), cut into 1cm/½in cubes
1–2 celery sticks, cut into 1cm/½in cubes
1 litre/1¾ pints/4 cups chicken stock
200g/7oz/1¾ cups frozen peas
90g/3½oz/scant 1 cup stellette or other dried tiny soup pasta
salt and ground black pepper
fresh basil leaves, to garnish
coarsely shaved Parmesan cheese, to serve

1 Heat the oil in a large frying pan, add the chicken thighs and fry for 5 minutes on each side. Remove with a slotted spoon and set aside.

2 Lower the heat, add the bacon, onion and herbs to the pan and stir well. Cook gently, stirring constantly, for about 5 minutes. Add all the vegetables, except the frozen peas, and cook for 5–7 minutes more, stirring frequently.

3 Return the chicken thighs to the pan, add the stock and then bring to the boil. Cover and cook over a low heat for 35–40 minutes, stirring the soup occasionally.

4 Remove the chicken thighs with a slotted spoon and place them on a board. Stir the peas and pasta into the soup and bring back to the boil. Simmer, stirring frequently until the pasta is *al dente*: 7–8 minutes or according to the instructions on the packet.

5 Meanwhile, remove and discard the chicken skin, then remove the meat from the bones and cut it into 1cm/½in pieces. Return the meat to the soup and heat through. Taste for seasoning. Serve hot in soup bowls; sprinkle over Parmesan shavings and garnish with one or two basil leaves.

Nutritional information per portion: Energy 198kcal/833kJ; Protein 15.6g; Carbohydrate 23.3g, of which sugars 3.9g; Fat 5.4g, of which saturates 1.4g; Cholesterol 30mg; Calcium 31mg; Fibre 3.2g; Sodium 224mg.

Meatball and **pasta soup**

Even though this soup comes from sunny Sicily, don't be fooled. It is substantial enough for a hearty meal on a chilly winter's day.

SERVES 4

2 x 300g/11oz cans condensed beef consommé
90g/3½oz/¾ cup dried very thin pasta, e.g. fidelini or spaghettini
fresh flat leaf parsley, to garnish
freshly grated Parmesan cheese, to serve

FOR THE MEATBALLS

1 very thick slice of white bread, crusts removed
30ml/2 tbsp milk
225g/8oz/1 cup minced (ground) beef
1 garlic clove, crushed
30ml/2 tbsp freshly grated Parmesan cheese
30–45ml/2–3 tbsp fresh flat leaf parsley leaves, coarsely chopped
1 egg
nutmeg
salt and ground black pepper

1 To make the meatballs, break the bread into a small bowl, then add the milk and set aside to soak. Meanwhile, put the minced beef, garlic, Parmesan, parsley and egg in another large bowl. Grate fresh nutmeg liberally over the top and add salt and pepper to taste.

2 Squeeze the bread with your hands to remove as much milk as possible, then add the bread to the meatball mixture and mix everything together well with your hands. Wash your hands, rinse them under the cold tap, then form the mixture into tiny balls about the size of small marbles.

3 Pour both cans of consommé into a large pan, add water as directed on the labels, then add an extra can of water. Stir in salt and pepper to taste and bring to the boil.

4 Drop in the meatballs, then break the pasta into small pieces and add it to the soup. Bring the soup to the boil, stirring gently. Simmer, stirring frequently, until the pasta is *al dente*: 7–8 minutes or according to the instructions on the packet. Taste for seasoning. Serve hot in warmed bowls, sprinkled with parsley and freshly grated Parmesan cheese.

Nutritional information per portion: Energy 277kcal/1158kJ; Protein 19.9g; Carbohydrate 20.5g, of which sugars 1.4g; Fat 14g, of which saturates 6.1g; Cholesterol 89mg; Calcium 133mg; Fibre 1g; Sodium 731mg.

Tomato sauces and cream sauces

It was the Neapolitans who first discovered the delights of tomato sauces. Simple and uncooked or simmered for a long while, they are typically southern Italian. They go best with the dried, commercially produced pasta of the south, and taste divine with wonderful southern ingredients – basil, garlic and olive oil. Northern Italians love cream sauce with pasta. Its deliciously rich texture complements fresh pasta perfectly.

Spaghetti with fresh tomato sauce

This is the famous Neapolitan sauce that is made in summer when tomatoes are very ripe and sweet. It is very simple, so that nothing detracts from the flavour of the tomatoes themselves. It is served here with spaghetti, which is the traditional choice of pasta.

SERVES 4

675g/1½lb ripe Italian plum tomatoes
60ml/4 tbsp olive oil
1 onion, finely chopped
350g/12oz fresh or dried spaghetti
1 small handful fresh basil leaves
salt and ground black pepper
coarsely shaved Parmesan cheese, to serve

1 Cut a cross in the bottom (flower) end of each tomato. Bring a medium pan of water to the boil and remove from the heat. Plunge a few of the tomatoes into the water, leave for 30 seconds, then lift out with a slotted spoon. Repeat with the remaining tomatoes, then peel off the skin and roughly chop the flesh.

2 Heat the oil in a large pan, add the onion and cook gently, stirring often, for about 5 minutes until softened and lightly coloured. Add the tomatoes, with salt and pepper to taste, bring to a simmer, then turn the heat down to low and cover the pan. Cook, stirring occasionally, for 30–40 minutes until thick.

3 Meanwhile, cook the pasta according to the instructions on the packet. Shred the basil leaves finely. Remove the sauce from the heat, add the basil and season. Drain the pasta, transfer it into a warmed bowl, pour the sauce over and toss well. Serve immediately, with shaved Parmesan handed around separately.

Nutritional information per portion: Energy 431kcal/1821kJ; Protein 12.1g; Carbohydrate 70.4g, of which sugars 8.4g; Fat 13.2g, of which saturates 1.9g; Cholesterol 0mg; Calcium 59mg; Fibre 4.9g; Sodium 22mg.

Rigatoni with winter tomato sauce

In winter, when fresh tomatoes are not at their best, this is the sauce the Italians make. Canned tomatoes combined with soffritto ***(the sautéed mixture of chopped onion, carrot, celery and garlic) and herbs give a better flavour than fresh winter tomatoes.***

SERVES 6–8

1 onion
1 carrot
1 celery stick
60ml/4 tbsp olive oil
1 garlic clove, thinly sliced
a few leaves each fresh basil, thyme and oregano or marjoram
2 x 400g/14oz cans chopped Italian plum tomatoes
15ml/1 tbsp sun-dried tomato paste
5ml/1 tsp sugar
about 90ml/6 tbsp dry red or white wine (optional)
350g/12oz/3 cups dried rigatoni
salt and ground black pepper
coarsely shaved Parmesan cheese, to serve

1 Chop the onion, carrot and celery stick finely, either in a food processor or by hand. Heat the olive oil in a medium pan, add the garlic slices and stir over a very low heat for 1–2 minutes.

2 Add the chopped vegetables and the fresh herbs. Cook over a low heat, stirring frequently, for 5–7 minutes until the vegetables have softened and are lightly coloured.

3 Add the canned tomatoes, tomato paste and sugar, then stir in the wine, if using. Add salt and pepper to taste. Bring to the boil, stirring, then lower to a gentle simmer. Cook, uncovered, for about 45 minutes, stirring occasionally.

4 Cook the pasta according to the instructions on the packet. Drain it and transfer it into a warmed bowl. Taste the sauce for seasoning, and pour over the pasta and toss well. Serve immediately, with shavings of Parmesan handed around separately. If you like, garnish with extra chopped herbs.

Nutritional information per portion: Energy 226kcal/956kJ; Protein 6.2g; Carbohydrate 37.8g, of which sugars 6.6g; Fat 6.6g, of which saturates 1g; Cholesterol 0mg; Calcium 25mg; Fibre 2.7g; Sodium 20mg.

Fusilli with **tomato** and **balsamic vinegar sauce**

This is a modern Cal-Ital recipe (Californian/Italian). The intense, sweet-sour flavour of balsamic vinegar gives a pleasant kick to a sauce made with canned tomatoes.

SERVES 6–8

2 x 400g/14oz cans chopped Italian plum tomatoes
2 pieces of drained sun-dried tomato in olive oil, thinly sliced
2 garlic cloves, crushed
45ml/3 tbsp olive oil
5ml/1 tsp sugar
350g/12oz/3 cups fresh or dried fusilli
45ml/3 tbsp balsamic vinegar
salt and ground black pepper
coarsely shaved Pecorino cheese and rocket (arugula) salad, to serve

1 Put the canned and sun-dried tomatoes in a medium pan with the garlic, olive oil and sugar. Add salt and pepper to taste. Bring to the boil, stirring. Lower the heat and simmer for about 30 minutes until reduced.

2 Meanwhile, cook the pasta in salted boiling water, according to the instructions on the packet.

3 Add the balsamic vinegar to the sauce and stir to mix evenly. Cook for 1–2 minutes, then remove from the heat and taste for seasoning.

4 Drain the pasta and turn it into a warmed bowl. Pour the sauce over the pasta and toss well. Serve immediately, with rocket salad and the shaved Pecorino handed around separately.

Nutritional information per portion: Energy 210kcal/891kJ; Protein 6.3g; Carbohydrate 36.9g, of which sugars 6g; Fat 5.2g, of which saturates 0.8g; Cholesterol 0mg; Calcium 20mg; Fibre 2.4g; Sodium 25mg.

Linguine with **sun-dried tomato pesto**

Tomato pesto was once a rarity, but is now becoming increasingly popular. To make it, use sun-dried tomatoes instead of basil. The result is absolutely delicious.

SERVES 4

25g/1oz/1/3 cup pine nuts
25g/1oz/1/3 cup freshly grated Parmesan cheese
50g/2oz/1/2 cup sun-dried tomatoes in olive oil
1 garlic clove, roughly chopped
60ml/4 tbsp olive oil
350g/12oz fresh or dried linguine
ground black pepper
coarsely shaved Parmesan cheese, to serve
basil leaves, to garnish

1 Put the pine nuts in a small non-stick frying pan and toss over a low to medium heat for 1–2 minutes or until the nuts are lightly toasted and golden.

2 Place the nuts into a food processor. Add the Parmesan, sun-dried tomatoes and garlic, with pepper to taste. Process until finely chopped.

3 With the machine running, gradually add the olive oil through the feeder tube until it has all been incorporated evenly and the ingredients have formed a smooth-looking paste.

4 Cook the pasta according to the packet instructions. Drain well, reserving a little of the cooking water. Transfer the pasta into a warmed bowl, add the pesto and a few spoonfuls of the hot water and toss well. Serve immediately garnished with basil leaves. Hand around shavings of Parmesan separately.

Nutritional information per portion: Energy 503kcal/2114kJ; Protein 14.4g; Carbohydrate 66.7g, of which sugars 4.7g; Fat 21.7g, of which saturates 3.4g; Cholesterol 6mg; Calcium 102mg; Fibre 3g; Sodium 98mg.

Spaghetti with tomatoes, anchovies, olives and capers

From Campania in the south of Italy, this classic sauce has a strong flavour.

SERVES 4

30ml/2 tbsp olive oil
1 small onion, finely chopped
1 garlic clove, finely chopped
4 canned anchovies, drained
50g/2oz/$^1/_2$ cup pitted black olives, sliced
15ml/1 tbsp capers
400g/14oz can chopped Italian plum tomatoes
45ml/3 tbsp water
15ml/1 tbsp chopped fresh flat leaf parsley
350g/12oz fresh or dried spaghetti
salt and ground black pepper

1 Heat the oil in a medium pan and add the onion, garlic and drained anchovies. Cook gently, stirring constantly, for 5–7 minutes or until the anchovies form a very soft pulp. Add the olives and capers and stir-fry for a minute.

2 Add the tomatoes, water, half the parsley, and salt and pepper to taste. Stir well and bring to the boil, then lower the heat and cover the pan. Simmer gently for 30 minutes, stirring occasionally. Meanwhile, cook the pasta according to the packet instructions.

3 Drain the pasta and transfer it into a warmed bowl. Taste the sauce for seasoning, pour it over the pasta and toss well. Serve garnished with the remaining parsley.

Nutritional information per portion: Energy 390kcal/1650kJ; Protein 12.3g; Carbohydrate 69.1g, of which sugars 6.8g; Fat 9.1g, of which saturates 1.3g; Cholesterol 2mg; Calcium 49mg; Fibre 4.1g; Sodium 411mg.

Bucatini with smoked pancetta, tomato and chilli sauce

This tomato sauce is known as* Amatriciana *in Italy, named after the town of Amatrice in Lazio.

SERVES 4

15ml/1 tbsp olive oil
1 small onion, finely sliced
115g/4oz smoked pancetta or rindless smoked streaky (fatty) bacon, diced
1 fresh red chilli, seeded and cut into thin strips
400g/14oz can chopped Italian plum tomatoes
30–45ml/2–3 tbsp dry white wine or water
350g/12oz dried bucatini
30–45ml/2–3 tbsp freshly grated Pecorino cheese, plus extra to serve (optional)
salt and ground black pepper

1 Heat the oil in a medium pan and cook the onion, pancetta and chilli over a low heat for 5–7 minutes, stirring. Add the tomatoes and wine or water, with salt and pepper to taste. Bring to the boil, stirring, then cover and simmer for 15–20 minutes, stirring occasionally. If the sauce is too dry, stir in a little of the pasta water.

2 Meanwhile, cook the pasta in a pan of salted boiling water, according to the packet instructions.

3 Drain the pasta and transfer it into a warmed bowl. Taste the sauce for seasoning, pour it over the pasta and add the grated Pecorino. Toss well. Serve immediately, with more grated Pecorino handed separately if you prefer.

Nutritional information per portion: Energy 467kcal/1972kJ; Protein 18.9g; Carbohydrate 69.2g, of which sugars 6.9g; Fat 13.9g, of which saturates 4.6g; Cholesterol 26mg; Calcium 125mg; Fibre 3.8g; Sodium 457mg.

Spaghetti with **meaty tomato sauce**

This Roman sauce hails from the days when meat was scarce and expensive, so cooks would put a little meat fat – or sometimes stock – in a tomato sauce to make it taste of meat.

SERVES 4

1 small onion
1 small carrot
2 celery sticks
2 garlic cloves
1 small handful fresh flat leaf parsley
50g/2oz ham or bacon fat, finely chopped
60–90ml/4–6 tbsp dry white wine, or more to taste
500g/1¼lb ripe Italian plum tomatoes, chopped
salt and ground black pepper

1 Chop the onion, carrot and celery in a food processor. Add the garlic cloves and parsley and process until finely chopped. Alternatively, chop everything by hand.

2 Put the vegetable mixture in a medium shallow pan or skillet with the ham fat and cook, stirring, over a low heat for 5 minutes. Add the wine, with salt and pepper to taste and simmer for 5 minutes, then stir in the tomatoes. Simmer for 40 minutes, stirring occasionally. Add a little hot water if the sauce seems too dry. Meanwhile, cook the pasta according to the instructions on the packet.

3 Have ready a large sieve (strainer) placed over a large bowl. Carefully pour in the sauce and press it through the sieve with the back of a metal spoon, leaving behind the tomato skins and any tough pieces of vegetable that won't go through.

4 Return the sauce to the clean pan and heat it through, adding a little more wine or hot water if it is too thick. Taste the sauce for seasoning, then toss with hot, freshly cooked pasta of your choice.

Nutritional information per portion: Energy 156kcal/645kJ; Protein 1.3g; Carbohydrate 6.8g, of which sugars 6.3g; Fat 12.9g, of which saturates 5.2g; Cholesterol 12mg; Calcium 25mg; Fibre 2.1g; Sodium 26mg.

Spaghetti with tomatoes and pancetta

This sauce comes from Spoleto in Umbria. It is a fresh, light sauce in which the tomatoes are cooked for a short time, so it should only be made in summer when tomatoes have the best flavour.

SERVES 4

350g/12oz ripe Italian plum tomatoes
150g/5oz pancetta or rindless streaky (fatty) bacon, diced
30ml/2 tbsp olive oil
1 onion, finely chopped
350g/12oz fresh or dried spaghetti
2–3 fresh marjoram sprigs, leaves stripped
salt and ground black pepper
freshly grated Pecorino cheese, to serve
shredded fresh basil, to garnish

1 With a sharp knife, cut a cross in the bottom (flower) end of each plum tomato. Bring a medium pan of water to the boil and remove from the heat. Plunge a few of the tomatoes into the water, leave for 30 seconds, lift out with a slotted spoon and set aside. Repeat with the remaining tomatoes, then peel off the skin and finely chop the flesh.

2 In a medium pan, gently heat the pancetta or bacon with the oil until the fat runs. Add the onion and stir to mix. Cook gently for 10 minutes, stirring.

3 Add the tomatoes, with salt and pepper to taste. Stir well and cook, uncovered, for 10 minutes. Meanwhile, cook the pasta according to the instructions on the packet.

4 Remove the sauce from the heat, stir in the marjoram and taste for seasoning. Drain the pasta and transfer it into a warmed bowl. Pour the sauce over the pasta and toss well. Serve immediately, sprinkled with shredded basil. Hand around grated Pecorino separately.

Nutritional information per portion: Energy 473kcal/1992kJ; Protein 17.2g; Carbohydrate 68.7g, of which sugars 6.5g; Fat 16.2g, of which saturates 4.1g; Cholesterol 24mg; Calcium 34mg; Fibre 3.6g; Sodium 484mg.

Penne with **tomato** and **chilli sauce**

This is one of Rome's most famous pasta dishes – penne tossed in a tomato sauce flavoured with chilli. Make the sauce as hot as you like by adding more chillies to taste.

SERVES 4

25g/1oz dried porcini mushrooms
90g/3½oz/7 tbsp butter
150g/5oz pancetta or rindless smoked streaky (fatty) bacon, diced
1–2 dried red chillies, to taste
2 garlic cloves, crushed
8 ripe Italian plum tomatoes, peeled and chopped
a few fresh basil leaves, torn, plus extra to garnish
350g/12oz/3 cups fresh or dried penne
50g/2oz/⅔ cup freshly grated Parmesan cheese
25g/1oz/⅓ cup freshly grated Pecorino cheese
salt

1 Soak the mushrooms in warm water for 15–20 minutes. Drain, squeeze dry with your hands and finely chop. Melt 50g/2oz/4 tbsp of the butter in a medium pan or skillet. Add the pancetta or bacon and stir-fry over a medium heat until golden and slightly crispy. Remove with a slotted spoon and set it aside.

2 Add the chopped mushrooms and cook in the same way. Remove and set aside with the pancetta or bacon. Crumble 1 chilli into the pan, add the garlic and cook, stirring, for a few minutes until the garlic turns golden. Add the tomatoes and basil and season with salt. Cook gently, stirring occasionally, for 10–15 minutes. Meanwhile, cook the penne in a pan of salted boiling water, according to the instructions on the packet.

3 Add the pancetta or bacon and the mushrooms to the sauce. Taste for seasoning, adding more chillies to taste. If the sauce is too dry, add a little of the pasta water. Drain the pasta and transfer it into a warmed bowl. Dice the remaining butter, add it to the pasta with the cheeses, then toss well. Pour the tomato sauce over the pasta, toss well and serve garnished with basil leaves.

Nutritional information per portion: Energy 681kcal/2856kJ; Protein 25.1g; Carbohydrate 69.7g, of which sugars 7.7g; Fat 35.5g, of which saturates 19g; Cholesterol 91mg; Calcium 264mg; Fibre 4.1g; Sodium 830mg.

Farfalle with **tomatoes** and **peas**

This pretty sauce should be served with plain white pasta so that the red, green and white make it tricolore, the three colours of the Italian flag. Here farfalle (bow-tie shaped pasta) is used, but other pasta shapes will work just as well.

SERVES 4

15ml/1 tbsp olive oil
5–6 rindless streaky (fatty) bacon rashers (strips), cut into small strips
400g/14oz can chopped Italian plum tomatoes
60ml/4 tbsp water
350g/12oz/3 cups dried farfalle
225g/8oz/2 cups frozen peas
50g/2oz/4 tbsp mascarpone
a few fresh basil leaves, shredded
salt and ground black pepper
basil leaves, to garnish
freshly grated Parmesan cheese, to serve

1 Heat the oil in a medium pan and add the bacon. Cook over a low heat, stirring frequently, for 5–7 minutes. Add the tomatoes and water, with salt and pepper to taste. Bring to the boil. Lower the heat, cover and simmer gently for about 15 minutes, stirring from time to time.

2 Meanwhile, cook the pasta in salted boiling water, according to the instructions on the packet.

3 Add the peas to the tomato sauce, stir well to mix and bring to the boil. Cover the pan and cook for 5–8 minutes until the peas are cooked and the sauce is quite thick. Taste the sauce for seasoning.

4 Turn off the heat under the pan and add the mascarpone and shredded basil. Mix well, cover and leave to stand for 1–2 minutes. Drain the pasta and transfer it into a warmed bowl. Pour over the sauce and toss well. Serve immediately, garnished with basil, and hand around some grated Parmesan separately.

Nutritional information per portion: Energy 548kcal/2306kJ; Protein 24.1g; Carbohydrate 74.7g, of which sugars 7.7g; Fat 19.1g, of which saturates 6.1g; Cholesterol 38mg; Calcium 44mg; Fibre 6.2g; Sodium 642mg.

Vermicelli with **lemon**

Fresh and tangy, this makes an excellent first course for a dinner party. It doesn't rely on fresh seasonal ingredients, so it is good at any time of year.

SERVES 4

350g/12oz dried vermicelli
juice of 2 large lemons
50g/2oz/1/4 cup butter
200ml/7fl oz/scant 1 cup panna da cucina or double (heavy) cream
115g/4oz/1 1/3 cups freshly grated Parmesan cheese
salt and ground black pepper

1 Cook the pasta in salted boiling water, according to the instructions on the packet. Pour the lemon juice into a medium pan. Add the butter, cream, and salt and pepper to taste.

2 Bring to the boil, then lower the heat and simmer for about 5 minutes, stirring occasionally, until the cream reduces slightly.

3 Drain the pasta and return it to the pan. Add the grated Parmesan, then taste the sauce for seasoning and pour it over the pasta.

4 Toss quickly over a medium heat until the pasta is evenly coated with the sauce, then divide the pasta among four warmed bowls and serve immediately.

Nutritional information per portion: Energy 706kcal/2934kJ; Protein 20.3g; Carbohydrate 70.4g, of which sugars 1.9g; Fat 37.9g, of which saturates 24.6g; Cholesterol 61mg; Calcium 406mg; Fibre 0.1g; Sodium 420mg.

Garganelli with asparagus and cream

This is a lovely recipe for late spring when bunches of fresh young asparagus are on sale in stores and markets everywhere.

SERVES 4

1 bunch fresh young asparagus, 250–300g/9–11oz
350g/12oz/3 cups dried garganelli
25g/1oz/2 tbsp butter
200ml/7fl oz/scant 1 cup panna da cucina or double (heavy) cream
30ml/2 tbsp dry white wine
90–115g/3½–4oz/1–1⅓ cups freshly grated Parmesan cheese
30ml/2 tbsp chopped fresh mixed herbs, such as basil, flat leaf parsley, chervil, marjoram and oregano
salt and ground black pepper

1 Trim off and discard the woody ends of the asparagus, leaving 200g/7oz asparagus spears. Cut diagonally into pieces the same length and shape as the garganelli.

2 Blanch the asparagus in salted boiling water for 2 minutes, adding the tips for the last minute only. Drain and rinse in cold water. Set aside.

3 Cook the pasta in a pan of salted boiling water according to the instructions on the packet.

4 Put the butter and cream in a medium pan, add salt and pepper to taste and bring to the boil. Simmer until the cream reduces and thickens, then add the asparagus, wine and half the grated Parmesan. Taste for seasoning and keep on a low heat.

5 Drain the pasta when cooked and transfer it into a warmed bowl. Pour the sauce over the pasta, sprinkle with the fresh herbs and toss well. Serve immediately, topped with the remaining grated Parmesan.

Nutritional information per portion: Energy 671kcal/2808kJ; Protein 22.1g; Carbohydrate 67.1g, of which sugars 5.1g; Fat 36.2g, of which saturates 21.6g; Cholesterol 91mg; Calcium 342mg; Fibre 3.8g; Sodium 261mg.

Alfredo's fettuccine

This traditional, simple recipe was invented by a Roman restaurateur called Alfredo, who became famous for serving it with a gold fork and spoon.

SERVES 4

50g/2oz/¼ cup butter
200ml/7fl oz/scant 1 cup panna da cucina or double (heavy) cream
50g/2oz/⅔ cup freshly grated Parmesan cheese, plus extra to serve
350g/12oz fresh fettuccine
salt and ground black pepper

1 Melt the butter in a large pan or skillet. Add the panna da cucina or double cream and bring it to the boil.

2 Simmer for 5 minutes, stirring, then add the Parmesan, with salt and pepper to taste, and turn off the heat under the pan.

3 Bring a large pan of salted water to the boil. Drop in all the pasta and quickly bring back to the boil, stirring occasionally. Cook until *al dente*: 2–3 minutes, or according to the instructions on the packet. Drain well.

4 Turn on the heat under the pan of cream to low, add all the pasta and toss until it is coated in the sauce. Taste for seasoning. Serve immediately, with extra grated Parmesan handed around separately.

Nutritional information per portion: Energy 697kcal/2912kJ; Protein 16.3g; Carbohydrate 65.8g, of which sugars 3.8g; Fat 42.8g, of which saturates 26g; Cholesterol 108mg; Calcium 199mg; Fibre 2.6g; Sodium 226mg.

Fusilli with **wild mushrooms**

A very rich dish with an earthy flavour and lots of garlic, this makes an ideal main course for vegetarians, especially if it is accompanied by a crisp green salad.

SERVES 4

1/2 x 275g/10oz jar bottled wild mushrooms in olive oil
25g/1oz/2 tbsp butter
225g/8oz/3 cups fresh wild mushrooms, sliced if large
5ml/1 tsp finely chopped fresh thyme
5ml/1 tsp finely chopped fresh marjoram or oregano, plus extra herbs to serve
4 garlic cloves, crushed
350g/12oz/3 cups fresh or dried fusilli
200ml/7fl oz/scant 1 cup panna da cucina or double (heavy) cream
salt and ground black pepper

1 Drain the oil from the bottled mushrooms, reserving about 15ml/1 tbsp in a medium pan. If large, slice or chop the bottled mushrooms into bitesize pieces.

2 Add the butter to the oil in the pan and place over a low heat until sizzling. Add the bottled and fresh mushrooms, chopped herbs and garlic, salt and pepper. Simmer over a medium heat, stirring frequently, for about 10 minutes or until the fresh mushrooms are soft and tender. Meanwhile, cook the pasta in salted boiling water, according to the instructions on the packet.

3 As soon as the mushrooms are cooked, increase the heat to high and toss the mixture with a wooden spoon to absorb any excess liquid. Pour in the cream and bring to the boil, stirring, then taste and add more salt and pepper if needed.

4 Drain the pasta and transfer it into a warmed bowl. Pour the sauce over the pasta and toss well. Serve immediately, sprinkled with extra fresh herb leaves.

Nutritional information per portion: Energy 656kcal/2741kJ; Protein 13g; Carbohydrate 66.1g, of which sugars 4g; Fat 39.5g, of which saturates 21g; Cholesterol 82mg; Calcium 53mg; Fibre 3.6g; Sodium 56mg.

Pink and green farfalle

In this modern recipe, pink prawns and green courgettes combine prettily with cream and pasta bows to make a substantial main course. Serve with chunks of warm ciabatta bread.

SERVES 4

50g/2oz/1/4 cup butter
2–3 spring onions (scallions), very thinly sliced diagonally
350g/12oz courgettes (zucchini), thinly sliced diagonally
60ml/4 tbsp dry white wine
300g/11oz/2 3/4 cups dried farfalle
75ml/5 tbsp crème fraîche
225g/8oz/1 1/3 cups peeled cooked prawns (shrimp), thawed and thoroughly dried if frozen
15ml/1 tbsp finely chopped fresh marjoram or flat leaf parsley, or a mixture
salt and ground black pepper

1 Melt the butter in a large pan, add the spring onions and cook gently, stirring often, for 5 minutes until softened. Add the courgettes, salt and ground black pepper, then stir-fry for 5 minutes. Pour over the wine and let it bubble, then cover and simmer for 10 minutes.

2 Cook the pasta in a pan of salted boiling water, according to the packet instructions. Add the crème fraîche to the courgette mixture and simmer for 10 minutes until well reduced.

3 Add the prawns, heat through gently, taste and season. Drain the pasta and transfer it into a warmed bowl. Add the sauce and chopped herbs and toss well. Serve immediately.

Nutritional information per portion: Energy 490kcal/2058kJ; Protein 21.1g; Carbohydrate 57.9g, of which sugars 4.7g; Fat 19.8g, of which saturates 11.9g; Cholesterol 158mg; Calcium 102mg; Fibre 3.1g; Sodium 191mg.

Penne with prawns and Pernod

This is a new and original Italian recipe, typical of those found on menus in the most innovative Italian restaurants. You could use white wine and basil, instead of the Pernod and dill, if you like.

SERVES 4

200ml/7fl oz/scant 1 cup panna da cucina or double (heavy) cream
250ml/8fl oz/1 cup fish stock
350g/12oz/3 cups dried penne
30–45ml/2–3 tbsp Pernod
225g/8oz/1 1/3 cups peeled cooked prawns (shrimp), thawed and thoroughly dried if frozen
30ml/2 tbsp chopped fresh dill, plus extra to garnish
salt and ground black pepper

1 Put the cream and the fish stock in a medium pan and bring to the boil. Lower the heat and simmer, stirring occasionally, for 10–15 minutes until reduced by about half.

2 Meanwhile, cook the dried pasta in a pan of salted boiling water, according to the instructions on the packet.

3 Add the Pernod and prawns to the cream sauce, with salt and pepper to taste. Heat the prawns through very gently.

4 Drain the pasta and transfer it into a warmed bowl. Pour the sauce over the pasta, add the dill and toss well. Serve immediately, sprinkled with chopped dill.

Nutritional information per portion: Energy 607kcal/2544kJ; Protein 21.2g; Carbohydrate 65.7g, of which sugars 3.7g; Fat 28.8g, of which saturates 16.9g; Cholesterol 178mg; Calcium 91mg; Fibre 2.6g; Sodium 121mg.

Tagliatelle with radicchio and cream

This is a fresh and elegant recipe that is very quick and easy to make. It is deliciously rich, and makes a good first course for a dinner party.

SERVES 4

225g/8oz dried tagliatelle
75–90g/3–3½oz pancetta or rindless streaky (fatty) bacon, diced
25g/1oz/2 tbsp butter
1 onion, finely chopped
1 garlic clove, crushed
1 head of radicchio, about 115–175g/4–6oz, finely shredded
150ml/¼ pint/⅔ cup panna da cucina or double (heavy) cream
50g/2oz/⅔ cup freshly grated Parmesan cheese
salt and ground black pepper

1 Cook the pasta in a large pan of salted boiling water according to the instructions on the packet.

2 Meanwhile, put the pancetta or bacon in a medium pan and heat gently until the fat runs. Increase the heat slightly and stir-fry the pancetta or bacon for 5 minutes.

3 Add the butter, onion and garlic to the pan and stir-fry for 5 minutes more. Add the radicchio and toss for 1–2 minutes until wilted.

4 Pour in the cream and add the grated Parmesan, with salt and pepper to taste. Stir for 1–2 minutes until the cream is bubbling and the ingredients are evenly mixed. Taste the sauce for seasoning.

5 Drain the pasta and transfer it into a warmed bowl. Pour the sauce over and toss well. Serve immediately.

Nutritional information per portion: Energy 543kcal/2264kJ; Protein 15.7g; Carbohydrate 44g, of which sugars 3.9g; Fat 35g, of which saturates 20g; Cholesterol 89mg; Calcium 197mg; Fibre 2.1g; Sodium 422mg.

Spaghetti with **eggs, bacon** and **cream**

Carbonara is an all-time favourite that needs no introducing. This version has plenty of pancetta or bacon and is not too creamy, but you can vary the amounts as you please.

SERVES 4

30ml/2 tbsp olive oil
1 small onion, finely chopped
8 pancetta or rindless smoked streaky (fatty) bacon rashers (strips), cut into 1cm/½in strips
350g/12oz fresh or dried spaghetti
4 eggs
60ml/4 tbsp crème fraîche
60ml/4 tbsp freshly grated Parmesan cheese, plus extra to serve
salt and ground black pepper

1 Heat the oil in a large pan or skillet, add the onion and cook gently, stirring often, for 5 minutes until softened but not coloured. Add the strips of pancetta or bacon to the onion in the pan and cook for about 10 minutes, stirring almost constantly. Meanwhile, cook the pasta in a pan of salted boiling water, according to the instructions on the packet until *al dente*.

2 Put the eggs, crème fraîche and grated Parmesan in a bowl. Grind in plenty of pepper, then beat everything together well.

3 Drain the pasta, transfer it into the pan with the pancetta or bacon and toss well to mix. Turn the heat off under the pan. Immediately add the egg mixture and toss vigorously so that it cooks lightly and coats the pasta.

4 Quickly taste for seasoning, then divide among four warmed bowls and sprinkle with black pepper. Serve immediately, with extra grated Parmesan handed around separately.

Nutritional information per portion: Energy 708kcal/2966kJ; Protein 30.7g; Carbohydrate 66.6g, of which sugars 4.2g; Fat 37.5g, of which saturates 15.5g; Cholesterol 261mg; Calcium 250mg; Fibre 2.8g; Sodium 824mg.

Linguine with **ham** and **mascarpone**

Mascarpone cheese masquerades as cream in this recipe. Its thick, unctuous consistency makes it perfect for sauces.

SERVES 6

25g/1oz/2 tbsp butter
150g/5oz/¾ cup mascarpone
90g/3½oz cooked ham, cut into thin strips
30ml/2 tbsp milk
45ml/3 tbsp freshly grated Parmesan cheese, plus extra to serve
500g/1¼lb fresh linguine
salt and ground black pepper

1 Melt the butter in a medium pan, add the mascarpone, ham and milk and stir well over a low heat until the mascarpone has melted. Add 15ml/1 tbsp of the grated Parmesan and plenty of pepper and stir well.

2 Cook the pasta in a large pan of salted boiling water for 2–3 minutes until *al dente*.

3 Drain the cooked pasta well and transfer it into a warmed bowl. Pour the sauce over the pasta, add the remaining Parmesan and toss well.

4 Taste for seasoning and serve the pasta immediately, with more ground black pepper and extra grated Parmesan handed around separately.

Nutritional information per portion: Energy 413kcal/1745kJ; Protein 18.2g; Carbohydrate 62.9g, of which sugars 3.9g; Fat 11.6g, of which saturates 6.4g; Cholesterol 36mg; Calcium 119mg; Fibre 2.4g; Sodium 292mg.

Farfalle with **gorgonzola cream**

Sweet and simple, this sauce has a nutty tang from the blue cheese. It is also good with long pasta, such as spaghetti or trenette.

SERVES 4

350g/12oz/3 cups dried farfalle
175g/6oz Gorgonzola cheese, any rind removed, diced
150ml/¼ pint/⅔ cup panna da cucina or double (heavy) cream
pinch of sugar
10ml/2 tsp finely chopped fresh sage, plus fresh sage leaves (some whole, some shredded) to garnish
salt and ground black pepper

1 Cook the pasta in a large pan of salted boiling water according to the instructions on the packet until *al dente*.

2 Meanwhile, put the Gorgonzola and cream in a medium pan. Add the sugar and plenty of ground black pepper and heat gently, stirring frequently, until the cheese has melted. Remove the pan from the heat.

3 Drain the cooked pasta well and return it to the pan in which it was cooked. Pour in the sauce.

4 Add the chopped sage to the pasta and toss over a medium heat until the pasta is evenly coated. Taste for seasoning, then divide among four warmed bowls. Garnish with sage and serve immediately.

Nutritional information per portion: Energy 423kcal/1773kJ; Protein 13.4g; Carbohydrate 43.7g, of which sugars 2.4g; Fat 22.9g, of which saturates 14.1g; Cholesterol 56mg; Calcium 169mg; Fibre 1.7g; Sodium 363mg.

Pipe rigate with peas and ham

Prettily flecked with pink and green, this is a lovely dish for a spring or summer dinner party. Though prosciutto is quite expensive, it really does make the dish.

SERVES 4

25g/1oz/2 tbsp butter
15ml/1 tbsp olive oil
150–175g/5–6oz/1¼–1½ cups frozen peas, thawed
1 garlic clove, crushed
150ml/¼ pint/⅔ cup chicken stock, dry white wine or water
30ml/2 tbsp chopped fresh flat leaf parsley
175ml/6fl oz/¾ cup panna da cucina or double (heavyy) cream
115g/4oz prosciutto crudo, shredded
350g/12oz/3 cups dried pipe rigate
salt and ground black pepper
chopped fresh herbs, to garnish

1 Melt half the butter with the olive oil in a medium pan until foaming. Add the thawed frozen peas and the crushed garlic to the pan, followed by the chicken stock, wine or water.

2 Sprinkle in the chopped parsley and add salt and pepper to taste. Cook over a medium heat, stirring frequently, for 5–8 minutes or until most of the liquid has been absorbed.

3 Add about half the cream, increase the heat to high and let the cream bubble, stirring constantly, until it thickens and coats the peas.

4 Remove from the heat, stir in the prosciutto and taste for seasoning.

5 Cook the pasta in a pan of salted boiling water according to the packet instructions. Drain well.

6 Immediately melt the remaining butter with the cream in the pan in which the pasta was cooked. Add the pasta and toss over a medium heat until it is evenly coated. Pour in the sauce, toss lightly to mix with the pasta and heat through. Serve immediately, sprinkled with fresh herbs.

Nutritional information per portion: Energy 414kcal/1738kJ; Protein 19.4g; Carbohydrate 48.6g, of which sugars 4g; Fat 15.1g, of which saturates 8.6g; Cholesterol 44mg; Calcium 259mg; Fibre 3.4g; Sodium 413mg.

Spaghetti with **saffron**

A quick and easy dish that makes a delicious midweek supper. The ingredients are all staples that you are likely to have in the refrigerator, so this recipe is perfect for impromptu meals.

SERVES 4

350g/12oz dried spaghetti
a few saffron strands
30ml/2 tbsp water
150g/5oz cooked ham, cut into thin strips
200ml/7fl oz/scant 1 cup panna da cucina or double (heavy) cream
50g/2oz/$^2/_3$ cup freshly grated Parmesan cheese, plus extra to serve
2 egg yolks
salt and ground black pepper

1 Cook the pasta in a pan of salted boiling water according to the packet instructions.

2 Put the saffron in a pan, add the water and bring to the boil. Remove from the heat and leave standing.

3 Add the strips of ham to the pan with the saffron. Stir in the cream and Parmesan, and a little salt and pepper. Heat gently, stirring all the time.

4 When the cream starts to bubble around the edges, remove the sauce from the heat and add the egg yolks. Beat well to mix, then taste for seasoning.

5 Drain the pasta and transfer it into a warmed bowl. Immediately pour the sauce over the pasta and toss together well. Serve immediately, with extra grated Parmesan handed around separately.

Nutritional information per portion: Energy 675kcal/2825kJ; Protein 24.6g; Carbohydrate 66.1g, of which sugars 4.1g; Fat 36.5g, of which saturates 20.6g; Cholesterol 204mg; Calcium 211mg; Fibre 2.5g; Sodium 605mg.

Fish and shellfish

Seafood sauces, both tomato- and cream-based, are served along the Italian coastline, and on the islands of Sicily and Sardinia, but they're very popular inland too. Intense flavours are found in Sicilian recipes, such as Spaghetti with Anchovies and Olives and Spaghetti with Bottarga, while Penne with Cream and Smoked Salmon is mild and creamy, and Orecchiette with Anchovies and Broccoli is fresh and light.

Spaghetti with **clam sauce**

This is one of Italy's most famous pasta dishes, Spaghetti alle Vongole, *sometimes translated as 'white clam sauce' to distinguish it from that other classic, clams in tomato sauce. This is how clams with pasta are served in Venice.*

SERVES 4

1kg/2¼lb fresh clams
60ml/4 tbsp olive oil
45ml/3 tbsp chopped fresh flat leaf parsley
120ml/4fl oz/½ cup dry white wine
350g/12oz dried spaghetti
2 garlic cloves
salt and ground black pepper

1 Scrub the clams under cold running water, discarding any that are open or that do not close when tapped sharply against the work surface.

2 Heat half the oil in a large pan, add the clams and 15ml/1 tbsp of the parsley and cook over a high heat for a few seconds. Pour in the wine, then cover tightly. Cook for 5 minutes, shaking often, until the clams have opened. Meanwhile, cook the pasta in salted boiling water, according to the packet instructions.

3 Using a slotted spoon, transfer the clams to a bowl, discarding any that have failed to open. Strain the liquid and set it aside. Reserve eight clams in their shells for the garnish, then remove the rest from their shells.

4 Heat the remaining oil in the clean pan. Fry the whole garlic cloves over a medium heat until golden, crushing them with the back of a spoon. Remove the garlic with a slotted spoon and discard.

5 Add the shelled clams to the oil remaining in the pan, gradually add some of their reserved strained liquid, then add plenty of pepper. Cook for 1–2 minutes, gradually adding more liquid as the sauce reduces. Add the remaining parsley and cook for 1–2 minutes.

6 Drain the pasta, add it to the pan and toss well. Serve in individual dishes, scooping the shelled clams from the bottom of the pan and placing some of them on top of each serving. Garnish with the reserved clams in their shells and serve immediately.

Nutritional information per portion: Energy 519kcal/2187kJ; Protein 30.9g; Carbohydrate 67.7g, of which sugars 3.4g; Fat 13.5g, of which saturates 2g; Cholesterol 84mg; Calcium 142mg; Fibre 3.2g; Sodium 1508mg.

Tagliolini with clams and mussels

Served on white china, this makes a stunning first course for a dinner party. The sauce can be prepared a few hours ahead of time, then the pasta cooked and the dish assembled at the last minute.

SERVES 4

450g/1lb fresh mussels
450g/1lb fresh clams
60ml/4 tbsp olive oil
1 small onion, finely chopped
2 garlic cloves, finely chopped
1 large handful fresh flat leaf parsley
175ml/6fl oz/¾ cup dry white wine
250ml/8fl oz/1 cup fish stock
1 small fresh red chilli, seeded and chopped
350g/12oz squid ink tagliolini or tagliatelle
salt and ground black pepper

1 Scrub the mussels and clams under cold running water. Discard any that are open or damaged, or that do not close when tapped against the work surface.

2 Heat half the oil in a large pan, add the onion and cook gently for about 5 minutes until softened. Sprinkle in the garlic, half the parsley, and salt and pepper to taste. Add the mussels, clams and the wine. Cover and bring to the boil over a high heat. Cook for 5 minutes, shaking often, until the shellfish have opened.

3 Transfer the mussels and clams into a fine sieve (strainer) set over a bowl and drain. Discard the aromatics in the sieve, together with any unopened mussels or clams. Return the liquid to the clean pan and add the fish stock. Chop the remaining parsley finely and add it to the liquid with the chopped chilli. Bring to the boil, then lower the heat and simmer, stirring, for a few minutes until slightly reduced. Turn off the heat.

4 Remove and discard the top shells from about half the mussels and clams, shelling the rest completely. Put all the mussels and clams in the pan of liquid and seasonings, then cover the pan tightly and set aside. Cook the pasta according to the instructions on the packet. Drain well, then return to the clean pan; toss with the remaining olive oil. Put the pan of shellfish over a high heat and toss to quickly heat the shellfish through and combine with the liquid and seasonings.

5 Divide the pasta among four warmed plates, spoon the shellfish mixture over and around, then serve immediately, sprinkled with parsley.

Nutritional information per portion: Energy 498kcal/2102kJ; Protein 24.7g; Carbohydrate 66.3g, of which sugars 3.4g; Fat 13.7g, of which saturates 2g; Cholesterol 47mg; Calcium 149mg; Fibre 3g; Sodium 679mg.

Trenette with **shellfish**

Colourful and delicious, this typical Genoese dish is ideal for a dinner party. The sauce is quite thin, so serve it with crusty bread and spoons as well as forks.

SERVES 4

45ml/3 tbsp olive oil
1 small onion, finely chopped
1 garlic clove, crushed
½ fresh red chilli, seeded and chopped
200g/7oz can chopped Italian plum tomatoes
30ml/2 tbsp chopped fresh flat leaf parsley
400g/14oz fresh clams
400g/14oz fresh mussels
60ml/4 tbsp dry white wine
400g/14oz/3½ cups dried trenette
a few fresh basil leaves
90g/3½oz/⅔ cup peeled cooked prawns (shrimp), thawed and thoroughly dried if frozen
salt and ground black pepper
chopped fresh herbs, to garnish

1 Heat 30ml/2 tbsp of the oil in a skillet or medium pan. Add the onion, garlic and chilli and cook over a medium heat for 1–2 minutes, stirring constantly. Stir in the tomatoes, half the parsley and pepper to taste. Bring to the boil, lower the heat, cover and simmer for 15 minutes.

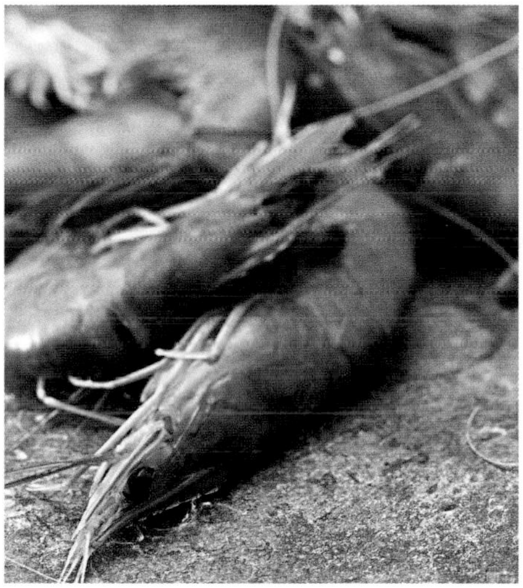

2 Scrub the clams and mussels under cold running water. Discard any that are open or that do not close when tapped. In a large pan, heat the remaining oil. Add the shellfish and the rest of the parsley. Toss over a high heat for a few seconds. Add the wine and cover tightly. Cook for 5 minutes, shaking often, until the clams and mussels have opened. Remove from the heat and transfer to a bowl, discarding any unopened shellfish.

3 Strain the cooking liquid into a measuring jug (cup) and set aside. Reserve eight clams and four mussels in their shells for the garnish, then remove the rest from their shells. Cook the pasta according to the instructions on the packet. Meanwhile, add 120ml/4fl oz/½ cup of the reserved shellfish liquid to the tomato sauce. Bring to the boil over a high heat, stirring. Lower the heat, tear in the basil leaves and add the prawns with the shelled clams and mussels. Stir well, then taste for seasoning.

4 Drain the pasta and transfer it into a warmed bowl. Add the sauce and toss well. Serve in individual bowls, sprinkle with herbs and garnish each portion with two reserved clams and one mussel.

Nutritional information per portion: Energy 524kcal/2218kJ; Protein 29.9g; Carbohydrate 78.1g, of which sugars 6g; Fat 11.4g, of which saturates 1.7g; Cholesterol 89mg; Calcium 163mg; Fibre 4g; Sodium 717mg.

Tagliatelle with **scallops**

Scallops and brandy make this a relatively expensive first course, but it is so delicious that you will find it well worth the cost.

SERVES 4

200g/7oz scallops, sliced
30ml/2 tbsp plain (all-purpose) flour
40g/1½oz/3 tbsp butter
2 spring onions (scallions), cut into thin rings
½–1 small fresh red chilli, seeded and very finely chopped
30ml/2 tbsp finely chopped fresh flat leaf parsley
60ml/4 tbsp brandy
105ml/7 tbsp fish stock
275g/10oz fresh spinach-flavoured tagliatelle
salt and ground black pepper

1 Toss the scallops in the flour, then shake off the excess.

2 Melt the butter in a skillet or large pan. Add the spring onions, finely chopped chilli and half the parsley and fry, stirring frequently, for 1–2 minutes over a medium heat. Add the scallops and toss over the heat for 1–2 minutes.

3 Pour the brandy over the scallops, then set it alight with a match. As soon as the flames die down, stir in the fish stock and salt and pepper to taste. Mix well. Simmer for 2–3 minutes, cover the pan and remove from the heat.

4 Cook the pasta in a pan of boiling water according to the instructions on the packet. Drain, add to the sauce and toss over a medium heat until mixed. Serve in warmed bowls sprinkled with the remaining parsley.

Nutritional information per portion: Energy 429kcal/1809kJ; Protein 20.7g; Carbohydrate 58.7g, of which sugars 2.6g; Fat 10.3g, of which saturates 5.6g; Cholesterol 45mg; Calcium 46mg; Fibre 2.3g; Sodium 153mg.

Spaghetti with **squid** and **peas**

In Tuscany, squid is often cooked with peas in a tomato sauce. This recipe is a variation on the theme, and it works very well.

SERVES 4

450g/1lb prepared squid
30ml/2 tbsp olive oil
1 small onion, finely chopped
400g/14oz can chopped Italian plum tomatoes
1 garlic clove, finely chopped
15ml/1 tbsp red wine vinegar
5ml/1 tsp sugar
10ml/2 tsp finely chopped fresh rosemary
115g/4oz/1 cup frozen peas
350g/12oz fresh or dried spaghetti
15ml/1 tbsp chopped fresh flat leaf parsley
salt and ground black pepper

1 Cut the prepared squid into strips about 5mm/¼in wide. Finely chop any tentacles.

2 Heat the oil in a skillet or medium pan, add the onion and cook, stirring, for about 5 minutes until softened. Add the squid, tomatoes, garlic, red wine vinegar and sugar.

3 Add the rosemary and season to taste. Bring to the boil, stirring, then cover and simmer gently for 20 minutes. Uncover the pan, add the peas and cook for 10 minutes.

4 Meanwhile, cook the pasta according to the instructions on the packet, then drain and transfer into a warmed bowl. Pour the sauce over, add the parsley, toss well and serve.

Nutritional information per portion: Energy 490kcal/2076kJ; Protein 30.7g; Carbohydrate 74.8g, of which sugars 8.5g; Fat 9.8g, of which saturates 1.6g; Cholesterol 253mg; Calcium 54mg; Fibre 5.1g; Sodium 136mg.

Penne with **prawns** and **artichokes**

This is a good dish to make in late spring or early summer, when greeny-purple baby artichokes appear in stores and on market stalls.

SERVES 4

juice of 1/2 lemon
4 baby globe artichokes
90ml/6 tbsp olive oil
2 garlic cloves, crushed
30ml/2 tbsp chopped fresh mint
30ml/2 tbsp chopped fresh flat leaf parsley
350g/12oz/3 cups dried penne
8–12 peeled cooked king or tiger prawns (jumbo shrimp), each cut into 2–3 pieces
25g/1oz/2 tbsp butter
salt and ground black pepper

1 Add the lemon juice to a bowl of water. Cut off the artichoke stalks and cut across the tops of the leaves, peeling and discarding any tough or discoloured outer leaves.

2 Cut the artichokes lengthways into quarters, removing any hairy chokes from the centres. Cut the pieces lengthways into 5mm/1/4in slices and put these in the bowl of water.

3 Drain the artichoke slices and pat dry. Heat the olive oil in a non-stick frying pan. Add the artichokes, garlic and half the mint and parsley.

4 Season generously and cook gently, stirring, for 10 minutes until tender.

5 Cook the pasta in a large pan of salted boiling water according to the packet instructions.

6 Add the prawns to the artichokes, stir well and heat through gently for 1–2 minutes.

7 Drain the pasta and transfer it into a warmed bowl. Add the butter and toss. Spoon the mixture over the pasta and toss well. Serve sprinkled with the remaining herbs.

Nutritional information per portion: Energy 519kcal/2181kJ; Protein 15.4g; Carbohydrate 65.5g, of which sugars 3.5g; Fat 23.6g, of which saturates 5.8g; Cholesterol 62mg; Calcium 78mg; Fibre 3.5g; Sodium 107mg.

Spaghetti with salmon and prawns

This is a lovely, fresh-tasting pasta dish, perfect for an* al fresco *meal in summer. Serve it as a main course lunch with warm ciabatta or focaccia bread and a dry white wine.

SERVES 4

300g/11oz salmon fillet
200ml/7fl oz/scant 1 cup dry white wine
a few fresh basil sprigs, plus extra basil leaves, to garnish
150ml/¼ pint/⅔ cup double (heavy) cream
6 ripe Italian plum tomatoes, peeled and finely chopped
350g/12oz/3 cups fresh or dried spaghetti
115g/4oz/⅔ cup peeled cooked prawns (shrimp), thawed and thoroughly dried if frozen
salt and ground black pepper

1 Put the salmon skin side up in a wide shallow pan. Pour the wine over, add the basil and sprinkle the fish with salt and pepper. Bring the wine to the boil, cover and simmer gently for no more than 5 minutes. Using a metal spatula, lift the fish out of the pan and set aside to cool a little.

2 Add the cream and tomatoes to the liquid remaining in the pan and bring to the boil. Stir well, lower the heat and simmer, uncovered, for 10–15 minutes.

3 Cook the pasta according to the instructions on the packet.

4 Flake the fish into large chunks, discarding the skin and any bones. Add the fish to the sauce with the prawns, tossing until the fish and shellfish are well coated. Taste the sauce for seasoning.

5 Drain the pasta and transfer it into a warmed bowl. Pour the sauce over and toss well. Serve, garnished with fresh basil leaves.

Nutritional information per portion: Energy 701kcal/2941kJ; Protein 32.4g; Carbohydrate 70.4g, of which sugars 8.5g; Fat 30.6g, of which saturates 14.3g; Cholesterol 145mg; Calcium 94mg; Fibre 4.1g; Sodium 115mg.

Paglia e fieno with **prawns** and **vodka**

The combination of prawns, vodka and pasta may seem unusual, but it has become something of a modern classic in Italy. Here, it is stylishly presented with two-coloured pasta.

SERVES 4

30ml/2 tbsp olive oil
1/4 large onion, finely chopped
1 garlic clove, crushed
15–30ml/1–2 tbsp sun-dried tomato paste
200ml/7fl oz/scant 1 cup panna da cucina or double (heavy) cream
350g/12oz fresh or dried paglia e fieno
12 raw tiger prawns (jumbo shrimp), peeled and chopped
30ml/2 tbsp vodka
salt and ground black pepper

1 Heat the oil in a medium pan, add the onion and garlic and cook gently, stirring, for 5 minutes until softened.

2 Add the tomato paste and stir for 1–2 minutes, then add the cream and bring to the boil, stirring. Season with salt and pepper to taste and let the sauce bubble until it starts to thicken slightly. Remove from the heat.

3 Cook the pasta according to the instructions on the packet. When it is almost ready, add the prawns and vodka to the sauce; toss quickly over a medium heat for 2–3 minutes until the prawns turn pink.

4 Drain the pasta and transfer it into a warmed bowl. Pour the sauce over and toss. Serve immediately.

Nutritional information per portion: Energy 650kcal/2722kJ; Protein 18.3g; Carbohydrate 67.4g, of which sugars 5.1g; Fat 34.2g, of which saturates 17.7g; Cholesterol 142mg; Calcium 81mg; Fibre 2.9g; Sodium 94mg.

Penne with **cream** and **smoked salmon**

This modern way of serving pasta is popular all over Italy. The three essential ingredients combine together beautifully, and the dish is very quick and easy to make.

SERVES 4

350g/12oz/3 cups dried penne
115g/4oz thinly sliced smoked salmon
2–3 fresh thyme sprigs
25g/1oz/2 tbsp butter
150ml/1/4 pint/2/3 cup extra-thick single (light) cream
salt and ground black pepper

1 Cook the pasta in a large pan of salted boiling water according to the instructions on the packet.

2 Meanwhile, using kitchen scissors, cut the smoked salmon into thin strips, about 5mm/1/4in wide. Strip the leaves from the thyme sprigs.

3 Melt the butter in a large pan. Stir in the cream with about a quarter of the salmon and thyme leaves, then season with pepper.

4 Heat gently for 3–4 minutes, stirring constantly. Do not allow to boil. Taste the sauce for seasoning.

5 Drain the pasta and toss it in the cream and salmon sauce. Divide among four warmed bowls and top with the remaining salmon and thyme leaves. Serve immediately.

Nutritional information per portion: Energy 459kcal/1936kJ; Protein 19.1g; Carbohydrate 65.7g, of which sugars 3.8g; Fat 15.2g, of which saturates 8.2g; Cholesterol 44mg; Calcium 62mg; Fibre 2.6g; Sodium 592mg.

Linguine with **crab**

This Roman recipe makes a very rich and tasty first course on its own, or can be served for a lunch or dinner with crusty Italian bread. Some cooks like a finer sauce, and strain the crab meat after pounding. If you fancy following their example, be warned – it's hard work.

SERVES 4

about 250g/9oz shelled crab meat
45ml/3 tbsp olive oil
1 small handful fresh flat leaf parsley, roughly chopped, plus extra to garnish
1 garlic clove, crushed
350g/12oz ripe Italian plum tomatoes, skinned and chopped
60–90ml/4–6 tbsp dry white wine
350g/12oz fresh or dried linguine
salt and ground black pepper

1 Pound the crab meat to a rough pulp with a mortar and pestle. Alternatively, use a sturdy bowl and the end of a rolling pin. Set aside.

2 Heat 30ml/2 tbsp of the oil in a large pan. Add the parsley and garlic, with salt and pepper, and fry for a few minutes until the garlic begins to brown. Add the tomatoes, crab meat and wine, cover the pan and simmer gently for 15 minutes, stirring occasionally.

3 Cook the pasta according to the instructions on the packet, draining it as soon as it is *al dente*, and reserving a little of the cooking water. Return the pasta to the clean pan, add the remaining oil and toss quickly over a medium heat until the pasta is well coated.

4 Add the tomato and crab mixture to the pasta and toss again, adding a little of the reserved cooking water, if needed. Adjust the seasoning to taste. Serve hot, in warmed bowls, sprinkled with parsley.

Nutritional information per portion: Energy 457kcal/1932kJ; Protein 22.8g; Carbohydrate 68g, of which sugars 6g; Fat 10.8g, of which saturates 1.5g; Cholesterol 45mg; Calcium 125mg; Fibre 3.9g; Sodium 359mg.

Capelli d'Angelo with lobster

This is a sophisticated, stylish dish, which is suitable for a special occasion. Some cooks make the sauce with champagne rather than sparkling white wine, especially when they are planning to serve champagne with the meal, for a truly indulgent treat.

SERVES 4

meat from the body, tail and claws of 1 cooked lobster
juice of ½ lemon
40g/1½oz/3 tbsp butter
4 fresh tarragon sprigs, leaves stripped and chopped
60ml/4 tbsp double (heavy) cream
90ml/6 tbsp sparkling dry white wine
60ml/4 tbsp fish stock
300g/11oz fresh capelli d'angelo
salt and ground black pepper
about 10ml/2 tsp lumpfish roe, to garnish (optional)

1 Cut the lobster meat into small pieces and place in a bowl. Sprinkle with the lemon juice.

2 Melt the butter in a skillet or large pan, add the lobster meat and tarragon and stir over the heat for a few seconds. Add the cream and stir for a few seconds more, then pour in the wine and stock, with salt and pepper to taste. Simmer for 2 minutes, then remove from the heat and cover.

3 Cook the pasta according to the instructions on the packet. Drain well, reserving a few spoonfuls of the cooking water.

4 Place the pan of lobster sauce over a medium to high heat, add the pasta and toss for just long enough to combine and heat through; moisten with a little of the reserved water from the pasta. Serve immediately in warmed bowls, sprinkled with lumpfish roe, if you like.

Nutritional information per portion: Energy 549kcal/2310kJ; Protein 37g; Carbohydrate 56g, of which sugars 2.9g; Fat 19.6g, of which saturates 10.6g; Cholesterol 179mg; Calcium 108mg; Fibre 2.2g; Sodium 480mg.

Orecchiette with anchovies and broccoli

This is a typical southern Italian or Sicilian dish. Anchovies, pine nuts, garlic and Pecorino cheese are all very popular ingredients. Serve with crusty Italian bread for a light lunch or dinner.

SERVES 4

300g/11oz/2 cups broccoli florets
40g/1½oz/½ cup pine nuts
350g/12oz/3 cups dried orecchiette
60ml/4 tbsp olive oil
1 small red onion, thinly sliced
50g/2oz jar anchovies in olive oil
1 garlic clove, crushed
50g/2oz/⅔ cup freshly grated Pecorino cheese
salt and ground black pepper

1 Break the broccoli florets into small sprigs and cut off the stalks. If the stalks are large, chop or slice them. Cook the florets and stalks in a pan of salted boiling water for 2 minutes, then drain and refresh under cold running water. Drain on kitchen paper.

2 Put the pine nuts in a dry non-stick frying pan and toss over a low to medium heat for 1–2 minutes or until the nuts are lightly toasted and golden. Remove and set aside.

3 Cook the pasta according to the instructions on the packet.

4 Heat the oil in a skillet, add the red onion and fry gently, stirring often, for 5 minutes until softened. Add the anchovies, with their oil, and garlic and fry over a medium heat, stirring often, for 1–2 minutes until it forms a paste. Add the broccoli and plenty of pepper and toss over the heat for a minute or two until the broccoli is hot. Taste for seasoning.

5 Drain the pasta and transfer it into a warmed bowl. Add the broccoli mixture and grated Pecorino and toss well to combine. Sprinkle the pine nuts over the top and serve.

Nutritional information per portion: Energy 578kcal/2425kJ; Protein 23.5g; Carbohydrate 67.8g, of which sugars 5.3g; Fat 25.5g, of which saturates 5.1g; Cholesterol 20mg; Calcium 256mg; Fibre 4.9g; Sodium 637mg.

Spaghetti with **tuna, mushrooms** and **bacon**

The Italian name for this dish,* Spaghetti alla Carrettiera, *means 'cart-driver's style'. The Romans lay claim to this recipe, but so do the Neapolitans and Sicilians, so there are many different versions of it.

SERVES 4

15g/1/2oz dried porcini mushrooms
175ml/6fl oz/3/4 cup warm water
30ml/2 tbsp olive oil
1 garlic clove
75g/3oz pancetta or rindless streaky (fatty) bacon, cut into 5mm/1/4in strips
225g/8oz/3 cups button (white) mushrooms, chopped
400g/14oz fresh or dried spaghetti
200g/7oz can tuna in olive oil, drained
salt and ground black pepper
freshly grated Parmesan cheese, to serve

1 In small a bowl, soak the porcini mushrooms in warm water for 15–20 minutes.

2 Heat the oil in a large pan, add the garlic clove and cook it gently for 2 minutes, crushing it with a wooden spoon. Remove the garlic and discard. Add the pancetta or bacon and cook for 3–4 minutes, stirring occasionally.

3 Drain the porcini mushrooms, reserving the liquid. Chop them finely. Add both types of mushroom to the pan and cook, stirring, for 1–2 minutes. Add 90ml/6 tbsp of the reserved liquid, with salt and pepper.

4 Simmer for 10 minutes, stirring often.

5 Cook the pasta according to the instructions on the packet, adding the remaining soaking liquid from the mushrooms to the cooking water.

6 Add the drained canned tuna to the mushroom sauce and fold it in gently. Taste for seasoning.

7 Drain the cooked pasta well and transfer into a warmed serving bowl. Pour the sauce over, toss and sprinkle liberally with freshly grated Parmesan. Serve immediately, with more Parmesan handed around separately.

Nutritional information per portion: Energy 545kcal/2301kJ; Protein 29.5g; Carbohydrate 74.3g, of which sugars 3.4g; Fat 16.5g, of which saturates 3.3g; Cholesterol 37mg; Calcium 36mg; Fibre 3.5g; Sodium 387mg

Spaghetti with anchovies and olives

The strong flavours of this dish are typical of traditional Sicilian cuisine.

SERVES 4

45ml/3 tbsp olive oil
1 large red (bell) pepper, seeded and finely chopped
1 small aubergine (eggplant), finely chopped
1 onion, finely chopped
8 ripe Italian plum tomatoes, peeled, seeded and finely chopped
2 garlic cloves, finely chopped
120ml/4fl oz/½ cup dry red or white wine
120ml/4fl oz/½ cup water
1 handful fresh herbs, such as basil, flat leaf parsley and rosemary
300g/11oz dried spaghetti
50g/2oz canned anchovies, roughly chopped, plus extra whole anchovies to garnish
12 pitted black olives
15–30ml/1–2 tbsp capers, to taste
salt and ground black pepper

1 Heat the oil in a pan and add all the vegetables and garlic. Cook gently, stirring, for 10–15 minutes until soft. Pour in the wine and water, add the fresh herbs and pepper to taste and bring to the boil. Lower the heat and simmer, stirring occasionally, for 10–15 minutes.

2 Meanwhile, cook the pasta in a large pan of salted boiling water according to the instructions on the packet.

3 Add the anchovies, olives and capers to the sauce, heat through for a few minutes and taste for seasoning. Drain the pasta and transfer it into a warmed bowl. Pour the sauce over the pasta, toss well and serve immediately.

Nutritional information per portion: Energy 754kcal/3162kJ; Protein 42.7g; Carbohydrate 65.5g, of which sugars 11.8g; Fat 35.4g, of which saturates 5.4g; Cholesterol 79mg; Calcium 419mg; Fibre 5.6g; Sodium 4933mg.

Spaghetti with tuna, anchovies and olives

This recipe from Capri is fresh, light and full of flavour. Serve immediately to enjoy it at its best.

SERVES 4

300g/11oz dried spaghetti
30ml/2 tbsp olive oil
6 ripe Italian plum tomatoes, chopped
5ml/1 tsp sugar
50g/2oz jar anchovies in olive oil, drained
about 60ml/4 tbsp dry white wine
200g/7oz can tuna in olive oil, drained
50g/2oz/½ cup pitted black olives, quartered lengthways
125g/4½oz packet mozzarella cheese, drained and diced
salt and ground black pepper
fresh basil leaves, to garnish

1 Cook the pasta in a large pan of salted boiling water, according to the instructions on the packet.

2 Meanwhile, heat the oil in a medium pan. Add the tomatoes, sugar and pepper to taste, and toss over a medium heat until the tomatoes soften and the juices run. Snip the anchovies into the pan with kitchen scissors.

3 Add the wine, tuna and olives and stir once or twice until they are just evenly mixed into the sauce. Add the mozzarella and heat through without stirring. Taste and add salt if necessary.

4 Drain the pasta and transfer into a warmed bowl. Pour the sauce over, toss gently, sprinkle with basil leaves and serve.

Nutritional information per portion: Energy 557kcal/2346kJ; Protein 32.7g; Carbohydrate 61.4g, of which sugars 8.3g; Fat 20.8g, of which saturates 6.6g; Cholesterol 51mg; Calcium 196mg; Fibre 4.1g; Sodium 1057mg.

Spaghetti with **bottarga**

Although this may seem an unusual recipe, with bottarga (salted and air-dried mullet or tuna roe) as the principal ingredient, it is very well known in Sardinia, Sicily and parts of southern Italy.

SERVES 4

350g/12oz fresh or dried spaghetti
60ml/4 tbsp olive oil
2–3 garlic cloves, peeled
ground black pepper
60–90ml/4–6 tbsp grated bottarga, to taste

1 Cook the pasta according to the instructions on the packet.

2 Meanwhile, heat half the olive oil in a large pan. Add the garlic and cook gently, stirring, for a few minutes. Remove the pan from the heat, scoop out the garlic with a slotted spoon and discard.

3 Drain the pasta. Return the pan of garlic-flavoured oil to the heat and add the pasta. Toss, season with pepper and moisten with the remaining oil.

4 Divide the pasta among warmed bowls, sprinkle the grated bottarga over the top and serve immediately.

Nutritional information per portion: Energy 419kcal/1769kJ; Protein 12.7g; Carbohydrate 66.1g, of which sugars 3g; Fat 13.4g, of which saturates 1.9g; Cholesterol 43mg; Calcium 25mg; Fibre 2.9g; Sodium 321mg.

Fregola with **fish**

This Sardinian speciality is a cross between a soup and a stew. For a filling dish, serve it with crusty Italian country bread to mop up the juices.

SERVES 4–6

75ml/5 tbsp olive oil
4 garlic cloves, finely chopped
1/2 small fresh red chilli, seeded and finely chopped
1 large handful fresh flat leaf parsley, roughly chopped
1 red snapper, about 450g/1lb, cleaned, with head and tail removed
1 red or grey mullet, about 500g/1 1/4 lb, cleaned, with head and tail removed
350–450g/12oz–1lb thick cod fillet
400g/14oz can chopped Italian plum tomatoes
175g/6oz/1 1/2 cups dried fregola
salt and ground black pepper

1 Heat 30ml/2 tbsp of the olive oil in a large flameproof casserole. Add the chopped garlic and chilli, with about half the chopped fresh parsley. Fry over a medium heat, stirring occasionally, for about 5 minutes.

2 Cut all of the fish into large chunks – including the skin and the bones in the case of the snapper and mullet – and add the pieces to the casserole as you cut them. Sprinkle the pieces with a further 30ml/2 tbsp of the olive oil and fry for a few minutes more.

3 Add the tomatoes, then fill the can with water and pour it into the pan. Bring to the boil, add salt and pepper, lower the heat and cook for 10 minutes, stirring occasionally.

4 Add the fregola and simmer for 5 minutes, then add 250ml/8fl oz/1 cup water and the remaining oil. Simmer for 15 minutes until the fregola is *al dente*.

5 If the sauce is too thick, add more water. Taste for seasoning. Serve hot, sprinkled with the remaining parsley.

Nutritional information per portion: Energy 300kcal/1256kJ; Protein 29.6g; Carbohydrate 17.3g, of which sugars 2.3g; Fat 12.9g, of which saturates 1.7g; Cholesterol 44mg; Calcium 79mg; Fibre 1.1g; Sodium 126mg.

Meat and poultry

Many meat sauces hail from northern Italy, especially the region of Emilia-Romagna. The egg-enriched pasta of the north holds meat sauces well, though for very rich sauces dried spaghetti or vermicelli may be a better option, as they hold less sauce with each forkful. Fresh meat and the famous hams, salami and sausages are enjoyed in abundance in northern Italy, chopped into small pieces and added to sauces.

Pappardelle with **rabbit sauce**

This rich-tasting dish comes from the north of Italy, where meats of all kinds are enjoyed in plenty and rabbit sauces for pasta are very popular.

SERVES 4

175ml/6fl oz/3/4 cup warm water
15g/1/2 oz dried porcini mushrooms
1 small onion
1/2 carrot
1/2 celery stick
2 bay leaves
25g/1oz/2 tbsp butter
15ml/1 tbsp olive oil
40g/11/2 oz pancetta or rindless streaky (fatty) bacon, chopped
15ml/1 tbsp roughly chopped fresh flat leaf parsley, plus extra to garnish
250g/9oz boneless rabbit meat
90ml/6 tbsp dry white wine
200g/7oz can chopped Italian plum tomatoes or 200ml/7fl oz/scant 1 cup passata (bottled strained tomatoes)
300g/11oz fresh or dried pappardelle
salt and ground black pepper

1 In a bowl, pour the warm water over the mushrooms and leave to soak for 15–20 minutes. Finely chop the vegetables. Make a tear in each bay leaf, so that they will release their flavour when added to the sauce. Heat the butter and oil in a skillet or medium pan until just sizzling. Add the vegetables, pancetta or bacon and the parsley and cook for about 5 minutes.

2 Add the pieces of rabbit and fry on both sides for 3–4 minutes. Pour the wine over and let it reduce for a few minutes, then add the tomatoes or passata. Drain the mushrooms and pour the soaking liquid into the pan. Chop the mushrooms, then add to the mixture, with the bay leaves and salt and pepper. Stir well, cover and simmer for 35–40 minutes until the rabbit is tender, stirring occasionally.

3 Remove from the heat and lift out the rabbit with a slotted spoon. Cut into bitesize chunks and stir into the sauce. Discard the bay leaves. Taste the sauce and season if needed. Cook the pasta in a pan of salted boiling water according to the packet instructions. Meanwhile, reheat the sauce. Drain the pasta and toss with the sauce in a warmed bowl. Serve immediately, sprinkled with parsley.

Nutritional information per portion: Energy 393kcal/1653kJ; Protein 23g; Carbohydrate 46g, of which sugars 4.9g; Fat 13.3g, of which saturates 5g; Cholesterol 46mg; Calcium 80mg; Fibre 1.1g; Sodium 128mg.

Farfalle with **chicken** and **cherry tomatoes**

Quick to prepare and easy to cook, this colourful dish is full of flavour. Serve it for a midweek meal, accompanied by a green salad.

SERVES 4

350g/12oz skinless chicken breast fillets, cut into bitesize pieces
60ml/4 tbsp Italian dry vermouth
10ml/2 tsp chopped fresh rosemary, plus 4 fresh rosemary sprigs, to garnish
15ml/1 tbsp olive oil
1 onion, finely chopped
90g/3½oz piece Italian salami, diced
275g/10oz/2½ cups dried farfalle
15ml/1 tbsp balsamic vinegar
400g/14oz can Italian cherry tomatoes
good pinch of crushed dried red chillies
salt and ground black pepper

1 Put the chicken pieces in a large bowl, pour in the dry vermouth and sprinkle with half the chopped rosemary and salt and pepper. Stir well and set aside.

2 Heat the oil in a large skillet or pan, add the onion and salami and fry over a medium heat for about 5 minutes, stirring frequently.

3 Cook the pasta in a large pan of salted boiling water according to the instructions on the packet.

4 Add the chicken and vermouth to the onion and salami, increase the heat to high and fry for 3 minutes or until the chicken is white on all sides. Sprinkle the vinegar over the chicken. Add the cherry tomatoes and dried chillies. Stir well and simmer for a few minutes more. Taste for seasoning.

5 Drain the pasta and transfer into the sauce. Add the remaining rosemary and toss well. Serve immediately, garnished with the rosemary sprigs.

Nutritional information per portion: Energy 490kcal/2067kJ; Protein 34.9g; Carbohydrate 55.8g, of which sugars 6.8g; Fat 14.1g, of which saturates 4.2g; Cholesterol 80mg; Calcium 36mg; Fibre 3.2g; Sodium 471mg.

Penne with **chicken, broccoli** and **cheese**

The combination of broccoli, garlic and Gorgonzola is very good, and goes especially well with chicken. You can also use leeks instead of broccoli, if you prefer.

SERVES 4

115g/4oz/scant 1 cup broccoli florets, divided into small sprigs
50g/2oz/¼ cup butter
2 skinless chicken breast fillets, cut into thin strips
2 garlic cloves, crushed
400g/14oz/3½ cups dried penne
120ml/4fl oz/½ cup dry white wine
200ml/7fl oz/scant 1 cup panna da cucina or double (heavy) cream
90g/3½oz Gorgonzola cheese, rind removed and diced small
salt and ground black pepper
freshly grated Parmesan cheese, to serve

1 Plunge the broccoli into a pan of boiling salted water. Bring back to the boil for 2 minutes, then drain in a colander and refresh under cold running water. Shake well to remove the water and set aside to drain completely.

2 Melt the butter in a large skillet or pan, add the chicken and garlic, with salt and pepper to taste, and stir well. Fry over a medium heat for 3 minutes or until the chicken turns white. Meanwhile, start cooking the pasta in a pan of salted boiling water according to the instructions on the packet.

3 Pour the wine and cream over the chicken mixture in the pan, stir to mix, then simmer, stirring occasionally, for about 5 minutes until the sauce has reduced and thickened. Add the broccoli, increase the heat and toss to heat it through and mix it with the chicken. Taste for seasoning.

4 Drain the pasta and transfer it into the sauce. Add the Gorgonzola and toss well. Serve immediately with grated Parmesan handed around seperately.

Nutritional information per portion: Energy 951kcal/3982kJ; Protein 47.8g; Carbohydrate 80.2g, of which sugars 8.6g; Fat 48.8g, of which saturates 28.5g; Cholesterol 165mg; Calcium 324mg; Fibre 10.2g; Sodium 433mg.

Pappardelle with **chicken** and **mushrooms**

Rich, creamy and filling, this is a good dinner party dish. If you prefer, you can use cremini mushrooms instead of porcini, which have a meaty texture and a pungent flavour.

SERVES 4

15g/½oz dried porcini mushrooms
175ml/6fl oz/¾ cup warm water
25g/1oz/2 tbsp butter
1 garlic clove, crushed
1 small handful fresh flat leaf parsley, roughly chopped
1 small leek or 4 spring onions (scallions), chopped
120ml/4fl oz/½ cup dry white wine
250ml/8fl oz/1 cup chicken stock
400g/14oz fresh or dried pappardelle
2 skinless chicken breast fillets, cut into thin strips
105ml/7 tbsp mascarpone cheese
salt and ground black pepper
fresh basil leaves, shredded, to garnish

1 Soak the dried mushrooms in the warm water in a bowl for 15–20 minutes. Place in a fine sieve (strainer) set over a bowl and squeeze the mushrooms to release as much liquid as possible. Chop finely and reserve the strained liquid.

2 Melt the butter in a medium skillet or pan, add the mushrooms, garlic, parsley and leek or spring onions, with seasoning to taste. Cook gently, stirring often, for 5 minutes, then pour in the wine and stock and bring to the boil. Lower the heat and simmer for 5 minutes or until the liquid has reduced and thickened.

3 Cook the pasta in a large pan of salted boiling water according to the packet instructions, adding the reserved liquid from the mushrooms.

4 Add the chicken strips to the sauce and simmer for 5 minutes or until just tender. Add the mascarpone a spoonful at a time, stirring well each time, and one or two spoonfuls of the water used to cook the pasta. Taste for seasoning.

5 Drain the pasta and transfer into a warmed large bowl. Add the sauce and toss. Serve immediately, topped with the shredded basil leaves.

Nutritional information per portion: Energy 921kcal/3881kJ; Protein 58.2g; Carbohydrate 133.1g, of which sugars 6.9g; Fat 16.9g, of which saturates 6.9g; Cholesterol 161mg; Calcium 206mg; Fibre 4.2g; Sodium 246mg.

Conchiglie with chicken livers and herbs

Fresh herbs and chicken livers are a good combination, often used together on crostini in Tuscany. Here they are tossed with pasta shells to make a very tasty main course dish.

SERVES 4

50g/2oz/$^1/_4$ cup butter
115g/4oz pancetta or rindless streaky (fatty) bacon, diced
250g/9oz frozen chicken livers, thawed, drained and diced
2 garlic cloves, crushed
10ml/2 tsp chopped fresh sage
300g/11oz/2$^3/_4$ cups dried conchiglie
150ml/$^1/_4$ pint/$^2/_3$ cup dry white wine
4 ripe Italian plum tomatoes, peeled and diced
15ml/1 tbsp chopped fresh flat leaf parsley
salt and ground black pepper

1 Melt half the butter in a medium skillet or pan, add the pancetta or bacon and fry over a medium heat for a few minutes until it is lightly coloured but not crisp.

2 Add the chicken livers, garlic, half the sage and plenty of pepper. Increase the heat and toss the livers for about 5 minutes, until they brown all over. Meanwhile, start cooking the pasta according to the instructions on the packet.

3 Pour the wine over the chicken livers in the pan and let it sizzle, then lower the heat and simmer gently for 5 minutes. Add the remaining butter to the pan. As soon as it has melted, add the diced tomatoes, toss to mix, then add the remaining sage and the parsley. Stir well. Taste and add salt if needed.

4 Drain the pasta and transfer it into a warmed bowl. Pour the sauce over and toss well. Serve immediately.

Nutritional information per portion: Energy 528kcal/2220kJ; Protein 25.4g; Carbohydrate 59g, of which sugars 5.9g; Fat 20.2g, of which saturates 9.6g; Cholesterol 283mg; Calcium 38mg; Fibre 3.2g; Sodium 498mg.

Fettuccine with **ham** and **peas**

This simple dish makes a good first course for six people, or a main course for three to four. The ingredients are easily available from the supermarket, so this makes an ideal impromptu meal.

SERVES 3–6

50g/2oz/1/4 cup butter
1 small onion, finely chopped
200g/7oz/1 3/4 cups fresh or frozen peas
100ml/3 1/2fl oz/scant 1/2 cup chicken stock
2.5ml/1/2 tsp sugar
175ml/6fl oz/3/4 cup dry white wine
350g/12oz fresh fettuccine
75g/3oz piece cooked ham, cut into bitesize chunks
115g/4oz/1 1/3 cups freshly grated Parmesan cheese
salt and ground black pepper

1 Melt the butter in a medium skillet or pan, add the onion and cook over a low heat for about 5 minutes until softened but not coloured. Add the peas, stock and sugar, with salt and pepper to taste.

2 Bring to the boil, then lower the heat and simmer for 3–5 minutes or until the peas are tender. Add the wine, increase the heat and boil until the wine has reduced.

3 Cook the pasta in a pan of salted boiling water according to the instructions on the packet. When it is almost ready, add the ham to the sauce, with about one third of the grated Parmesan. Heat through, stirring, then season to taste.

4 Drain the pasta and transfer it into a large warmed bowl. Pour the sauce over the pasta and toss well. Serve immediately, sprinkled with the remaining grated Parmesan.

Nutritional information per portion: Energy 463kcal/1945kJ; Protein 21.7g; Carbohydrate 54.4g, of which sugars 4.5g; Fat 16.9g, of which saturates 9.7g; Cholesterol 49mg; Calcium 290mg; Fibre 3.8g; Sodium 462mg.

Bucatini with **sausage** and **pancetta**

This is a very rich and satisfying main course dish. It hardly needs grated Parmesan cheese as an accompaniment, but you can hand some around in a separate bowl, if you wish.

SERVES 4

115g/4oz pork sausage meat (bulk sausage)
400g/14oz can Italian plum tomatoes
15ml/1 tbsp olive oil
1 garlic clove, crushed
115g/4oz pancetta or rindless streaky (fatty) bacon, roughly chopped
30ml/2 tbsp chopped fresh flat leaf parsley
400g/14oz dried bucatini
60–75ml/4–5 tbsp panna da cucina or double (heavy) cream
2 egg yolks
salt and ground black pepper

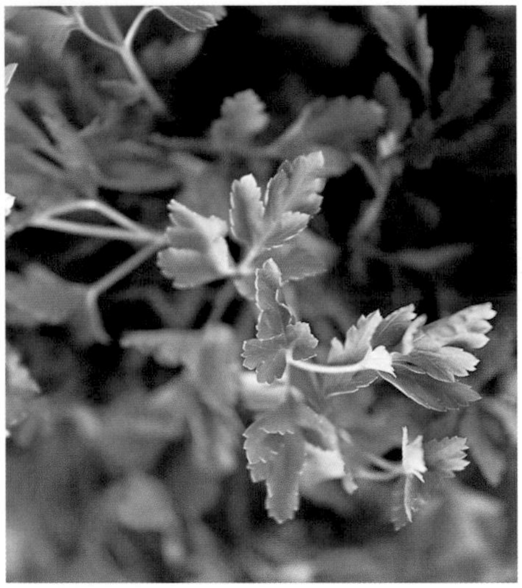

1 Remove any skin from the sausage meat and break the meat up roughly with a knife. Purée the tomatoes in a food processor or blender.

2 Heat the oil in a medium skillet or pan, add the garlic and fry over a low heat for 1–2 minutes. Remove the garlic with a slotted spoon and discard it.

3 Add the pork sausage meat and pancetta or bacon and cook over a medium heat for 3–4 minutes. Stir constantly with a wooden spoon to break up the sausage meat – it will turn brown and take on a crumbly consistency.

4 Add the puréed tomatoes to the pan with half the parsley and salt and pepper to taste. Stir well and bring to the boil, scraping up any sediment from the sausage meat that has stuck to the bottom of the pan.

5 Lower the heat, cover and simmer for 30 minutes, stirring occasionally. Taste for seasoning.

6 Meanwhile, cook the pasta according to the packet instructions. Put the cream and egg yolks in a large warmed bowl; mix with a fork. When the pasta is *al dente*, drain and add it to the cream mixture. Toss well, then pour the sausage meat sauce over and toss again. Serve sprinkled with the remaining parsley.

COOK'S TIPS

- ***To save time puréeing the tomatoes, use passata (bottled strained tomatoes).***
- ***For authenticity, buy* salsiccia a metro*, a pure pork sausage sold by the metre at Italian delicatessens.***

Nutritional information per portion: Energy 657kcal/2760kJ; Protein 22.4g; Carbohydrate 80.2g, of which sugars 7.5g; Fat 29.6g, of which saturates 11.5g; Cholesterol 157mg; Calcium 83mg; Fibre 4.2g; Sodium 629mg.

Rigatoni with pork

This excellent sauce uses minced pork rather than minced beef. Here, it is served with rigatoni, but you could serve it with tagliatelle or spaghetti to make a pork version of Bolognese.

SERVES 4

1 small onion
1/2 carrot
1/2 celery stick
2 garlic cloves
25g/1oz/2 tbsp butter
30ml/2 tbsp olive oil
150g/5oz minced (ground) pork
60ml/4 tbsp dry white wine
400g/14oz can chopped Italian plum tomatoes
a few fresh basil leaves, plus extra to garnish
400g/14oz/3 1/2 cups dried rigatoni
salt and ground black pepper
freshly shaved Parmesan cheese, to serve

1 Chop all the fresh vegetables and garlic finely. Heat the butter and oil in a large skillet or pan until just sizzling, add the chopped vegetables and garlic and cook over a medium heat, stirring frequently, for 3–4 minutes. Add the minced pork and cook gently for 2–3 minutes, breaking up any lumps in the meat with a wooden spoon.

2 Lower the heat and fry for a further 2–3 minutes, stirring frequently, then stir in the wine. Mix in the tomatoes, whole basil leaves, salt to taste and add plenty of pepper. Bring to the boil, then lower the heat, cover and simmer for 40 minutes, stirring from time to time.

3 Cook the pasta in a large pan of salted boiling water according to the instructions on the packet. Just before draining it, add a ladleful or two of the cooking water to the sauce. Stir well, then taste the sauce for seasoning.

4 Drain the pasta, add it to the pan of sauce and toss well. Serve immediately, sprinkled with the basil and shaved Parmesan.

Nutritional information per portion: Energy 537kcal/2265kJ; Protein 20.2g; Carbohydrate 79.6g, of which sugars 8.3g; Fat 16.5g, of which saturates 5.7g; Cholesterol 38mg; Calcium 46mg; Fibre 4.5g; Sodium 85mg.

Eliche with sausage and radicchio

Sausage and radicchio may seem odd companions, but the combined flavour of these ingredients is really delicious. This robust and hearty dish makes a good main course.

SERVES 4

30ml/2 tbsp olive oil
1 onion, finely chopped
200g/7oz Italian pure pork sausage
175ml/6fl oz/3/4 cup passata (bottled strained tomatoes)
90ml/6 tbsp dry white wine
300g/11oz/2 3/4 cups dried eliche
50g/2oz radicchio leaves
salt and ground black pepper

1 Heat the olive oil in a large, deep skillet or pan. Add the onion and cook over a low heat, stirring frequently, for about 5 minutes until softened.

2 Snip the end off the sausage skin, squeeze the sausage meat into the pan and stir to mix it with the oil and onion, breaking it up into small pieces. Continue to fry the mixture, increasing the heat if necessary, until the sausage meat has browned and looks crumbly. Stir in the passata, then sprinkle in the wine, with salt and pepper to taste. Simmer over a low heat, stirring occasionally, for 10–12 minutes.

3 Meanwhile, cook the pasta in a pan of salted boiling water according to the instructions on the packet. Before draining the pasta, add a ladleful or two of the cooking water to the sausage sauce and stir well. Season the sauce to taste.

4 Finely shred the radicchio leaves. Drain the cooked pasta and transfer it into the pan of sausage sauce. Add the shredded radicchio and toss well to combine everything together. Serve immediately.

Nutritional information per portion: Energy 518kcal/2174kJ; Protein 15g; Carbohydrate 63.2g, of which sugars 5.7g; Fat 23g, of which saturates 7.1g; Cholesterol 24mg; Calcium 53mg; Fibre 3g; Sodium 485mg.

Malloreddus with Sardinian sausage

In Sardinia they call this dish simply 'malloreddus', which is the local name for the type of pasta traditionally used to make it.

SERVES 4–6

30ml/2 tbsp olive oil
6 garlic cloves
200g/7oz Italian pure pork sausage, diced small
2 small handfuls fresh basil leaves
400g/14oz can chopped Italian plum tomatoes
a good pinch of saffron threads
15ml/1 tbsp sugar
350g/12oz/3 cups dried malloreddus (gnocchi sardi)
75g/3oz/1 cup freshly grated Pecorino Sardo cheese
salt and ground black pepper

1 Heat the oil in a medium skillet or pan. Add the garlic, sausage and half the basil leaves. Fry, stirring frequently, until the sausage is browned all over. Remove and discard the garlic. Add the tomatoes. Fill the empty can with water, pour it into the pan, then stir in the saffron, sugar, 5ml/1 tsp salt and pepper to taste. Bring to the boil, lower the heat and simmer for 20–30 minutes, stirring occasionally.

2 Meanwhile, cook the pasta in a pan of salted boiling water according to the packet instructions.

3 Drain the pasta and transfer it into a warmed bowl. Taste the sauce for seasoning, pour it over the pasta and toss well. Add about one-third of the grated Pecorino and the remaining basil and toss well to mix again. Serve immediately, with the remaining Pecorino sprinkled on top.

Nutritional information per portion: Energy 433kcal/1817kJ; Protein 15.9g; Carbohydrate 51.1g, of which sugars 7.1g; Fat 19.7g, of which saturates 7.3g; Cholesterol 28mg; Calcium 184mg; Fibre 2.5g; Sodium 398mg.

Rigatoni with bresàola and peppers

Bresàola – *cured raw beef – is usually served thinly sliced as an antipasto. Here its strong, almost gamey, flavour is used to good effect.*

SERVES 6

30ml/2 tbsp olive oil
1 small onion, finely chopped
150g/5oz bresàola, cut into thin strips
4 (bell) peppers (red and orange or yellow), diced
120ml/4fl oz/½ cup dry white wine
400g/14oz can chopped plum tomatoes
450g/1lb/4 cups dried rigatoni
50g/2oz/⅔ cup freshly shaved Parmesan cheese
1 small handful fresh basil leaves
salt and ground black pepper

1 Heat the oil in a medium pan, add the onion and bresàola, cover the pan and cook gently for 5–8 minutes until softened. Add the peppers, wine, 5ml/1 tsp salt and plenty of pepper. Stir well and simmer for 10–15 minutes.

2 Add the tomatoes and bring to the boil, stirring, then lower the heat. Replace the lid. Simmer for 20 minutes, stirring occasionally, until the peppers are soft.

3 Meanwhile, cook the pasta in a pan of salted boiling water according to the packet instructions.

4 Drain the pasta and transfer it into a warmed bowl. Taste the sauce for seasoning, then pour it over the pasta and add half the Parmesan. Toss well and serve, with the basil leaves and the remaining Parmesan sprinkled on top.

Nutritional information per portion: Energy 391kcal/1651kJ; Protein 17.7g; Carbohydrate 60.1g, of which sugars 12.3g; Fat 9.1g, of which saturates 2.8g; Cholesterol 23mg; Calcium 137mg; Fibre 4.6g; Sodium 405mg.

Spaghetti with **lamb** and **sweet pepper sauce**

This simple sauce is a speciality of the Abruzzo-Molise region, east of Rome, where it is traditionally served with **maccheroni alla chitarra** ***– square-shaped long macaroni.***

SERVES 4–6

60ml/4 tbsp olive oil
250g/9oz boneless lamb neck (US shoulder or breast) fillet, diced quite small
2 garlic cloves, finely chopped
2 bay leaves, torn
250ml/8fl oz/1 cup dry white wine
4 ripe Italian plum tomatoes, peeled and chopped
2 large red (bell) peppers, seeded and diced
400–450g/14oz–1lb dried spaghetti
salt and ground black pepper

1 Heat half the olive oil in a medium skillet or pan, add the small pieces of lamb and sprinkle with a little salt and pepper. Cook the meat over a medium to high heat for about 10 minutes, stirring often, until it is browned on all sides.

2 Sprinkle in the garlic and add the bay leaves, then pour in the wine and let it bubble until reduced.

3 Add the remaining oil, the tomatoes and the peppers; stir to mix with the lamb. Season again. Cover with the lid and simmer over a low heat for 45–55 minutes or until the lamb is very tender.

4 Meanwhile, cook the spaghetti in a large pan of salted boiling water, according to the instructions of the packet.

5 Stir the sauce occasionally during cooking and moisten with water if it becomes too dry. Remove the bay leaves before serving it with the pasta.

Nutritional information per portion: Energy 172kcal/717kJ; Protein 14g; Carbohydrate 6.1g, of which sugars 5.9g; Fat 7.3g, of which saturates 3g; Cholesterol 44mg; Calcium 51mg; Fibre 1.6g; Sodium 319mg.

Spaghetti with **minced beef sauce**

Spaghetti Bolognese was 'invented' by Italians in America in response to demand for a spaghetti dish with a meat sauce. The classic meat sauce – ragù – from Bologna is served with tagliatelle.

SERVES 4–6

30ml/2 tbsp olive oil
1 onion, finely chopped
1 garlic clove, crushed
5ml/1 tsp dried mixed herbs
1.25ml/1/4 tsp cayenne pepper
350–450g/12oz–1lb minced (ground) beef
400g/14oz can chopped plum tomatoes
45ml/3 tbsp tomato ketchup
15ml/1 tbsp sun-dried tomato paste
5ml/1 tsp Worcestershire sauce
5ml/1 tsp dried oregano
450ml/3/4 pint/13/4 cups beef or vegetable stock
45ml/3 tbsp red wine
400–450g/14oz–1lb dried spaghetti
salt and ground black pepper
freshly grated Parmesan cheese, to serve

1 Heat the oil in a medium pan, add the onion and garlic and cook gently, stirring often, for 5 minutes until softened. Stir in the mixed herbs and cayenne and cook for 2–3 minutes. Add the minced beef and cook gently for 5 minutes, stirring often, breaking up any lumps with a wooden spoon.

2 Stir in the canned tomatoes, ketchup, sun-dried tomato paste, Worcestershire sauce, oregano and plenty of black pepper. Pour in the stock and red wine and bring to the boil, stirring. Cover the pan, lower the heat and leave the sauce to simmer for 30 minutes, stirring occasionally.

3 Cook the pasta according to the instructions on the packet. Drain well and divide among warmed bowls. Taste the sauce and add a little salt if necessary, then spoon it on top of the pasta and sprinkle with a little grated Parmesan. Serve immediately, with grated Parmesan handed around separately.

Nutritional information per portion: Energy 396kcal/1682kJ; Protein 30.2g; Carbohydrate 62.3g, of which sugars 8.8g; Fat 2.8g, of which saturates 0.6g; Cholesterol 43mg; Calcium 43mg; Fibre 4.8g; Sodium 82mg.

Tortellini with ham

This is a very easy recipe that can be made quickly from store-cupboard ingredients.

SERVES 4

250g/9oz packet tortellini alla carne (meat-filled tortellini)
30ml/2 tbsp olive oil
1/4 large onion, finely chopped
115g/4oz cooked ham, diced
150ml/1/4 pint/2/3 cup strained crushed Italian plum tomatoes
100ml/3 1/2 fl oz/scant 1/2 cup panna da cucina or double (heavy) cream
about 90g/3 1/2 oz/generous 1 cup freshly grated Parmesan cheese
salt and ground black pepper

1 Cook the pasta in a large pan of salted boiling water according to the instructions on the packet.

2 Meanwhile, heat the oil in a large skillet or pan, add the onion and cook over a low heat, stirring frequently, for about 5 minutes until softened. Add the ham and cook, stirring occasionally, until it darkens.

3 Add the strained crushed tomatoes. Fill the empty carton with water and pour into the pan. Stir well. Season to taste.

4 Bring to the boil, lower the heat and simmer for a few minutes, stirring occasionally, until it has reduced slightly. Stir in the cream. Drain the pasta and add to the sauce.

5 Add a handful of grated Parmesan to the pan. Stir, toss well and taste for seasoning. Serve in warmed bowls, topped with the remaining Parmesan.

Nutritional information per portion: Energy 509kcal/2118kJ; Protein 19.9g; Carbohydrate 26.2g, of which sugars 4.1g; Fat 36.8g, of which saturates 17.5g; Cholesterol 85mg; Calcium 353mg; Fibre 1.9g; Sodium 696mg.

Pasta with beef sauce

This red wine Bolognese sauce should be served with tagliatelle for an authentic Italian dish.

SERVES 4–6

45ml/3 tbsp olive oil
1 onion, finely chopped
1 small carrot, finely chopped
1 celery stick, finely chopped
2 garlic cloves, finely chopped
400g/14oz minced (ground) beef
120ml/4fl oz/1/2 cup red wine
200ml/7fl oz/scant 1 cup passata (bottled strained tomatoes)
15ml/1 tbsp tomato purée (paste)
5ml/1 tsp dried oregano
15ml/1 tbsp chopped fresh flat leaf parsley
about 350ml/12fl oz/1 1/2 cups beef stock
8 baby Italian tomatoes (optional)
400–450g/14oz–1lb dried spaghetti, tagliatelle, penne or fusilli
salt and ground black pepper

1 Heat the oil in a large pan, add the chopped vegetables and cook gently, stirring often, for 5–7 minutes. Add the beef and cook for 5 minutes, stirring often, breaking up any lumps with a wooden spoon. Stir in the wine and mix well.

2 Cook for 1–2 minutes. Add the passata, tomato purée, herbs and 60ml/4 tbsp of the stock. Season to taste. Stir well and bring to the boil. Cover, and cook for 30 minutes, stirring occasionally. Add more stock as necessary. Add the tomatoes, if using, and simmer for 5–10 minutes more.

3 Meanwhile, cook the pasta in a large pan of salted water according the instructions on the packet, until *al dente*. Taste the sauce for seasoning and toss with the pasta.

Nutritional information per portion: Energy 228kcal/946kJ; Protein 13.8g; Carbohydrate 3.2g, of which sugars 2.9g; Fat 16.4g, of which saturates 5.4g; Cholesterol 40mg; Calcium 19mg; Fibre 0.8g; Sodium 144mg.

Tagliatelle with **meat sauce**

This recipe is an authentic meat sauce – ragù – from the city of Bologna in Emilia-Romagna. It is very rich, and is always served with tagliatelle. Spaghetti Bolognese is a different dish.

SERVES 6–8

25g/1oz/2 tbsp butter
15ml/1 tbsp olive oil
1 onion, finely chopped
2 carrots, finely chopped
2 celery sticks, finely chopped
2 garlic cloves, finely chopped
130g/4½oz pancetta or rindless streaky (fatty) bacon, diced
250g/9oz lean minced (ground) beef
250g/9oz lean minced (ground) pork
120ml/4fl oz/½ cup dry white wine
2 x 400g/14oz cans crushed plum tomatoes
475–750ml/16fl oz–1¼ pints/2–3 cups beef stock
100ml/3½fl oz/scant ½ cup panna da cucina or double (heavy) cream
350–450g/12oz–1lb fresh or dried tagliatelle
salt and ground black pepper
freshly grated Parmesan cheese, to serve

1 Heat the butter and oil in a large skillet or pan until sizzling. Add the vegetables and the pancetta or bacon and cook over a medium heat, stirring often, for 10 minutes until the vegetables are soft.

2 Add the minced beef and pork and cook gently for 10 minutes, stirring often, breaking up any lumps with a wooden spoon. Stir in salt, pepper and the wine and stir again. Simmer for 5 minutes, or until reduced.

3 Add the canned tomatoes and 250ml/8fl oz/1 cup of the beef stock and bring to the boil.

4 Stir the sauce well, then lower the heat. Half cover the pan with a lid and leave to simmer very gently for 2 hours, stirring occasionally. Add more stock as it becomes absorbed.

5 Pour the cream into the sauce, stir well, then simmer, without a lid, for another 30 minutes, stirring often.

6 Meanwhile, cook the pasta according to the packet instructions.

7 Taste the sauce for seasoning. Drain the pasta and transfer into a warm bowl. Pour the sauce over and toss. Serve sprinkled with grated Parmesan.

Nutritional information per portion: Energy 432kcal/1796kJ; Protein 24.9g; Carbohydrate 13.6g, of which sugars 5g; Fat 28.6g, of which saturates 10g; Cholesterol 79mg; Calcium 40mg; Fibre 1.5g; Sodium 229mg.

Spaghetti with **meatballs**

Meatballs simmered in a sweet and spicy tomato sauce are truly delicious with spaghetti. Children love them and you can easily leave out the chillies.

SERVES 6–8

350g/12oz minced (ground) beef
1 egg
60ml/4 tbsp roughly chopped fresh flat leaf parsley
2.5ml/½ tsp crushed dried red chillies
1 thick slice white bread, crusts removed, torn into small pieces
30ml/2 tbsp milk
about 30ml/2 tbsp olive oil
300ml/½ pint/1¼ cups passata (bottled strained tomatoes)
400ml/14fl oz/1¾ cups vegetable stock
5ml/1 tsp sugar
350–450g/12oz–1lb fresh or dried spaghetti
salt and ground black pepper
freshly grated Parmesan cheese, to serve

1 In a large bowl, mix the minced beef, egg, half the parsley, half the chillies and plenty of salt and pepper.

2 In a small bowl, soak the pieces of bread in milk for a few minutes. Squeeze out the excess and crumble the bread over the meat mixture. Mix everything together with a wooden spoon, then knead the mixture until smooth and sticky.

3 Wash your hands, rinse them under the cold tap, then roll small pieces of the mixture between your palms to make 40–60 small balls. Chill on a tray in the refrigerator for 30 minutes.

4 Heat the oil in a large non-stick frying pan. Cook the meatballs in batches until browned on all sides. Gently heat the passata and stock in a large pan, then add the remaining chillies, the sugar and salt and pepper. Add the meatballs to the mixture and bring to the boil. Lower the heat and cover. Simmer for 20 minutes.

5 Cook the pasta according to the packet instructions. When it is *al dente*, drain and transfer it into a warmed large bowl. Pour over the sauce, toss gently, sprinkle with the remaining parsley and serve with grated Parmesan handed around separately.

Nutritional information per portion: Energy 324kcal/1364kJ; Protein 17.1g; Carbohydrate 40.3g, of which sugars 7.7g; Fat 11.6g, of which saturates 3.8g; Cholesterol 50mg; Calcium 51mg; Fibre 2.7g; Sodium 156mg.

Vegetables and vegetarian

With pasta, the simpler a vegetable sauce, the better. Modern recipes are often little more than chopped or sliced raw vegetables, 'cooked' by the heat of freshly drained pasta, retaining colour, crunch, flavour and maximum nutritional value. The recipes in this chapter can mostly be cooked quickly, and some simply consist of butter and herbs, cheese and pepper or garlic and oil, and are the easiest of all to make.

Orecchiette with **rocket**

Serve this hearty dish from Puglia in the south-east of Italy as a main course with country bread. A farmhouse-style Italian loaf called* pugliese *would be most appropriate.

SERVES 4–6

45ml/3 tbsp olive oil
1 small onion, finely chopped
300g/11oz canned chopped Italian plum tomatoes or passata (bottled strained tomatoes)
2.5ml/½ tsp dried oregano
pinch of chilli powder or cayenne pepper
about 30ml/2 tbsp red or white wine (optional)
2 potatoes, total weight about 200g/7oz, diced
300g/11oz/2¾ cups dried orecchiette
2 garlic cloves, finely chopped
150g/5oz rocket (arugula) leaves, stalks removed, shredded
90g/3½oz/scant ½ cup ricotta cheese
salt and ground black pepper
freshly grated Pecorino cheese, to serve

1 Heat 15ml/1 tbsp of the olive oil in a medium pan, add half the onion and cook gently, stirring often, for 5 minutes until soft. Add the tomatoes or passata, oregano and chilli powder or cayenne pepper. Pour the wine over, if using, and add a little salt and pepper. Cover and simmer for 15 minutes, stirring occasionally.

2 Add the potatoes and pasta to a large pan of boiling salted water. Stir well and let the water return to the boil. Lower the heat and simmer for 15 minutes, or according to the packet instructions, until the pasta is cooked.

3 Heat the remaining oil in a large skillet or pan, add the remaining onion and the garlic and fry for 2–3 minutes, stirring occasionally. Add the rocket, toss over the heat for 2 minutes until wilted. Stir in the tomato sauce and ricotta. Mix well.

4 Drain the pasta and potatoes, add both to the pan of sauce and toss to mix. Taste for seasoning and serve immediately in warmed bowls, with grated Pecorino handed around separately.

Nutritional information per portion: Energy 584kcal/2451kJ; Protein 18.9g; Carbohydrate 65.4g, of which sugars 3.5g; Fat 29.2g, of which saturates 7.1g; Cholesterol 19mg; Calcium 311mg; Fibre 3.3g; Sodium 260mg.

Trenette with **pesto, green beans** and **potatoes**

In Liguria, pesto is served with trenette, green beans and diced potatoes. The ingredients for fresh pesto are quite expensive, so the green beans and potatoes help it go further.

SERVES 4

about 40 fresh basil leaves
2 garlic cloves, thinly sliced
25ml/1½ tbsp pine nuts
45ml/3 tbsp freshly grated Parmesan cheese, plus extra to serve
30ml/2 tbsp freshly grated Pecorino cheese, plus extra to serve
60ml/4 tbsp extra virgin olive oil
2 potatoes, total weight about 250g/9oz
100g/3½oz green beans
350g/12oz dried trenette
salt and ground black pepper

1 Process the basil leaves, garlic, pine nuts and cheeses in a blender or food processor for 5 seconds. Add half the olive oil and a pinch of salt and process for 5 seconds more. Stop the machine, remove the lid and scrape down the side of the bowl. Add the remaining oil and process for 5–10 seconds.

2 Cut the potatoes in half lengthways. Slice each half crossways into 5mm/¼in thick slices. Top and tail the beans, then cut them into 2cm/¾in pieces. Plunge the potatoes and beans into a large pan of salted boiling water and boil, uncovered, for 5 minutes.

3 Add the pasta, bring the water back to the boil, stir well, then cook for 5–7 minutes or until the pasta is *al dente*. Put the pesto in a large bowl and add 45–60ml/3–4 tbsp of the water used for cooking the pasta. Mix well.

4 Drain the pasta and vegetables, add them to the pesto and toss. Serve on warmed plates, with extra Parmesan and Pecorino handed around separately.

Nutritional information per portion: Energy 579kcal/2436kJ; Protein 20.6g; Carbohydrate 76.2g, of which sugars 4.8g; Fat 23.4g, of which saturates 6g; Cholesterol 19mg; Calcium 280mg; Fibre 4.3g; Sodium 217mg.

Penne with artichokes

Artichokes have been a very popular vegetable in Italy since their introduction into Naples around the ninth century and are often used in sauces for pasta. This sauce is garlicky and richly flavoured, the perfect first course for a dinner party during the globe artichoke season.

SERVES 6

juice of 1/2–1 lemon
2 globe artichokes
30ml/2 tbsp olive oil
1 small fennel bulb, thinly sliced, with feathery tops reserved
1 onion, finely chopped
4 garlic cloves, finely chopped
1 handful fresh flat leaf parsley, roughly chopped
400g/14oz can chopped Italian plum tomatoes
150ml/1/4 pint/2/3 cup dry white wine
350g/12oz/3 cups dried penne
10ml/2 tsp capers, chopped
salt and ground black pepper
freshly grated Parmesan cheese, to serve

1 Have ready a bowl of cold water to which you have already added the juice of half of one lemon. Cut off the artichoke stalks, then discard the outer leaves until only the pale inner leaves that are almost white at the base remain.

2 Cut off the tops of these pale inner leaves so that only the base remains. Cut the base in half lengthways, then prise the hairy choke out of the centre with the tip of the knife and discard. Cut the artichokes lengthways into 5mm/1/4 in slices, adding them immediately to the bowl of acidulated water.

3 Bring a large pan of water to the boil. Add a good pinch of salt, then drain the artichokes and add them immediately to the water. Boil for 5 minutes, drain and set aside.

4 Heat the oil in a large skillet or pan and add the sliced fennel, finely chopped onion and garlic and the roughly chopped parsley. Cook over a low to medium heat, stirring frequently, for about 10 minutes until the fennel has softened and is lightly coloured.

5 Add the tomatoes and wine, with salt and pepper to taste. Bring to the boil, stirring, then lower the heat, cover the pan and simmer for 10–15 minutes. Stir in the artichokes, replace the lid and simmer for 10 minutes more. Meanwhile, cook the pasta in salted boiling water, according to the instructions on the packet.

6 Drain the pasta, reserving a little of the cooking water. Stir the capers into the sauce, then taste for seasoning and add the remaining lemon juice if you like.

7 Transfer the pasta into a warmed large bowl, pour the sauce over and toss well to mix, adding a little of the reserved cooking water if you like a thinner sauce. Serve immediately, garnished with the reserved fennel fronds. Hand around a bowl of grated Parmesan separately.

Nutritional information per portion: Energy 268kcal/1133kJ; Protein 7.9g; Carbohydrate 46.7g, of which sugars 5.2g; Fat 5g, of which saturates 0.7g; Cholesterol 0mg; Calcium 38mg; Fibre 3.2g; Sodium 22mg.

Conchiglie with **roasted vegetables**

Nothing could be simpler – or more delicious – than tossing freshly cooked pasta with roasted vegetables. The flavour is simply superb.

SERVES 4–6

1 red (bell) pepper, seeded
1 yellow or orange (bell) pepper, seeded
1 small aubergine (eggplant), roughly diced
2 courgettes (zucchini), roughly diced
75ml/5 tbsp extra virgin olive oil
15ml/1 tbsp chopped flat leaf parsley
5ml/1 tsp dried oregano or marjoram
250g/9oz baby Italian plum tomatoes
2 garlic cloves, roughly chopped
350–400g/12–14oz/3–3½ cups dried conchiglie
salt and ground black pepper
4–6 fresh marjoram or oregano flowers, to garnish

1 Preheat the oven to 190°C/375°F/ Gas 5. Cut the peppers into 4cm/ 1½in squares. Rinse the aubergine and courgettes in a colander under cold running water, drain, then transfer into a large roasting pan.

2 Pour 45ml/3 tbsp of the olive oil over the vegetables and sprinkle with the fresh and dried herbs. Season to taste and stir well. Roast for about 30 minutes, stirring occasionally.

3 Hull the tomatoes and halve them lengthways. Add the tomatoes and garlic to the roasting pan and roast for 20 minutes more, stirring occasionally.

4 Meanwhile, cook the pasta according to the packet instructions.

5 Drain the pasta and transfer into a warm bowl. Add the vegetables and the remaining oil and toss well. Serve sprinkled with a few herb flowers.

Nutritional information per portion: Energy 277kcal/1171kJ; Protein 9.5g; Carbohydrate 50.3g, of which sugars 8.7g; Fat 5.5g, of which saturates 0.8g; Cholesterol 0mg; Calcium 52mg; Fibre 4.6g; Sodium 11mg.

Rigatoni with **wild mushrooms**

This is a good sauce to make from store-cupboard ingredients because it doesn't rely on anything fresh, apart from the herbs.

SERVES 4–6

30g/1oz dried porcini mushrooms
175ml/6fl oz/$^{3}/_{4}$ cup warm water
30ml/2 tbsp olive oil
2 shallots, finely chopped
2 garlic cloves, crushed
a few sprigs of fresh marjoram, leaves stripped and finely chopped, plus extra to garnish
1 handful fresh flat leaf parsley, chopped
25g/1oz/2 tbsp butter, diced
400g/14oz can chopped Italian plum tomatoes
400g/14oz/3$^{1}/_{2}$ cups dried rigatoni
25g/1oz/$^{1}/_{3}$ cup freshly grated Parmesan cheese, plus extra to serve
salt and ground black pepper

1 Put the dried mushrooms in a bowl, pour the warm water over and soak for 15–20 minutes. Pour into a fine sieve (strainer) set over a bowl and squeeze the mushrooms to release as much liquid as possible. Reserve the mushrooms and the strained liquid.

2 Heat the oil in a medium skillet and fry the shallots, garlic and herbs over a low heat, stirring frequently, for about 5 minutes. Add the mushrooms and butter and stir until the butter has melted. Season well with salt and pepper.

3 Stir in the tomatoes and the reserved liquid from the mushrooms. Bring to the boil, cover, lower the heat and simmer for 20 minutes, stirring occasionally. Meanwhile, cook the pasta according to the packet instructions.

4 Taste the sauce for seasoning. Drain the pasta, reserving some water, and transfer it into a warmed large bowl. Add the sauce and grated Parmesan. Toss to mix. Add a little cooking water if you prefer a thinner sauce. Serve garnished with marjoram and more Parmesan handed around separately.

Nutritional information per portion: Energy 438kcal/1857kJ; Protein 15.7g; Carbohydrate 78.8g, of which sugars 7.6g; Fat 8.9g, of which saturates 3.8g; Cholesterol 14mg; Calcium 137mg; Fibre 4.7g; Sodium 108mg.

Tagliolini with sun-dried tomatoes and radicchio

This is a light, modern pasta dish often served in fashionable restaurants. It is the presentation that sets it apart, not the preparation, which is very quick and easy.

SERVES 4

45ml/3 tbsp pine nuts
175g/6oz dried egg tagliolini
175g/6oz dried spinach tagliolini
45ml/3 tbsp extra virgin olive oil
30ml/2 tbsp sun-dried tomato paste
2 pieces sun-dried tomatoes in olive oil, drained and very finely sliced
2 pieces sun-dried tomatoes in olive oil, drained and very finely sliced
40g/1½oz radicchio leaves, finely shredded
4–6 spring onions (scallions), thinly sliced into rings
salt and ground black pepper

1 Put the pine nuts in a non-stick frying pan and toss over a low to medium heat for 1–2 minutes or until they are lightly toasted and golden. Remove and set aside.

2 Cook the pasta according to the packet instructions, keeping the colours separate by using two pans.

3 While the pasta is cooking, heat 15ml/1 tbsp of the oil in a medium skillet or pan. Add the sun-dried tomato paste and the sun-dried tomatoes, then stir in two ladlefuls of the water used for cooking the pasta. Simmer until the sauce is slightly reduced, stirring constantly.

4 Mix in the shredded radicchio, then taste and season if necessary. Keep on a low heat. Drain the pasta, keeping the colours separate, and return to the pans in which they were cooked. Add about 15ml/1 tbsp oil to each pan and toss over a medium to high heat until the pasta is well coated.

5 Arrange a portion of green and white pasta in each of four warmed bowls, then spoon the sun-dried tomato and radicchio mixture in the centre. Sprinkle the spring onions and toasted pine nuts over the top and serve immediately. Before eating, each diner should toss the sauce ingredients with the pasta to mix well.

Nutritional information per portion: Energy 475kcal/1998kJ; Protein 12.6g; Carbohydrate 66.5g, of which sugars 4.5g; Fat 19.5g, of which saturates 2.2g; Cholesterol 0mg; Calcium 34mg; Fibre 3.3g; Sodium 6mg.

Pasta with **mushrooms**

Served with warm ciabatta, this makes an excellent vegetarian supper dish. Fresh wild mushrooms can be used instead of chestnut mushrooms but they are seasonal and often expensive.

SERVES 4

15g/1/2 oz dried porcini mushrooms
175ml/6fl oz/3/4 cup warm water
45ml/3 tbsp olive oil
2 garlic cloves, finely chopped
1 handful fresh flat leaf parsley, roughly chopped
2 large pieces drained sun-dried tomato in olive oil, sliced into thin strips
120ml/4fl oz/1/2 cup dry white wine
225g/8oz/2 cups chestnut mushrooms, thinly sliced
475ml/16fl oz/2 cups vegetable stock
450g/1lb/4 cups dried short pasta shapes, e.g. ruote, penne, fusilli or eliche
salt and ground black pepper
rocket (arugula) and/or fresh flat leaf parsley, to garnish

1 Put the dried porcini mushrooms in a bowl, pour the warm water over and leave to soak for 15–20 minutes. Pour into a fine sieve (strainer) set over a bowl and squeeze the porcini with your hands to release as much liquid as possible. Reserve the strained soaking liquid. Chop the porcini finely.

2 Heat the oil and cook the garlic, parsley, sun-dried tomato strips and porcini over a low heat, stirring often, for 5 minutes. Stir in the wine, simmer for a few minutes until reduced, then stir in the chestnut mushrooms. Pour in the stock and simmer, uncovered, for 15–20 minutes more until the liquid has reduced and the sauce is quite thick and rich.

3 Cook the pasta in a large pan of salted boiling water according to the instructions on the packet. Taste the mushroom sauce for seasoning. Drain the pasta, reserving a little of the cooking liquid, and transfer it into a large warmed bowl. Add the mushroom sauce and toss well, thinning the sauce if necessary with some of the pasta cooking water. Serve immediately, sprinkled liberally with chopped rocket and/or parsley.

Nutritional information per portion: Energy 420kcal/1787kJ; Protein 15.1g; Carbohydrate 84.9g, of which sugars 5.1g; Fat 2.6g, of which saturates 0.3g; Cholesterol 0mg; Calcium 61mg; Fibre 4.8g; Sodium 14mg.

Spaghettini with roasted garlic

Roasted garlic is sweet and milder than you would expect. Although you can buy it in supermarkets, it's best to roast it yourself, so that it melts into the olive oil and coats the pasta beautifully.

SERVES 4

1 whole head of garlic
400g/14oz fresh or dried spaghettini
120ml/4fl oz/½ cup extra virgin olive oil
salt and ground black pepper
coarsely shaved Parmesan cheese, to serve

1 Preheat the oven to 180°C/350°F/Gas 4. Place the garlic in an oiled roasting pan and roast it for 30 minutes.

2 Meanwhile, cook the pasta in a pan of salted boiling water, according to the instructions on the packet.

3 Leave the garlic to cool, then lay it on its side and slice off the top third. Hold the garlic over a bowl and dig out the flesh from each clove with the point of the knife. Pour in the oil and add plenty of black pepper. Mix well.

4 Drain the pasta and return it to the clean pan. Pour in the oil and garlic mixture and toss the pasta vigorously over a medium heat until thoroughly coated. Serve immediately, with shavings of Parmesan handed around separately.

VARIATION

For a fiery finish, sprinkle crushed, dried red chillies over when tossing the pasta and oil.

Nutritional information per portion: Energy 545kcal/2296kJ; Protein 14.5g; Carbohydrate 84.9g, of which sugars 4.1g; Fat 18.7g, of which saturates 2.6g; Cholesterol 0mg; Calcium 55mg; Fibre 4.2g; Sodium 8mg.

Spaghetti with **garlic** and **oil**

The Italian name for this dish is* Spaghetti Aglio e Olio*, but in Rome, they run the words together and pronounce this dish as 'spaghetti-ayo-e-oyo' or just 'ayo-e-oyo'. It is sometimes given its full name of* Spaghetti Aglio, Olio e Peperoncino *because chilli is always included to give the dish some bite.

SERVES 4

400g/14oz fresh or dried spaghetti
90ml/6 tbsp extra virgin olive oil
2–4 garlic cloves, crushed
1 dried red chilli
1 small handful fresh flat leaf parsley, roughly chopped
salt

1 Cook the pasta in a large pan of salted boiling water, according to the packet instructions.

2 Heat the oil very gently in a small frying pan or pan. Add the crushed garlic and whole dried chilli.

3 Stir over a low heat until the garlic begins to brown. Discard the chilli.

4 Drain the pasta and transfer into a large bowl warmed. Pour on the oil and garlic mixture, add the parsley and toss well. Serve immediately.

Nutritional information per portion: Energy 505kcal/2126kJ; Protein 12.8g; Carbohydrate 76.4g, of which sugars 3.5g; Fat 18.6g, of which saturates 2.6g; Cholesterol 0mg; Calcium 27mg; Fibre 3.3g; Sodium 3mg.

Spaghetti with aubergines

This famous dish, known as Spaghetti alla Bellini *in Italy, is named after the Sicilian composer. You may also come across it called* Spaghetti alla Norma, *after Bellini's opera.*

SERVES 4–6

60ml/4 tbsp olive oil
1 garlic clove, roughly chopped
450g/1lb ripe Italian plum tomatoes, peeled and chopped
vegetable oil for shallow frying
350g/12oz aubergines (eggplants), diced small
400g/14oz fresh or dried spaghetti
1 handful fresh basil leaves, shredded
115g/4oz ricotta salata cheese, coarsely grated
salt and ground black pepper

1 Heat the olive oil, add the garlic and cook over a low heat, stirring constantly, for 1–2 minutes. Stir in the tomatoes, then season to taste. Cover and simmer for 20 minutes.

2 Meanwhile, pour oil into a deep frying pan to a depth of about 1cm/½in. Heat the oil until hot but not smoking, then fry the aubergine cubes in batches for 4–5 minutes until tender and lightly browned. Remove the aubergine with a slotted spoon and drain on kitchen paper.

3 Cook the pasta in a large pan of salted water according to the instructions on the packet.

4 Meanwhile, stir the fried aubergines into the tomato sauce and warm through. Taste for seasoning.

5 Drain the pasta and transfer it into a warmed bowl. Add the sauce, with the shredded basil and a generous handful of ricotta salata. Toss well and serve immediately, with the remaining ricotta sprinkled on top.

Nutritional information per portion: Energy 399kcal/1680kJ; Protein 10.8g; Carbohydrate 53.6g, of which sugars 6.3g; Fat 17.3g, of which saturates 3.7g; Cholesterol 8mg; Calcium 28mg; Fibre 3.9g; Sodium 10mg.

Pasta with **spicy aubergine sauce**

This flavoursome vegetarian sauce goes well with any short pasta shape. It can also be layered with sheets of pasta and béchamel or cheese sauce to make a delicious vegetarian lasagne.

SERVES 4–6

30ml/2 tbsp olive oil
1 small fresh red chilli
2 garlic cloves
2 handfuls flat leaf parsley, chopped
450g/1lb aubergines (eggplants), roughly chopped
1 handful fresh basil leaves
200ml/7fl oz/scant 1 cup water
1 vegetable stock (bouillon) cube
8 ripe plum tomatoes, peeled
60ml/4 tbsp red wine
5ml/1 tsp sugar
1 sachet saffron powder
2.5ml/$^1/_2$ tsp ground paprika
400g/14oz/3$^1/_2$ cups dried lumaconi
salt and ground black pepper

1 Heat the oil in a large skillet or pan and add the whole chilli, whole garlic cloves and half the chopped parsley. Smash the garlic cloves with a wooden spoon to release their flavour, cover the pan and cook the mixture over a low to medium heat for 10 minutes, stirring occasionally.

2 Remove and discard the chilli. Add the aubergines, the rest of the parsley, all the basil, and half the water. Add the stock cube and stir until dissolved.

3 Cover and cook, stirring often, for 10 minutes. Finely chop the tomatoes and add to the pan with the wine, sugar, saffron and paprika. Season and add the remaining water. Cover and cook for 30–40 minutes, stirring often.

4 Meanwhile, cook the pasta in a pan of salted boiling water, according to the instructions on the packet.

5 Season the sauce to taste, and serve immediately with the pasta.

Nutritional information per portion: Energy 277kcal/1174kJ; Protein 8.8g; Carbohydrate 49.7g, of which sugars 8.3g; Fat 5.5g, of which saturates 0.8g; Cholesterol 0mg; Calcium 45mg; Fibre 4.7g; Sodium 18mg.

Elicoidali with **cheese** and **cream**

Mezzanotte means 'middle of the night', which is when this dish,* Elicoidali di Mezzanotte, *is eaten – after a night on the tiles. When you arrive home hungry, it's just the thing to sober you up.

SERVES 4

400g/14oz/3½ cups dried elicoidali
3 egg yolks
105ml/7 tbsp freshly grated Parmesan cheese
200g/7oz/scant 1 cup ricotta cheese
60ml/4 tbsp panna da cucina or double (heavy) cream
nutmeg
40g/1½oz/3 tbsp butter
salt and ground black pepper

1 Cook the pasta in a large pan of salted boiling water according to the instructions on the packet.

2 Meanwhile, mix the egg yolks, grated Parmesan and ricotta together in a bowl. Add the cream and mix with a fork.

3 Grate in nutmeg to taste, then season with plenty of black pepper and a little salt.

4 Drain the pasta thoroughly when cooked. Return the clean pan to the heat. Melt the butter, add the drained pasta and toss vigorously over a medium heat.

5 Turn off the heat under the pan and add the ricotta mixture. Stir well with a large spoon for 10–15 seconds until all the pasta is coated in sauce. Serve immediately, in warmed individual bowls.

Nutritional information per portion: Energy 670kcal/2816kJ; Protein 29.2g; Carbohydrate 75.7g, of which sugars 4.9g; Fat 30g, of which saturates 16.5g; Cholesterol 220mg; Calcium 359mg, Fibre 2.9g; Sodium 357mg.

Chitarra spaghetti with butter and herbs

For this recipe, use just one favourite herb or several – basil, flat leaf parsley, rosemary, thyme, marjoram or sage all work well.

SERVES 4

400g/14oz fresh or dried spaghetti alla chitarra
2 good handfuls mixed fresh herbs, plus extra herb leaves and flowers, to garnish
115g/4oz/½ cup butter
salt and ground black pepper
freshly grated Parmesan cheese, to serve

1 Cook the pasta in a large pan of salted water according to the instructions on the packet.

2 Chop the herbs roughly or finely, whichever you prefer.

3 When the pasta is almost *al dente*, melt the butter in a large skillet or pan. As soon as it sizzles, drain the pasta and add it to the pan, then sprinkle in the herbs and salt and pepper to taste.

4 Toss over a medium heat until the pasta is coated in the oil and herbs. Serve immediately in warmed bowls, sprinkled with extra herb leaves and flowers. Hand around freshly grated Parmesan separately.

Nutritional information per portion: Energy 565kcal/2371kJ; Protein 12.9g; Carbohydrate 75g, of which sugars 4.1g; Fat 25.8g, of which saturates 15.2g; Cholesterol 61mg; Calcium 80mg; Fibre 4.2g; Sodium 186mg.

Spaghetti with cheese and pepper

This is a Roman dish, always made with spaghetti. It is remarkably easy to cook, and tastes wonderful.

SERVES 4

400g/14oz fresh or dried spaghetti
115g/4oz/1⅓ cups freshly grated Pecorino (preferably Pecorino Romano) cheese
5ml/1 tsp coarsely ground black pepper
extra virgin olive oil, to taste
salt

1 Cook the pasta in a large pan of salted water according to the instructions on the packet.

2 As soon as the pasta is *al dente*, drain it, leaving it a little moister than usual, and transfer it into a large warmed bowl.

3 Add the cheese, pepper and salt to taste. Toss well to mix, then moisten with as much olive oil as you like. Serve immediately.

Nutritional information per portion: Energy 472kcal/1997kJ; Protein 23.3g; Carbohydrate 74.1g, of which sugars 3.3g; Fat 11.2g, of which saturates 6.1g; Cholesterol 29mg; Calcium 370mg; Fibre 2.9g; Sodium 316mg.

Black pasta with **ricotta**

This is designer pasta at its most dramatic. Serve it for a smart first course at a dinner party – it will be a great talking point.

SERVES 4

300g/11oz dried squid ink pasta
60ml/4 tbsp ricotta cheese, as fresh as possible
60ml/4 tbsp extra virgin olive oil
1 small fresh red chilli, seeded and finely chopped
1 small handful fresh basil leaves
salt and ground black pepper

1 Cook the pasta in a large pan of salted boiling water according to the instructions on the packet.

2 Meanwhile, put the ricotta in a bowl, season to taste and use a little of the hot water from the pasta pan to mix it to a smooth, creamy consistency. Taste for seasoning.

3 Drain the pasta. Heat the oil gently in the clean pan and add the pasta with the chilli and salt and pepper to taste. Toss quickly over a high heat to combine.

4 Divide the pasta among four warmed bowls, then top with the ricotta. Sprinkle with basil leaves and serve immediately. Let each diner toss their own portion of pasta and cheese.

COOK'S TIP

Black pasta is made with squid ink. If you prefer, use green spinach-flavoured pasta or red tomato-flavoured pasta.

Nutritional information per portion: Energy 387kcal/1631kJ; Protein 10.8g; Carbohydrate 56.5g, of which sugars 3.3g; Fat 14.7g, of which saturates 3.1g; Cholesterol 6mg; Calcium 49mg; Fibre 2.9g; Sodium 7mg.

Paglia e fieno with **walnuts** and **Gorgonzola**

Cheese and nuts are popular ingredients for pasta sauces. The combination is very rich, so reserve this dish for a dinner party first course.

SERVES 4

275g/10oz dried paglia e fieno
25g/1oz/2 tbsp butter
5ml/1 tsp finely chopped fresh sage or 2.5ml/½ tsp dried sage, plus fresh sage leaves, to garnish (optional)
115g/4oz torta di Gorgonzola cheese, diced
45ml/3 tbsp mascarpone cheese
75ml/5 tbsp milk
50g/2oz/½ cup walnut halves, ground
30ml/2 tbsp freshly grated Parmesan cheese
ground black pepper

1 Cook the pasta in a large pan of salted boiling water, according to the packet instructions. Melt the butter in a large skillet or pan over a low heat and stir in the sage. Sprinkle in the Gorgonzola and add the mascarpone. Stir with a wooden spoon until the cheeses start to melt. Pour in the milk and keep stirring.

2 Add the walnuts, Parmesan and plenty of black pepper. Continue to stir over a low heat to form a creamy sauce. Do not allow to boil or the nuts will taste bitter. Cook for only a few minutes or the nuts will discolour the sauce.

3 Drain the pasta, transfer it into a warmed bowl, then add the sauce and toss well. Serve immediately, with more black pepper ground on top. Garnish with sage leaves, if you wish.

Nutritional information per portion: Energy 529kcal/2216kJ; Protein 20.7g; Carbohydrate 52.6g, of which sugars 3.9g; Fat 27.7g, of which saturates 12.4g; Cholesterol 48mg; Calcium 283mg; Fibre 2.4g; Sodium 481mg.

Baked pasta

Lasagne, macaroni cheese and cannelloni have become so popular outside of Italy that we seldom consider their origins. A layered pasta was mentioned by a Roman gastronome in the first century AD, so lasagne, at least, has a very long history. Today baked pasta dishes, known as Pasta al Forno, *are eaten at large family meals as they can be prepared in advance and are easy to serve. This chapter includes classic dishes and modern favourites.*

Mushroom and courgette lasagne

This is the perfect main-course lasagne for vegetarians. Adding dried porcini to fresh chestnut mushrooms intensifies the flavour and gives the whole dish more substance. To round things off perfectly, serve with crusty Italian bread.

SERVES 6

15g/½oz dried porcini mushrooms
175ml/6fl oz/¾ cup warm water
30ml/2 tbsp olive oil
75g/3oz/6 tbsp butter
450g/1lb courgettes (zucchini), thinly sliced
1 onion, finely chopped
450g/1lb/6 cups chestnut mushrooms, thinly sliced
2 garlic cloves, crushed
1 quantity Winter tomato sauce (see page 29)
10ml/2 tsp chopped fresh marjoram or 5ml/1 tsp dried marjoram, plus extra fresh leaves, to garnish
6–8 dried lasagne sheets
50g/2oz/⅔ cup freshly grated Parmesan cheese
salt and ground black pepper

FOR THE WHITE SAUCE

40g/1½oz/3 tbsp butter
40g/1½oz/⅓ cup plain (all-purpose) flour
900ml/1½ pints/3¾ cups hot milk
nutmeg

1 Soak the porcini mushrooms in a bowl of warm water for 15–20 minutes. Pour into a fine sieve (strainer) set over a bowl and squeeze the mushrooms with your hands to release as much liquid as possible. Chop the mushrooms finely and set aside. Strain the soaking liquid through a fine sieve and reserve half for the sauce.

2 Preheat the oven to 190°C/375°F/Gas 5. Heat the olive oil in a large skillet or pan with 25g/1oz/2 tbsp of the butter.

3 Add half the courgette slices to the pan and season with salt and pepper. Cook over a medium heat, turning often, for 5–8 minutes until lightly coloured on both sides. Remove from the pan with a slotted spoon and allow to drain on kitchen paper. Repeat with the remaining courgettes.

4 Melt half the remaining butter in the fat remaining in the pan, then cook the finely chopped onion, stirring, for 1–2 minutes. Add half of the chestnut mushrooms and the crushed garlic to the pan and sprinkle with a little salt and pepper to taste.

5 Toss the mushrooms over a high heat for 5 minutes until they are juicy and tender. Transfer to a bowl with a slotted spoon, then repeat with the remaining butter and mushrooms.

6 Make the white sauce. Melt the butter in a large pan, add the flour and cook, stirring, over a medium heat for 1–2 minutes. Add the hot milk a little at a time, whisking well after each addition. Bring to the boil and cook, stirring, until the sauce is smooth and thick. Grate in fresh nutmeg to taste and season with a little salt and pepper. Whisk well, then remove the sauce from the heat.

7 In a food processor or blender, blend the tomato sauce and reserved porcini soaking liquid to a pureé. Add the courgettes to the bowl of fried mushrooms, then stir in the porcini and marjoram. Adjust the seasoning to taste, then spread a third of the tomato sauce in a baking dish. Add half the vegetable mixture, spreading it evenly.

8 Top with a third of the white sauce, then half the lasagne sheets. Repeat these layers, then top with the remaining tomato sauce and white sauce and sprinkle with the grated Parmesan cheese.

9 Bake the lasagne for 35–40 minutes, or until the pasta feels tender when pierced with a skewer. Allow to stand for about 10 minutes before serving. If you like, sprinkle each serving with marjoram leaves.

Nutritional information per portion: Energy 421kcal/1757kJ; Protein 15.5g; Carbohydrate 32.9g, of which sugars 15g; Fat 26.2g, of which saturates 12.4g; Cholesterol 49mg; Calcium 346mg; Fibre 3.8g; Sodium 310mg.

Stuffed shells

Perfect for a dinner party, these pasta shells, stuffed with a tasty spinach and ricotta filling, make an appetizer for six, or a main course for four, in which case you should fill 20 shells, rather than 18.

SERVES 4–6

18–20 large pasta shells for stuffing
25g/1oz/2 tbsp butter
1 small onion, finely chopped
275g/10oz fresh spinach leaves, washed, trimmed and shredded
1 garlic clove, crushed
1 sachet of saffron powder
nutmeg
250g/9oz/generous 1 cup ricotta cheese
1 egg
1 quantity Winter Tomato Sauce (see page 29)
about 150ml/¼ pint/⅔ cup dry white wine, vegetable stock or water
100ml/3½fl oz/scant ½ cup panna da cucina or double (heavy) cream
50g/2oz/⅔ cup freshly grated Parmesan cheese
salt and ground black pepper

1 Preheat the oven to 190°C/375°F/Gas 5. Bring a large pan of salted water to the boil. Add the pasta shells and cook for 10 minutes. Drain the shells, fill half the pan with cold water and place the shells in the water.

2 Melt the butter in a pan, add the onion and cook gently, stirring, for 5 minutes until softened. Add the spinach, garlic and saffron, grate in plenty of nutmeg and add salt and pepper. Stir well, increase the heat to medium and cook for 5–8 minutes, stirring often, until the spinach is wilted and tender.

3 Increase the heat to high and stir until the water is absorbed and the spinach is quite dry. Transfer the spinach into a bowl, add the ricotta and beat well to mix. Taste for seasoning, then add the egg and beat well again.

4 Purée the tomato sauce in a blender or food processor, pour it into a measuring jug (cup) and make it up to 750ml/1¼ pints/3 cups with the wine, stock or water. Add the cream, stir well and taste for seasoning.

5 Spread half the sauce over the bottom of six individual gratin dishes. Remove the pasta shells one at a time from the water, shake well and fill with the spinach and ricotta mixture, using a teaspoon. Arrange three shells in the centre of each dish, spoon over the remaining sauce, then cover with the grated Parmesan. Oven bake for 10–12 minutes or until hot. Leave to stand for about 5 minutes before serving.

Nutritional information per portion: Energy 358kcal/1505kJ; Protein 11.6g; Carbohydrate 43.3g, of which sugars 7.7g; Fat 16.7g, of which saturates 5.6g; Cholesterol 20mg; Calcium 56mg; Fibre 2.9g; Sodium 542mg.

Pasta pie

This is an excellent vegetarian dish, and children love it. All the ingredients will probably be in your store cupboard or refrigerator, so it's a good 'standby' meal.

SERVES 4

30ml/2 tbsp olive oil
1 small onion, finely chopped
400g/14oz can chopped Italian plum tomatoes
15ml/1 tbsp sun-dried tomato paste
5ml/1 tsp dried mixed herbs
5ml/1 tsp dried oregano or basil
5ml/1 tsp sugar
175g/6oz/1 1/2 cups dried conchiglie or rigatoni
30ml/2 tbsp freshly grated Parmesan cheese
30ml/2 tbsp dried breadcrumbs
salt and ground black pepper

FOR THE WHITE SAUCE
25g/1oz/2 tbsp butter
25g/1oz/1/4 cup plain (all-purpose) flour
600ml/1 pint/2 1/2 cups milk
1 egg

1 Heat the olive oil in a large skillet or pan and cook the onion over a gentle heat, stirring frequently, for 5 minutes until softened. Stir in the tomatoes. Fill the empty can with water and add it to the tomato mixture, with the tomato paste, herbs and sugar. Add salt and pepper to taste and bring to the boil, stirring. Cover the pan, lower the heat and simmer, stirring occasionally, for 10–15 minutes.

2 Preheat the oven to 190°C/375°F/Gas 5. Cook the pasta according to the packet instructions. Meanwhile, make the white sauce. Melt the butter in a pan, add the flour and cook, stirring, for 1 minute. Add the milk a little at a time, whisking well after each addition. Bring to the boil and cook, stirring, until smooth and thick. Season, then remove from the heat.

3 Drain the pasta and transfer it into a baking dish. Taste the tomato sauce and add salt and pepper. Pour the sauce into the dish and stir well to mix with the pasta.

4 Beat the egg into the white sauce, then pour the sauce over the pasta mixture. Separate the pasta with a fork so that the sauce fills any gaps. Level the surface, sprinkle it with grated Parmesan and breadcrumbs and bake for 15–20 minutes or until golden brown and bubbling. Allow to stand for 10 minutes before serving.

Nutritional information per portion: Energy 444kcal/1870kJ; Protein 17.4g; Carbohydrate 56g, of which sugars 14.3g; Fat 18.4g, of which saturates 7.8g; Cholesterol 77mg; Calcium 320mg; Fibre 3g; Sodium 279mg.

Cannelloni Sorrentina-style

For this fresh-tasting version of the Italian classic dish, sheets of cooked lasagne are rolled around a tomato filling to make a delicious main course for a summer dinner party. The filling ingredients are quite similar to those used on a Neapolitan pizza.

SERVES 4–6

60ml/4 tbsp olive oil
1 small onion, finely chopped
900g/2lb ripe Italian plum tomatoes, peeled and finely chopped
2 garlic cloves, crushed
1 large handful fresh basil leaves, shredded, plus extra whole basil leaves, to garnish
250ml/8fl oz/1 cup vegetable stock
250ml/8fl oz/1 cup dry white wine
30ml/2 tbsp sun-dried tomato paste
2.5ml/½ tsp sugar
16–18 fresh or dried lasagne sheets
250g/9oz/generous 1 cup ricotta cheese
130g/4½oz packet mozzarella cheese, drained and diced small
8 bottled anchovy fillets in olive oil, drained and halved lengthways
50g/2oz/⅔ cup freshly grated Parmesan cheese
salt and ground black pepper

1 Heat the oil in a medium pan, add the onion and cook gently, stirring frequently, for about 5 minutes until softened. Stir in the tomatoes, garlic and half the basil. Season with salt and pepper to taste and toss over a medium to high heat for 5 minutes.

2 Scoop about half the tomato mixture out of the pan, place in a bowl and set it aside to cool.

3 Stir the vegetable stock, white wine, tomato paste and sugar into the tomato mixture remaining in the pan and simmer for about 20 minutes, stirring occasionally.

4 Meanwhile, cook the lasagne sheets in batches in a pan of salted boiling water, according to the instructions on the packet. Drain and separate the sheets of lasagne and lay them out flat on a clean dish towel.

5 Preheat the oven to 190°C/375°F/Gas 5. Add the ricotta and mozzarella to the tomato mixture in the bowl. Stir in the remaining basil and season to taste with salt and pepper.

6 Spread a little of the mixture over each lasagne sheet. Place an anchovy fillet across the width of each sheet, close to one of the short ends. Starting from the end with the anchovy, roll each lasagne sheet up like a Swiss roll (jelly roll).

7 Purée the tomato sauce in a blender or food processor. Spread a little of the tomato sauce over the bottom of a large baking dish. Arrange the cannelloni seam side down in a single layer in the dish and spoon the remaining sauce over them.

8 Sprinkle the Parmesan over the top and bake for 20 minutes or until the topping is golden brown and bubbling. Serve hot, garnished with basil leaves.

Nutritional information per portion: Energy 476kcal/1995kJ; Protein 19.9g; Carbohydrate 45g, of which sugars 9.3g; Fat 22.4g, of which saturates 9.8g; Cholesterol 41mg; Calcium 238mg; Fibre 3.7g; Sodium 365mg.

Macaroni with **four cheeses**

Rich and creamy, this is a deluxe macaroni cheese that can be served for an informal lunch or dinner party. It goes well with either a tomato and basil salad or a leafy green salad.

SERVES 4

250g/9oz/2¼ cups short-cut macaroni
50g/2oz/¼ cup butter
50g/2oz/½ cup plain (all-purpose) flour
600ml/1 pint/2½ cups milk
100ml/3½ fl oz/scant ½ cup panna da cucina or double (heavy) cream
100ml/3½ fl oz/scant ½ cup dry white wine
50g/2oz/½ cup grated Gruyère or Emmenthal cheese
50g/2oz Fontina cheese, diced small
50g/2oz Gorgonzola cheese, crumbled
75g/3oz/1 cup freshly grated Parmesan cheese
salt and ground black pepper

1 Preheat the oven to 180°C/350°F/Gas 4. Cook the pasta in a large pan of salted boiling water according to the instructions on the packet.

2 Meanwhile, gently melt the butter in a medium pan, add the flour and cook, stirring, for 1–2 minutes. Add the milk a little at a time, whisking vigorously after each addition. Stir in the cream, followed by the dry white wine. Bring to the boil. Cook, stirring continuously, until the sauce thickens, then remove the sauce from the heat.

3 Add the Gruyère or Emmenthal, Fontina, Gorgonzola and about a third of the grated Parmesan to the sauce. Stir well to mix in the cheeses, then taste for seasoning and add salt and pepper if necessary.

4 Drain the pasta well and transfer it into a baking dish. Pour the sauce over the pasta and mix well, then sprinkle the remaining Parmesan over the top. Bake for 25–30 minutes or until golden brown. Serve hot.

Nutritional information per portion: Energy 523kcal/2202kJ; Protein 20.6g; Carbohydrate 69.7g, of which sugars 6.6g; Fat 19.3g, of which saturates 11.7g; Cholesterol 51mg; Calcium 349mg; Fibre 2.5g; Sodium 349mg.

Mixed meat cannelloni

A creamy, rich filling and sauce make this an unusual cannelloni. If you prefer, instead of pasta tubes, you could roll fresh lasagne sheets around the filling.

SERVES 4

1 onion
1 carrot
2 ripe plum tomatoes, peeled
60ml/4 tbsp olive oil
2 garlic cloves, crushed
130g/4½oz minced (ground) beef
130g/4½oz minced (ground) pork
250g/9oz minced (ground) chicken
30ml/2 tbsp brandy
25g/1oz/2 tbsp butter
90ml/6 tbsp panna da cucina or double (heavy) cream
50g/2oz/¼ cup butter
50g/2oz/½ cup plain (all-purpose) flour
900ml/1½ pints/3¾ cups milk
nutmeg
16 dried cannelloni tubes
75g/3oz/1 cup Parmesan cheese, grated
salt and ground black pepper
green salad, to serve

1 Finely chop the onion, carrot and tomatoes. Heat the oil in a medium skillet, add the onion, carrot, garlic and tomatoes and cook gently, stirring, for 10 minutes, until soft. Add the meats and cook gently for 10 minutes, stirring to break up any lumps. Add the brandy, increase the heat and stir until reduced. Add the butter and cream. Cook gently, stirring often, for 10 minutes. Allow to cool.

2 Heat the oven to 190°C/375°F/Gas 5. Make the white sauce. Melt the butter in a medium pan, add the flour and cook, stirring, for 1–2 minutes. Add the milk a little at a time, whisking vigorously after each addition. Bring to the boil and cook, stirring, until the sauce is smooth and thick. Grate in fresh nutmeg, season with salt and pepper and whisk well. Remove the pan from the heat.

3 Spoon a little of the white sauce into a baking dish. Fill the cannelloni tubes with the meat mixture and place in a single layer in the dish. Pour the remaining white sauce over them, then sprinkle with the Parmesan. Bake for 35–40 minutes or until the pasta feels tender when pierced with a skewer. Allow to stand for 10 minutes before serving with green salad.

Nutritional information per portion: Energy 1025kcal/4284kJ; Protein 52.5g; Carbohydrate 71.3g, of which sugars 17.1g; Fat 59.1g, of which saturates 28.9g; Cholesterol 188mg; Calcium 563mg; Fibre 3.4g; Sodium 517mg.

Sicilian lasagne

Lasagne is not traditional in Sicily as it is in northern Italy, but the Sicilians have their own version. Though some think it a bit complicated, it really takes just a little patience.

SERVES 6

1 small onion
1/2 carrot
1/2 celery stick
45ml/3 tbsp olive oil
250g/9oz boneless pork, diced
60ml/4 tbsp dry white wine
400g/14oz can chopped Italian plum tomatoes or 400ml/14fl oz/1 2/3 cups passata (bottled strained tomatoes)
200ml/7fl oz/scant 1 cup chicken stock
15ml/1 tbsp tomato purée (paste)
2 bay leaves
15ml/1 tbsp chopped fresh flat leaf parsley
250g/9oz fresh lasagne sheets, pre-cooked if necessary
2 hard-boiled eggs, sliced
130g/4 1/2 oz packet mozzarella cheese, drained and sliced
60ml/4 tbsp freshly grated Pecorino cheese
salt and ground black pepper

1 Finely chop the vegetables. Heat 30ml/2 tbsp of oil in a large skillet or pan, add the vegetables and cook over a medium heat, stirring frequently, for 10 minutes. Add the pork and fry for 5 minutes, stirring occasionally, until well browned all over.

2 Add the wine and let it bubble and reduce for a few minutes. Add the tomatoes or passata, the stock and tomato purée. Make a tear in each bay leaf and add to the pan with the parsley and salt and pepper, mixing well. Cover and cook for 30–40 minutes until the pork is tender, stirring occasionally. Take off the heat and remove the bay leaves.

3 Using a slotted spoon, lift the meat out of the sauce, chop roughly and return to the sauce. Stir well.

4 Heat the oven to 190°C/375°F/Gas 5. Cut the lasagne sheets into 2.5cm/1in strips and add to a pan of salted boiling water. Cook for 3–4 minutes until just *al dente*. Drain, then stir the strips into the sauce.

5 Spread out half the pasta and sauce in a shallow baking dish and cover with half the egg and mozzarella slices and half the Pecorino. Repeat the layers, then drizzle the remaining oil over the top. Bake for 30–35 minutes until golden brown and bubbling. Leave standing for 10 minutes before serving.

Nutritional information per portion: Energy 308kcal/1297kJ; Protein 21g; Carbohydrate 37g, of which sugars 6.7g; Fat 8.8g, of which saturates 4.1g; Cholesterol 102mg; Calcium 116mg; Fibre 2.7g; Sodium 153mg.

Lasagne with meatballs

This unusual recipe for lasagne, which includes both a meat sauce and meatballs, is an ideal dish for a winter lunch or supper. It takes some time to make, so prepare it the day before.

SERVES 6–8

300g/11oz minced (ground) beef
300g/11oz minced (ground) pork
1 large egg
50g/2oz/1 cup fresh white breadcrumbs
75ml/5 tbsp freshly grated Parmesan cheese
30ml/2 tbsp chopped fresh flat leaf parsley, plus extra to garnish
2 garlic cloves, crushed
60ml/4 tbsp olive oil
1 onion, finely chopped
1 carrot, finely chopped
1 celery stick, finely chopped
2 x 400g/14oz cans chopped plum tomatoes
10ml/2 tsp dried oregano or basil
6–8 fresh lasagne sheets, pre-cooked, if necessary
salt and ground black pepper

FOR THE BÉCHAMEL SAUCE

750ml/1$\frac{1}{4}$ pints/3 cups milk
1 bay leaf
1 fresh thyme sprig
50g/2oz/$\frac{1}{4}$ cup butter
50g/2oz/$\frac{1}{2}$ cup plain (all-purpose) flour
nutmeg

1 Put 175g/6oz each of the minced beef and pork in a large bowl. Add the egg, breadcrumbs, 30ml/2 tbsp of the grated Parmesan, half the parsley and garlic and plenty of salt and pepper.

2 Mix everything together with a wooden spoon, then use your hands to squeeze and knead the mixture so that it becomes smooth and quite sticky. Wash your hands, rinse under the cold tap, then roll small pieces of the mixture between your palms to make about 60 very small balls. Place the balls on a tray and chill in the refrigerator for about 30 minutes.

3 Meanwhile, put the milk for the béchamel sauce in a pan. Make a tear in the bay leaf, add it and a sprig of thyme to the milk and bring it to the boil. Remove from the heat, cover and leave to infuse.

4 Make the meat sauce. Heat half the oil in a medium skillet or pan, add the onion, carrot, celery and remaining garlic and stir over a low heat for 5 minutes until softened. Add the remaining minced beef and pork and cook gently for 10 minutes, stirring frequently and breaking up any lumps in the meat.

5 Stir in salt and pepper to taste, then add the tomatoes, remaining parsley and the oregano or basil. Stir well, cover and simmer gently for 45 minutes to 1 hour, stirring occasionally.

6 Heat the remaining oil in a large, non-stick frying pan. Cook the meatballs in batches over a medium to high heat for 5–8 minutes until browned on all sides. Shake the pan from time to time so that the meatballs roll around as they cook. Transfer the meatballs to kitchen paper to drain.

7 Heat the oven to 190°C/375°F/Gas 5. Make the béchamel sauce. Strain the milk to remove the bay leaf and thyme. Melt the butter in a medium pan, add the flour and cook, stirring, for 1–2 minutes. Add the milk a little at a time, whisking vigorously after each addition. Bring to the boil and cook, stirring constantly, until the sauce is smooth and thick. Grate in a little nutmeg and add salt and pepper. Whisk well, then remove from the heat.

8 Spread a third of the meat sauce in the bottom of a large, shallow baking dish. Add half the meatballs, spread with a third of the béchamel and cover with half the lasagne sheets. Repeat these layers, then top with the remaining meat sauce and béchamel. Sprinkle the remaining grated Parmesan evenly over the surface and bake for 30–40 minutes or until golden brown and bubbling. Leave to stand for 10 minutes before serving. Garnish each serving with extra chopped parsley.

Nutritional information per portion: Energy 553kcal/2320kJ; Protein 29.7g; Carbohydrate 51g, of which sugars 10.4g; Fat 27g, of which saturates 11.3g; Cholesterol 99mg; Calcium 277mg; Fibre 3g; Sodium 308mg.

Cannelloni stuffed with meat

This rich, substantial dish takes quite a long time to prepare but can be made a day ahead up to the baking stage. It's well worth the effort – the tomato and creamy white sauces go perfectly together.

SERVES 6

15ml/1 tbsp olive oil
1 small onion, finely chopped
450g/1lb minced (ground) beef
1 garlic clove, finely chopped
5ml/1 tsp dried mixed herbs
120ml/4fl oz/½ cup beef stock
1 egg
75g/3oz cooked ham or mortadella sausage, finely chopped
45ml/3 tbsp fine fresh white breadcrumbs
150g/5oz/1⅔ cups freshly grated Parmesan cheese
18 dried cannelloni tubes
salt and ground black pepper

FOR THE TOMATO SAUCE
30ml/2 tbsp olive oil
1 small onion, finely chopped
½ carrot, finely chopped
1 celery stick, finely chopped
1 garlic clove, crushed
400g/14oz can chopped Italian plum tomatoes
a few sprigs of fresh basil
2.5ml/½ tsp dried oregano

FOR THE WHITE SAUCE
50g/2oz/¼ cup butter
50g/2oz/½ cup plain (all-purpose) flour
900ml/1½ pints/3¾ cups milk
nutmeg

1 Heat the olive oil in a medium pan and cook the onion over a gentle heat, stirring occasionally, for 5 minutes until softened. Add the minced beef and garlic and cook gently, stirring, for 10 minutes, breaking up any lumps with a wooden spoon. Add the mixed herbs, season to taste, then moisten with half the stock.

2 Cover the pan and simmer for 25 minutes, stirring occasionally and adding more stock as the mixture reduces. Spoon into a bowl and leave to cool.

3 Meanwhile, make the tomato sauce. Heat the olive oil in a medium pan, add the vegetables and garlic and cook over a medium heat, stirring frequently, for about 10 minutes. Add the canned tomatoes. Fill the empty can with water, pour it into the pan, then stir in the herbs, with seasoning to taste. Bring to the boil, lower the heat, cover and simmer for 25–30 minutes, stirring occasionally.

4 Purée the tomato sauce in a blender or food processor until smooth.

5 Add the egg, ham or mortadella, breadcrumbs and 90ml/6 tbsp of the grated Parmesan to the meat and stir well to mix. Taste for seasoning.

6 Spread a little of the tomato sauce over the bottom of a baking dish. Using a teaspoon, fill the cannelloni tubes with the meat mixture and place them in a single layer in the dish on top of the tomato sauce. Pour the remaining tomato sauce over the top.

7 Preheat the oven to 190°C/375°F/Gas 5. Make the white sauce. Melt the butter in a pan, add the flour and cook, stirring, for 1–2 minutes. Add the milk a little at a time, whisking vigorously after each addition. Bring to the boil and cook, stirring, until the sauce is smooth and thick. Grate in fresh nutmeg to taste and season with a little salt and pepper. Whisk well, then remove from the heat.

8 Pour the white sauce over the stuffed cannelloni, then sprinkle with the remaining Parmesan. Place in the oven and bake for 40–45 minutes or until the cannelloni tubes feel tender when pierced with a skewer. Allow the cannelloni to stand for about 10 minutes before serving.

Nutritional information per portion: Energy 455kcal/1905kJ; Protein 25.5g; Carbohydrate 41.7g, of which sugars 6.4g; Fat 21.8g, of which saturates 7.8g; Cholesterol 76mg; Calcium 203mg; Fibre 1.6g; Sodium 571mg.

Vermicelli omelette

A frittata is a flat baked omelette. Here it is made with vegetables and herbs, but you can use anything you like, such as ham, sausage, salami, chicken and mushrooms.

SERVES 4–6

50g/2oz dried vermicelli
6 eggs
60ml/4 tbsp panna da cucina or double (heavy) cream
1 handful fresh basil leaves, chopped
1 handful fresh flat leaf parsley, chopped
75g/3oz/1 cup freshly grated Parmesan cheese
25g/1oz/2 tbsp butter
15ml/1 tbsp olive oil
1 onion, finely sliced
3 large pieces bottled roasted red (bell) pepper, drained, rinsed, dried and cut into strips
1 garlic clove, crushed
salt and ground black pepper
rocket (arugula) leaves, to serve

1 Preheat the oven to 190°C/375°F/Gas 5. Cook the pasta in a pan of salted boiling water for 8 minutes. Meanwhile, break the eggs into a bowl and add the cream and herbs. Whisk in two-thirds of the Parmesan and season to taste.

2 Drain the pasta well and allow to cool; snip it into short lengths with scissors. Add to the egg mixture and whisk again. Set aside.

3 Melt the butter in the oil in a large, ovenproof non-stick frying pan. Add the sliced onion and cook gently, stirring often, for 5 minutes until softened. Add the peppers and garlic.

4 Pour the egg and pasta mixture into the pan and stir well. Cook over a low to medium heat, without stirring, for 3–5 minutes or until just set underneath.

5 Sprinkle over the remaining Parmesan and bake in the oven for 5 minutes or until set and golden brown. Before serving, leave to stand for at least 5 minutes. Cut into wedges and serve warm or cold, with the rocket.

Nutritional information per portion: Energy 270kcal/1118kJ; Protein 12.5g; Carbohydrate 9.4g, of which sugars 2.5g; Fat 20.4g, of which saturates 9.9g; Cholesterol 225mg; Calcium 191mg; Fibre 0.6g; Sodium 236mg.

Lasagne from **Bologna**

This is the classic* lasagne al forno. *It is an authentic Bolognese recipe based on a rich, meaty filling. The Bolognese sauce can be made up to 3 days in advance and stored in the refrigerator.

SERVES 6

1 quantity Bolognese Meat Sauce (see pages 87–90 for various recipes)
150–250ml/5–8fl oz/2/3–1 cup hot beef stock
12 dried lasagne sheets
50g/2oz/2/3 cup freshly grated Parmesan cheese

FOR THE WHITE SAUCE
50g/2oz/1/4 cup butter
50g/2oz/1/2 cup plain (all-purpose) flour
900ml/1 1/2 pints/3 3/4 cups hot milk
salt and ground black pepper

1 Preheat the oven to 190°C/375°F/Gas 5. If the Bolognese sauce is cold, reheat it. Once it is hot, stir in enough stock to make it quite thin.

2 Make the white sauce. Melt the butter in a medium pan, add the flour and cook, stirring, for 1–2 minutes. Add the milk a little at a time, whisking vigorously after each addition. Bring to the boil and cook, stirring, until the sauce is smooth and thick. Add salt and pepper to taste, whisk well to mix, then remove from the heat.

3 Spread a third of the Bolognese sauce over the bottom of a baking dish. Cover with about a quarter of the white sauce, followed by four sheets of lasagne. Repeat the layers twice more, then cover the top layer of lasagne with the remaining white sauce and sprinkle the grated Parmesan evenly over the top.

4 Bake for 40–45 minutes or until the pasta feels tender when pierced with a skewer. Allow to stand for about 10 minutes before serving.

Nutritional information per portion: Energy 472kcal/1994kJ; Protein 20.5g; Carbohydrate 66g, of which sugars 10.4g; Fat 16g, of which saturates 8.8g; Cholesterol 43mg; Calcium 316mg; Fibre 2g; Sodium 296mg.

Lasagne with **three cheeses**

Rich and filling, this is the type of lasagne that is popular in America. It was invented by Italian immigrants who made full use of the abundant ingredients available to them.

SERVES 6–8

25g/1oz/2 tbsp butter
15ml/1 tbsp olive oil
225–250g/8–9oz/3–3¼ cups button (white) mushrooms, quartered lengthways
30ml/2 tbsp chopped fresh flat leaf parsley
1 quantity Beef Sauce (see page 88)
250–350ml/8–12fl oz/1–1½ cups hot beef stock
9–12 fresh lasagne sheets, pre-cooked if necessary
450g/1lb/2 cups ricotta cheese
1 large egg
3 x 130g/4½oz packets mozzarella cheese, drained and thinly sliced
115g/4oz/1⅓ cups freshly grated Parmesan cheese
salt and ground black pepper

1 Preheat the oven to 190°C/375°F/Gas 5. Melt the butter and the oil in a frying pan. Add the mushrooms, with salt and pepper to taste, and toss over a medium to high heat for 5–8 minutes until the mushrooms are tender and quite dry. Remove the pan from the heat and stir in the parsley.

2 Make the Beef Sauce or, if it is cold, reheat it. Once it is hot, stir in enough hot beef stock to make the sauce quite thin.

3 Stir in the mushroom and parsley mixture, then spread about a quarter of this sauce over the bottom of a baking dish. Cover with three or four sheets of lasagne.

4 Beat together the ricotta and egg in a bowl, with salt and pepper to taste, then spread about a third of the mixture over the lasagne sheets. Cover with a third of the mozzarella slices, then sprinkle with about a quarter of the grated Parmesan. Repeat these layers twice, using half the remaining Beef Sauce each time, and finishing with the remaining Parmesan.

5 Bake the lasagne for 30–40 minutes or until the cheese topping is golden brown and bubbling. Allow to stand for about 10 minutes before serving.

Nutritional information per portion: Energy 533kcal/2226kJ; Protein 32.5g; Carbohydrate 29.7g, of which sugars 3.1g; Fat 32.4g, of which saturates 18.7g; Cholesterol 121mg; Calcium 370mg; Fibre 1.4g; Sodium 402mg.

Stuffed pasta

Originally from the north of Italy, stuffed pasta is now a speciality in every town. The recipes in this chapter are for a variety of shapes, but they all use the same basic pasta dough. The pasta is always made with eggs, which strengthens the dough and helps to hold the filling in during cooking. Making your own pasta is not that difficult, especially if you have a pasta machine, which will save you time and effort.

Ravioli with pumpkin

This is a very simple version of a Christmas Eve speciality from Lombardy. In traditional recipes the pumpkin filling is flavoured with* mostarda di frutta *(a kind of sweet fruit pickle), crushed amaretti and sugar. Here the pumpkin is seasoned with Parmesan and nutmeg.

SERVES 8

1 quantity Pasta with Eggs (see page 205)
115g/4oz/½ cup butter
freshly grated Parmesan cheese, to serve

FOR THE FILLING
450g/1lb piece of pumpkin
15ml/1 tbsp olive oil
40g/1½oz/scant ¼ cup freshly grated Parmesan cheese
nutmeg
salt and ground black pepper

1 Make the filling. Preheat the oven to 220°C/425°F/Gas 7. Cut the piece of pumpkin into chunks and remove the seeds and fibres. Put the chunks, skin side down, in a roasting pan and drizzle the oil over the pumpkin flesh. Roast in the oven for 30 minutes, turning the pieces over once or twice.

2 Leave the roasted pumpkin until it is cool enough to handle, then scrape the flesh out into a bowl and discard the pumpkin skin. Mash the roasted pumpkin flesh with a fork, then add the grated Parmesan, freshly grated nutmeg and salt and pepper to taste. Stir well to mix, then set aside until cold.

3 Using a pasta machine, roll out one-quarter of the pasta into a 90–100cm/36–40in strip. Cut the strip with a sharp knife into two 45–50cm/18–20in lengths (you can do this during rolling if the strip gets too long to manage).

4 Using a teaspoon, put 10–12 small mounds of the filling along one side of one of the pasta strips, spacing them evenly.

5 Brush a little water around each mound, then fold the plain side of the pasta strip over the mounds of filling. Starting from the folded edge, press down gently with your fingertips around each mound, pushing the air out at the unfolded edge. Sprinkle lightly with flour.

6 With a fluted pasta wheel, cut along each long side, then in between each mound to make small square shapes. Put the ravioli on floured dish towels, sprinkle lightly with flour and leave to dry, while repeating the process with the remaining pasta to get 80–95 ravioli altogether.

7 Drop the ravioli into a large pan of salted boiling water, bring back to the boil and boil for 4–5 minutes. Meanwhile, melt the butter in a small pan until it is sizzling.

8 Drain the ravioli and divide them equally among eight warmed dinner plates or large bowls. Drizzle the sizzling butter over the ravioli and serve immediately, sprinkled with grated Parmesan. Hand more grated Parmesan around separately.

Nutritional information per portion: Energy 342kcal/1435kJ; Protein 9.2g; Carbohydrate 43g, of which sugars 2.9g; Fat 16g, of which saturates 8.9g; Cholesterol 36mg; Calcium 93mg; Fibre 2.2g; Sodium 143mg.

Pansotti with **herbs** and **cheese**

In Liguria, the dough for pansotti *is flavoured with white wine, and the stuffing is made of cheese and* preboggion, *a mixture of many different types of fresh herbs and wild leaves. The dish is traditionally served with a complex pesto made from walnuts. The recipe given here is a simple but tasty version.*

SERVES 6–8

1 quantity Herb-flavoured Pasta with Eggs (see pages 205 and 214)
50g/2oz/1/4 cup butter
freshly grated Parmesan cheese, to serve

FOR THE FILLING
1 large handful fresh basil leaves,
1 large handful fresh flat leaf parsley
250g/9oz/generous 1 cup ricotta cheese
150g/5oz/1 2/3 cups freshly grated Parmesan cheese
a few sprigs fresh marjoram or oregano, leaves removed and finely chopped
1 garlic clove, crushed
1 small egg
salt and ground black pepper

FOR THE SAUCE
90g/3 1/2 oz shelled walnuts
1 garlic clove
60ml/4 tbsp extra virgin olive oil
125ml/4fl oz/1/2 cup panna da cucina or double (heavy) cream

1 First make the filling. Finely chop the basil and parsley, then place in a bowl with the ricotta, Parmesan, garlic and egg. Season and beat well to mix.

2 To make the sauce, put the walnuts, garlic clove and oil in a food processor and blend to a paste, adding up to 125ml/4fl oz/1/2 cup warm water through the feeder tube to slacken the consistency. Spoon the mixture into a large bowl and add the cream. Beat well to mix, then add salt and pepper to taste.

3 Using a pasta machine, roll out one-quarter of the pasta into a 90–100cm/36–40in strip. Cut the strip with a sharp knife into two 45–50cm/18–20in lengths (you can do this during rolling if the strip gets too long to manage).

4 Using a 5cm/2in square ravioli cutter, cut eight to ten squares from one of the pasta strips. Using a teaspoon, put a mound of filling in the centre of each square.

5 Brush a little water around the edge of each square, then fold the square diagonally in half over the filling to make a triangular shape. Press gently to seal.

6 Spread out the pansotti on clean floured dish towels, sprinkle lightly with flour and leave to dry, while repeating the process with the remaining dough to make 64–80 pansotti altogether.

7 Cook the pansotti in a large pan of salted boiling water for 4–5 minutes. Meanwhile, put the walnut sauce in a large warmed bowl and add a ladleful of the pasta cooking water to thin it down. Melt the butter in a small pan until sizzling.

8 Drain the pansotti and transfer them into the bowl of walnut sauce. Drizzle the butter over them, toss well, then sprinkle with grated Parmesan. Alternatively, toss the pansotti in the melted butter, spoon into warmed individual bowls and drizzle over the sauce. Serve immediately, with more grated Parmesan handed around separately.

Nutritional information per portion: Energy 593kcal/2475kJ; Protein 19.7g; Carbohydrate 43.3g, of which sugars 3.4g; Fat 39.1g, of which saturates 16.9g; Cholesterol 90mg; Calcium 262mg; Fibre 2g; Sodium 257mg.

Stuffed pasta roll

This impressive first course for a dinner party looks stunning when served. It takes quite a long time to make, but it can be made up to the baking stage the day before.

SERVES 6

75g/3oz/6 tbsp butter
1 small onion, finely chopped
150g/5oz fresh spinach leaves, washed and trimmed
250g/9oz/generous 1 cup ricotta cheese
1 egg
60ml/4 tbsp freshly grated Parmesan cheese
60ml/4 tbsp freshly grated Pecorino cheese
nutmeg, freshly grated
2/3 quantity Pasta with Eggs (see page 205)
salt and ground black pepper

FOR THE TOMATO SAUCE
1 onion, finely chopped
1 carrot, finely chopped
1 celery stick, finely chopped
60ml/4 tbsp olive oil
1 garlic clove, thinly sliced
a few leaves each fresh basil, thyme and oregano or marjoram, plus extra basil leaves, to garnish
2 x 400g/14oz cans chopped plum tomatoes
15ml/1 tbsp sun-dried tomato paste
5ml/1 tsp sugar
75–105ml/5–7 tbsp dry white wine

1 Melt 25g/1oz/2 tbsp of the butter in a pan, add the onion and cook gently, stirring, for 5 minutes until softened. Add the spinach and season, then cook over a medium heat for 5–8 minutes, stirring, until the spinach is wilted and tender. Increase the heat and stir until the water is absorbed.

2 Finely chop the spinach mixture, transfer to a bowl and add the ricotta, egg and half the Parmesan and Pecorino. Season with nutmeg, salt and pepper. Beat well.

3 Roll out the pasta dough to a 50 x 40cm/20 x 16in rectangle. Place on a large piece of muslin (cheesecloth), with one of the short sides nearest you. Spread the spinach over the pasta, leaving a 2cm/3/4in margin along the long sides and a 5cm/2in margin along the far short side. Moisten the long sides with water.

4 Starting from the short side nearest you, pick up the muslin and roll the pasta away from you. Don't press it, just let it roll to form a 40cm/16in long 'sausage'. Press the two open ends to seal the pasta, then roll the muslin around the rotolo a couple of times and tie the two ends tightly with string.

5 Fill half a fish kettle or large oval flameproof casserole with water and bring to the boil. Add a pinch of salt, then the rotolo. Half cover, and simmer for 45 minutes, turning twice. Remove it from the water and place on a board. Prop the board up at one end so excess water drains away into the sink. Leave to cool.

6 Make the tomato sauce. Heat the oil in a pan, add the garlic slices and stir over a very low heat for 1–2 minutes. Add the chopped vegetables and fresh herbs. Cook over a low heat, stirring for 5–7 minutes until the vegetables are soft and lightly coloured. Add the tomatoes, tomato paste, sugar, salt and pepper to taste. Bring to the boil, stirring constantly, then lower the heat and simmer gently, uncovered, for about 45 minutes, stirring occasionally.

7 Heat the oven to 200°C/400°F/Gas 6. Unwrap the rotolo and cut it into 12 thick slices. Melt the remaining butter and brush a little over the inside of six ovenproof dishes or a large shallow baking dish. Arrange the slices slightly overlapping in the dishes or dish and drizzle the remaining butter over. Sprinkle with the remaining Parmesan and Pecorino and bake in the oven for 10–15 minutes until golden brown.

8 Meanwhile, blend the tomato sauce in a food processor until smooth. Transfer the sauce to a pan and add enough wine to thin it down to a pouring consistency, then heat until bubbling. Serve the rotolo slices on individual plates, on a pool of tomato sauce, and sprinkle with basil leaves.

Nutritional information per portion: Energy 584kcal/2449kJ; Protein 22.4g; Carbohydrate 57.3g, of which sugars 9.6g; Fat 31.3g, of which saturates 16.5g; Cholesterol 106mg; Calcium 299mg; Fibre 4.3g; Sodium 765mg.

Agnolotti with **taleggio** and **marjoram**

The filling for these little half-moons is very simple – it consists of only two ingredients – but the combination of flavours is absolutely delicious.

SERVES 6–8

1 quantity Pasta with Eggs (see page 205)
350–400g/12–14oz taleggio cheese
about 30ml/2 tbsp finely chopped fresh marjoram, plus extra to garnish
115g/4oz/½ cup butter
salt and ground black pepper
freshly grated Parmesan cheese, to serve

1 Using a pasta machine, roll out a quarter of the pasta into a 90–100cm/36–40in strip. Using a sharp knife, cut it into two 45–50cm/18–20in lengths (do this during rolling if the strip gets too long to manage).

2 Cut eight to ten small cubes of taleggio and place them along one side of one of the pasta strips, evenly spaced. Sprinkle each cube with a little marjoram and pepper to taste. Brush a little water around each cube of cheese, then fold the plain side of the pasta strip over them.

3 Starting from the folded edge, press down gently with your fingertips around each cube, pushing the air out at the unfolded edge. Sprinkle lightly with flour.

4 Using only half of a 5cm/2in fluted round ravioli or pastry (cookie) cutter, cut around each cube of cheese to make a half-moon shape (the folded edge should be the straight edge). If you like, press the cut edges of the agnolotti with the tines of a fork to give a decorative effect.

5 Put the agnolotti on floured dish towels, sprinkle lightly with flour and leave to dry while repeating the process with the remaining ingredients to get 65–80 agnolotti altogether. Drop them into a large pan of salted boiling water, bring back to the boil and boil for 4–5 minutes until *al dente*.

6 Melt the butter in a small pan until it is sizzling. Drain the agnolotti and divide them equally among six to eight warmed large bowls. Drizzle the sizzling butter over them and serve immediately, sprinkled with freshly grated Parmesan and chopped fresh marjoram. Hand around more Parmesan separately.

Nutritional information per portion: Energy 483kcal/2021kJ; Protein 18.1g; Carbohydrate 42g, of which sugars 2.1g; Fat 27.2g, of which saturates 17.1g; Cholesterol 73mg; Calcium 351mg; Fibre 1.9g; Sodium 407mg.

Spinach and **ricotta ravioli**

The literal translation of this recipe name, Ravioli di Magro, *is 'lean ravioli'. It is used to describe meat-free ravioli, usually those with a spinach and ricotta filling.* Ravioli di Magro *is served on Christmas Eve, a time when meat-filled pasta should not be eaten.*

SERVES 8

1 quantity Pasta with Eggs (see page 205)
freshly grated Parmesan cheese, to serve

FOR THE FILLING
40g/1½oz/3 tbsp butter
175g/6oz fresh spinach leaves, washed, trimmed and shredded
200g/7oz/scant 1 cup ricotta cheese
25g/1oz/⅓ cup freshly grated Parmesan cheese
nutmeg
1 small egg
salt and ground black pepper

FOR THE SAUCE
50g/2oz/¼ cup butter
250ml/8fl oz/1 cup panna da cucina or double (heavy) cream
50g/2oz/⅔ cup freshly grated Parmesan cheese

1 Make the filling. Melt the butter in a medium pan, add the spinach and salt and pepper to taste and cook over a medium heat for 5–8 minutes, stirring frequently, until the spinach is wilted and tender. Increase the heat to high and stir until the water is absorbed and the spinach is quite dry.

2 Transfer the spinach into a bowl and leave until cold, then add the ricotta, grated Parmesan and freshly grated nutmeg to taste. Beat well to mix, taste for seasoning, then add the egg and beat well again.

3 Using a pasta machine, roll out one-quarter of the pasta into a 90–100cm/36–40in strip. Cut the strip with a sharp knife into two 45–50cm/18–20in lengths (do this during rolling if it gets too long to manage).

4 Using a teaspoon, put 10–12 small mounds of the filling along one side of one of the pasta strips, spacing them evenly. Brush a little water around each mound, then fold the plain side of the pasta strip over the filling.

5 Starting from the folded edge, press down gently with your fingertips around each mound of filling, pushing the air out at the unfolded edge. Sprinkle lightly with flour.

6 With a fluted pasta wheel, cut along each long side, then in between each mound to make small square shapes.

7 Put the ravioli on floured dish towels, sprinkle lightly with flour and leave to dry while repeating the process with the remaining pasta to get 80–95 ravioli altogether.

8 Drop the ravioli into a large pan of salted boiling water and boil for 4–5 minutes.

9 Meanwhile, make the sauce. Gently heat the butter, cream and Parmesan in a medium pan until the butter and Parmesan have melted. Increase the heat and simmer for a minute or two until the sauce is slightly reduced, then add salt and pepper to taste.

10 Drain the ravioli and divide them equally among eight warmed large bowls. Drizzle the sauce over them and serve immediately, sprinkled with grated Parmesan.

Nutritional information per portion: Energy 547kcal/2283kJ; Protein 15.9g; Carbohydrate 43.4g, of which sugars 3.6g; Fat 35.6g, of which saturates 21.5g; Cholesterol 114mg; Calcium 222mg; Fibre 2.1g; Sodium 252mg.

Ravioli with **crab**

This modern recipe for a dinner party appetizer uses chilli-flavoured pasta, which looks and tastes good with crab, but you can use plain pasta if you prefer.

SERVES 4

1 quantity Chilli-flavoured Pasta with Eggs (see pages 205 and 214)
90g/3½oz/7 tbsp butter
juice of 1 lemon
fresh flat leaf parsley and crushed dried chillies, to garnish (optional)

FOR THE FILLING
175g/6oz/¾ cup mascarpone
175g/6oz/¾ cup crab meat
30ml/2 tbsp finely chopped fresh flat leaf parsley
finely grated rind of 1 lemon
pinch of crushed dried chillies (optional)
salt and ground black pepper

1 Make the filling. Put the mascarpone in a bowl and mash it with a fork. Add the crab meat, parsley, lemon rind, crushed dried chillies, if using, and salt and pepper to taste. Stir well.

2 Using a pasta machine, roll out one-quarter of the pasta into a 90–100cm/36–40in strip. Cut the strip with a sharp knife into two 45–50cm/18–20in lengths (do this during rolling if the strip gets too long to manage).

3 With a 6cm/2½in fluted pastry (cookie) cutter, cut out eight squares from each strip. Using a teaspoon, put a mound of filling in the centre of half the discs. Brush a little water around the edge of the mounds, top with the plain discs and press the edges to seal. To finish, press the edges with the tines of a fork.

4 Put the ravioli on floured dish towels, sprinkle lightly with flour and leave to dry while repeating the process with the remaining dough to make around 30 ravioli altogether. If you have any stuffing left, you can re-roll the pasta trimmings and make more ravioli.

5 Cook the ravioli in a large pan of salted boiling water for 4–5 minutes. Meanwhile, melt the butter and lemon juice in a small pan until sizzling. Drain the ravioli and divide among four warmed bowls.

6 Serve, drizzled with lemon butter and garnished with flat leaf parsley and dried chillies, if you like.

Nutritional information per portion: Energy 581kcal/2437kJ; Protein 22.6g; Carbohydrate 66.3g, of which sugars 4.4g; Fat 26.8g, of which saturates 15.9g; Cholesterol 98mg; Calcium 79mg; Fibre 2.6g; Sodium 380mg.

Cheese and ham ravioli with tomato sauce

Typical of southern Italian cuisine, these ravioli are very tasty and substantial enough for a main course, served with a salad. As a first course, there are enough ravioli for eight servings.

SERVES 4–6

1 quantity Pasta with Eggs (see page 205)
60ml/4 tbsp freshly grated Pecorino cheese, plus extra to serve

FOR THE FILLING
175g/6oz/3/4 cup ricotta cheese
30ml/2 tbsp freshly grated Parmesan cheese
115g/4oz prosciutto, finely chopped
150g/5oz packet mozzarella cheese, drained and finely chopped
1 small egg
15ml/1 tbsp fresh flat leaf parsley, chopped, plus extra to garnish

FOR THE TOMATO SAUCE
30ml/2 tbsp olive oil
1 onion, finely chopped
400g/14oz can chopped Italian plum tomatoes
15ml/1 tbsp sun-dried tomato paste
5–10ml/1–2 tsp dried oregano, to taste
salt and ground black pepper

1 Make the sauce. Heat the oil in a medium pan, add the onion and cook gently, stirring frequently, for about 5 minutes until softened.

2 Add the tomatoes. Fill the empty can with water, pour it into the pan, then stir in the tomato paste, oregano and salt and pepper to taste. Bring to the boil and stir well, then cover the pan and simmer gently for 30 minutes, stirring occasionally and adding more water if the sauce becomes too thick.

3 Meanwhile, make the filling. Put all the filling ingredients in a bowl with salt and pepper to taste. Mix well with a fork, breaking up any lumps in the ricotta.

4 Using a pasta machine, roll out one-quarter of the pasta into a 90–100cm/36–40in strip. Cut the strip with a sharp knife into two 45–50cm/18–20in lengths (you can do this during rolling if the strip gets too long to manage).

5 Using two teaspoons, put 10–12 small mounds of the filling along one side of one of the pasta strips, spacing them evenly. The filling will be quite moist. Brush a little water around each mound, then fold the plain side of the pasta strip over the filling.

6 Starting from the folded edge, press down gently with your fingertips around each mound, pushing the air out at the unfolded edge. Sprinkle lightly with flour. With a fluted pasta wheel, cut along each long side, then in between each mound to make small square shapes.

7 Put the ravioli on floured dish towels; sprinkle lightly with flour. Leave to dry while repeating the process with the remaining pasta to get 80–95 ravioli altogether. Drop the ravioli into a large pan of salted boiling water, bring back to the boil and boil for 4–5 minutes.

8 Drain the ravioli well and pour about a third of them into a warmed bowl. Sprinkle 15ml/1 tbsp freshly grated Pecorino over the ravioli. Pour over a third of the tomato sauce.

9 Repeat the layers twice, then top with the remaining grated Pecorino. Serve immediately, garnished with chopped parsley. Hand around more grated Pecorino separately.

Nutritional information per portion: Energy 521kcal/2194kJ; Protein 27.4g; Carbohydrate 59.5g, of which sugars 6.2g; Fat 21g, of which saturates 10.4g; Cholesterol 85mg; Calcium 303mg; Fibre 3g; Sodium 513mg.

Tortellini from Emilia-Romagna

These are the tortellini that are served on the day after Christmas in Emilia-Romagna. Traditionally they were made with minced leftover capon from Christmas Day, but today turkey or chicken is often used instead.

SERVES 6–8

1 quantity Pasta with Eggs (see page 205)
2 litres/3½ pints/8 cups beef stock made with stock (bouillon) cubes or diluted canned consommé
freshly grated Parmesan cheese, to serve

FOR THE FILLING
25g/1oz/2 tbsp butter
250g/9oz minced (ground) turkey or chicken
5ml/1 tsp chopped fresh rosemary
5ml/1 tsp chopped fresh sage
nutmeg
250ml/8fl oz/1 cup chicken stock
60ml/4tbsp freshly grated Parmesan cheese
90g/3½oz mortadella sausage, very finely chopped
1 small egg
salt and ground black pepper

1 Make the filling. Melt the butter in a medium skillet, then add the minced turkey or chicken and chopped herbs. Grate in a little nutmeg and add salt and pepper to taste. Cook gently for 5–6 minutes, stirring frequently and breaking up any lumps in the meat with a wooden spoon.

2 Add the stock and stir well to mix, then simmer gently, uncovered, for 15–20 minutes until the meat is cooked and quite dry. Transfer the meat to a bowl with a slotted spoon and leave to cool. Add the grated Parmesan, mortadella and egg to the meat and stir well to mix.

3 Using a pasta machine, roll out one-quarter of the pasta into a 90–100cm/36–40in strip. Cut the strip with a sharp knife into two 45–50cm/18–20in lengths (you can do this during rolling if the strip gets too long to manage).

4 With a 5cm/2in fluted ravioli or pastry (cookie) cutter, cut out eight to ten discs from one of the pasta strips. Using a teaspoon, put a small mound of filling in the centre of each disc. Brush a little water around the edge of each mound.

5 Fold the disc in half over the filling so that the edges do not quite meet. Press to seal. Wrap the tortellini shape around your index finger and pinch the bottom corners together to seal.

6 Put the tortellini in a single layer on floured dish towels, sprinkle lightly with flour and leave to dry while repeating the process with the remaining dough to make 65–80 tortellini altogether. If you have any stuffing left, re-roll the pasta trimmings and make more tortellini.

7 Bring the beef stock to the boil in a large pan. Drop in the tortellini, then bring back to the boil and boil for 4–5 minutes. Taste the stock and season with salt and pepper if necessary.

8 Pour the tortellini and stock into a warmed large soup tureen, sprinkle with a little grated Parmesan and serve immediately. Hand around more Parmesan separately.

Nutritional information per portion: Energy 216kcal/905kJ; Protein 15.9g; Carbohydrate 15.2g, of which sugars 0.5g; Fat 10.8g, of which saturates 5.1g; Cholesterol 95mg; Calcium 205mg; Fibre 0.9g; Sodium 396mg.

Ravioli with pork and turkey

This Roman-style ravioli, stuffed with minced meat and cheese is scented with fresh herbs, and makes a substantial first course. Alternatively, you can use veal instead of pork or turkey.

SERVES 8

1 quantity Pasta with Eggs (see page 205)
50g/2oz/1/4 cup butter
a large bunch of fresh sage, leaves removed and roughly chopped
60ml/4 tbsp freshly grated Parmesan cheese
extra sage leaves and freshly grated Parmesan cheese, to serve

FOR THE FILLING

25g/1oz/2 tbsp butter
150g/5oz minced (ground) pork
115g/4oz minced (ground) turkey
4 fresh sage leaves, finely chopped
1 sprig of fresh rosemary, leaves removed and finely chopped
30ml/2 tbsp dry white wine
65g/2 1/2 oz/generous 1/4 cup ricotta cheese
45ml/3 tbsp freshly grated Parmesan cheese
1 egg
nutmeg
salt and ground black pepper

1 Make the filling. Melt the butter in a medium pan, add the minced pork and turkey and the herbs and cook gently for 5–6 minutes, stirring frequently, breaking up any lumps in the meat with a wooden spoon. Add salt and pepper to taste and stir well to mix thoroughly.

2 Add the wine to the pan and stir again. Simmer for 1–2 minutes until reduced slightly, then cover the pan and simmer gently for 20 minutes, stirring occasionally. With a slotted spoon, transfer the meat to a bowl and leave to cool.

3 Add the ricotta and Parmesan cheeses to the bowl with the egg and freshly grated nutmeg to taste. Stir well to mix the ingredients thoroughly.

4 Using a pasta machine, roll out one-quarter of the pasta into a 90–100cm/36–40in strip. Cut the strip with a sharp knife into two 45–50cm/18–20in lengths (you can do this during rolling if the strip gets too long to manage).

5 Using a teaspoon, put 10–12 small mounds of the filling along one side of one of the pasta strips, spacing them evenly. Brush a little water on to the pasta strip around each mound, then fold the plain side of the pasta strip over the filling.

6 Starting from the folded edge, press down gently with your fingertips around each mound of filling, pushing the air out at the unfolded edge. Sprinkle lightly with flour.

7 With a fluted pasta wheel, cut along each long side, then in between each mound to make small square shapes. Dust lightly with flour.

8 Put the ravioli in a single layer on floured dish towels and leave to dry while repeating the process with the remaining pasta to make 80–95 ravioli altogether. Drop the ravioli into a large pan of salted boiling water and boil for 4–5 minutes.

9 While the ravioli are cooking, melt the butter in a small pan, add the fresh sage leaves and stir over a medium to high heat until the sage leaves are sizzling in the butter.

10 Drain the ravioli and pour half into a large warmed bowl. Sprinkle with half the grated Parmesan, then half the sage butter. Repeat with the remaining ravioli, Parmesan and sage butter.

11 Serve immediately, garnished with fresh sage leaves. Hand around more grated Parmesan separately.

Nutritional information per portion: Energy 393kcal/1653kJ; Protein 20g; Carbohydrate 42g, of which sugars 2.2g; Fat 17.1g, of which saturates 9.4g; Cholesterol 85mg; Calcium 180mg; Fibre 1.6g; Sodium 236mg.

Meat-filled agnolotti with vodka sauce

In this dish, dainty half-moon shapes are filled with spiced minced meat and bacon and served with a cream and blue-cheese sauce that is spiked with vodka. This very special dish would make an impressive dinner party first course.

SERVES 6–8

1 quantity Pasta with Eggs (see page 205)
freshly grated Parmesan cheese, to serve

FOR THE FILLING
15ml/1 tbsp olive oil
75g/3oz pancetta, streaky (fatty) bacon or ham, finely diced
250g/9oz minced (ground) pork or veal
2 garlic cloves, crushed
good pinch of ground cinnamon
120ml/4fl oz/1/2 cup red wine
60ml/4 tbsp chopped fresh flat leaf parsley
1 small egg
salt and ground black pepper

FOR THE SAUCE
50g/2oz/1/4 cup butter
250ml/8fl oz/1 cup panna da cucina or double (heavy) cream
115g/4oz Gorgonzola cheese, diced
45ml/3 tbsp vodka

1 Make the filling. Heat the oil in a medium pan, add the pancetta, bacon or ham and stir-fry for a few minutes until lightly coloured. Add the minced pork or veal, the garlic, cinnamon and salt and pepper to taste and cook gently for 5–6 minutes, stirring frequently and breaking up any lumps.

2 Pour in the wine and stir well to mix, then simmer gently, stirring occasionally, for 15–20 minutes until the meat is cooked and quite dry. Transfer the meat to a bowl with a slotted spoon and leave to cool. Add the parsley and egg to the meat mixture and stir well to mix.

3 Using a pasta machine, roll out one quarter of the pasta into a 90–100cm/36–40in strip. Cut the strip with a sharp knife into two 45–50cm/18–20in lengths (you can do this during rolling if the strip gets too long to manage).

4 Using a teaspoon, space eight to ten small mounds of the filling evenly along one side of one pasta strip. Brush a little water around each mound, then fold the plain side of the pasta strip over the filling.

5 Starting from the folded edge, press gently around each mound with your fingertips, pushing out the air. Using only half of a 5cm/2in fluted round ravioli or pastry (cookie) cutter, cut around each mound of filling to make a half-moon shape. The folded edge should be the straight edge. If you like, press the cut edges of the agnolotti with the tines of a fork to give a decorative effect.

6 Put the agnolotti on floured dish towels, spreading them out in a single layer, so that they don't stick together. Sprinkle them lightly with flour and leave to dry while repeating the process with the remaining pasta to get 65–80 agnolotti altogether.

7 Drop the agnolotti into a large pan of salted boiling water, bring back to the boil for 4–5 minutes until *al dente*.

8 Meanwhile, make the sauce. Melt the butter in a medium pan, add the cream and cheese and heat through, stirring, until the cheese has melted. Add the vodka, season to taste with pepper and stir well to mix.

9 Drain the agnolotti and divide them among six to eight warmed bowls. Spoon the sauce over them and sprinkle liberally with grated Parmesan. Serve immediately.

Nutritional information per portion: Energy 543kcal/2266kJ; Protein 17.8g; Carbohydrate 37.7g, of which sugars 2.3g; Fat 34.3g, of which saturates 18.8g; Cholesterol 117mg; Calcium 108mg; Fibre 1.5g; Sodium 370mg.

Cheese cappellacci with Bolognese sauce

In Emilia-Romagna it is traditional to serve these cappellacci *with a rich meat sauce, but if you prefer you can serve them with a tomato sauce, or just melted butter.*

SERVES 6

1 quantity Pasta with Eggs (see page 205)
2 litres/3½ pints/8 cups beef stock made with stock (bouillon) cubes or diluted canned consommé
freshly grated Parmesan cheese, to serve
basil leaves, to garnish

FOR THE FILLING

250g/9oz/generous 1 cup ricotta cheese
90g/3½oz taleggio cheese, rind removed, diced finely
60ml/4 tbsp freshly grated Parmesan cheese
1 small egg
nutmeg
salt and ground black pepper

FOR THE BOLOGNESE MEAT SAUCE

25g/1oz/2 tbsp butter
15ml/1 tbsp olive oil
1 onion
2 carrots
2 celery sticks
2 garlic cloves
130g/4½oz pancetta or rindless streaky (fatty) bacon, diced
250g/9oz lean minced (ground) beef
250g/9oz lean minced (ground) pork
120ml/4fl oz/½ cup dry white wine
2 x 400g/14oz cans crushed Italian plum tomatoes
475–750ml/16fl oz–1¼ pints/2–3 cups beef stock
100ml/3½fl oz/scant ½ cup panna da cucina or double (heavy) cream

1 Make the filling. Put the ricotta, taleggio and grated Parmesan in a bowl and mash together with a fork. Add the egg and freshly grated nutmeg and salt and pepper to taste and stir well to mix.

2 Using a pasta machine, roll out one-quarter of the pasta into a 90–100cm/36–40in strip. Cut the strip with a sharp knife into two 45–50cm/18–20in lengths (you can do this during rolling if the strip gets too long to manage).

3 Using a 6–7.5cm/2½–3in square ravioli cutter, cut six or seven squares from one of the pasta strips. Using a teaspoon, put a mound of filling in the centre of each square. Brush a little water around the edge of each square, then fold the square diagonally in half over the filling to make a triangular shape. Press to seal.

4 Wrap the triangle around one of your index fingers, bringing the bottom two corners together. Pinch the ends together to seal, then press around the top edge of the filling to make an indentation so that the 'hat' looks like a bishop's mitre.

5 Place the cappellacci on floured dish towels, sprinkle them lightly with flour and leave to dry while repeating the process with the remaining dough to make 50–55 cappellacci altogether.

6 Make the meat sauce. Heat the butter and oil in a large skillet or pan until sizzling. Add the vegetables, garlic, and the pancetta or bacon and cook over a medium heat, stirring often, for 10 minutes. Add the minced beef and pork, lower the heat and cook gently for 10 minutes, stirring frequently and breaking up any lumps in the meat with a wooden spoon. Stir in salt and pepper to taste, then add the wine and stir again. Simmer for about 5 minutes, or until reduced.

7 Add the tomatoes and 250ml/8fl oz/1 cup of the stock and bring to the boil. Stir well, then lower the heat, half cover the pan with a lid and leave to simmer very gently for 2 hours. Stir occasionally during this time and add more stock as it becomes absorbed.

8 Add the panna da cucina or double cream to the meat sauce. Stir well to mix, then simmer the sauce, without a lid, for another 30 minutes, stirring frequently.

9 Bring the stock to the boil in a large pan. Drop the cappellacci into the stock, bring back to the boil and boil for 4–5 minutes; drain the cappellacci and divide them among six warmed bowls. Spoon the hot Bolognese sauce over the cappellacci and sprinkle with Parmesan and basil leaves. Serve immediately.

Nutritional information per portion: Energy 802kcal/3349kJ; Protein 42g; Carbohydrate 50.9g, of which sugars 9.3g; Fat 47.8g, of which saturates 24.4g; Cholesterol 174mg; Calcium 308mg; Fibre 3.5g; Sodium 742mg.

Light and easy

Chargrilled vegetables, designer salad leaves and a variety of pestos are a few of the ingredients being introduced to pasta by today's chefs. They are not traditional dishes – many originated in restaurants in response to the current taste for lighter, healthier food – but they are so quick and easy, there's no reason why you can't make them yourself at home. Invent your own combinations using fresh, seasonal vegetables and herbs.

Penne with **rocket** and **mozzarella**

Like a warm salad, this pasta dish is very quick and easy to make – perfect for an* al fresco *summer lunch.

SERVES 4

400g/14oz/3½ cups fresh or dried penne
6 ripe Italian plum tomatoes, peeled, seeded and diced
2 x 150g/5oz packets mozzarella cheese, drained and diced
2 large handfuls of rocket (arugula), total weight about 150g/5oz
75ml/5 tbsp extra virgin olive oil
salt and ground black pepper

1 Cook the pasta in a large pan of salted boiling water, according to the packet instructions.

2 Meanwhile, put the tomatoes, mozzarella, rocket and olive oil into a large bowl with a little salt and pepper to taste and toss well to mix.

3 Drain the cooked pasta and transfer it into the bowl. Toss well to mix and serve immediately.

VARIATION

For a less peppery taste, use basil leaves instead of rocket, or a mixture of the two.

Nutritional information per portion: Energy 693kcal/2913kJ; Protein 28.1g; Carbohydrate 79.4g, of which sugars 8.5g; Fat 31.5g, of which saturates 12.7g; Cholesterol 44mg; Calcium 371mg; Fibre 5.2g; Sodium 365mg.

Eliche with **chargrilled peppers**

Chargrilled peppers are good with pasta because they have a soft juicy texture and a wonderful smoky flavour.

SERVES 4

3 large whole (bell) peppers (red, yellow and orange)
350g/12oz/3 cups fresh or dried eliche or fusilli
1–2 garlic cloves, to taste, finely chopped
60ml/4 tbsp extra virgin olive oil
4 ripe Italian plum tomatoes, peeled, seeded and diced
50g/2oz/½ cup pitted black olives, halved or quartered lengthways
1 handful of fresh basil leaves
salt and ground black pepper

1 Grill (broil) the peppers at a high temperature for 10 minutes, turning frequently until charred all over. Put in a plastic bag, seal it and set aside until cool.

2 Remove the peppers from the bag and hold them one at a time under cold running water. Peel off the charred skins with your fingers, split the peppers open and pull out the cores. Rub off all the seeds under the running water, then pat the peppers dry on kitchen paper.

3 Cook the pasta in a large pan of salted boiling water, according to the packet instructions until *al dente*.

4 Thinly slice the peppers and place them in a large bowl with the remaining ingredients and salt and pepper. Drain the cooked pasta and transfer it into the bowl. Toss well to mix and serve immediately.

Nutritional information per portion: Energy 402kcal/1688kJ; Protein 10.1g; Carbohydrate 51.6g, of which sugars 7.1g; Fat 18.7g, of which saturates 2.9g; Cholesterol 3mg; Calcium 75mg; Fibre 3.7g; Sodium 36mg.

Tagliatelle with **broccoli** and **spinach**

This is an excellent vegetarian dish. It is nutritious and filling, and needs no accompaniment. If you like, you can use tagliatelle flecked with herbs.

SERVES 4

2 heads of broccoli
450g/1lb fresh spinach, stalks removed
nutmeg
450g/1lb fresh or dried egg tagliatelle
about 45ml/3 tbsp extra virgin olive oil
juice of 1/2 lemon, or to taste
salt and ground black pepper
freshly grated Parmesan cheese, to serve

1 Put the broccoli in the basket of a steamer, cover and steam over boiling water for 10 minutes. Add the spinach to the broccoli, cover and steam for 4–5 minutes or until both are tender. Towards the end of the cooking time, sprinkle the vegetables with freshly grated nutmeg and salt and pepper to taste. Transfer the vegetables to a colander.

2 Add salt to the water in the steamer and fill the steamer pan with boiling water, then add the pasta and cook according to the instructions on the packet. Meanwhile, chop the broccoli and spinach in the colander.

3 Drain the pasta. Heat 45ml/3tbsp oil in the pasta pan, add the pasta and chopped vegetables and toss over a medium heat until evenly mixed. Sprinkle in the lemon juice and plenty of black pepper, then taste and add more lemon juice, oil, salt and nutmeg if you like. Serve immediately, sprinkled liberally with freshly grated Parmesan and black pepper.

Nutritional information per portion: Energy 504kcal/2130kJ; Protein 22.2g; Carbohydrate 87.4g, of which sugars 7.3g; Fat 9.6g, of which saturates 1.4g; Cholesterol 0mg; Calcium 289mg; Fibre 8.9g; Sodium 171mg.

Macaroni with broccoli and cauliflower

This dish originates from the south of Italy, and is full of flavour and very filling. If you leave out the anchovies, it can be served to vegetarians.

SERVES 4

175g/6oz cauliflower florets, cut into small sprigs
175g/6oz broccoli florets, cut into small sprigs
350g/12oz/3 cups short-cut macaroni
45ml/3 tbsp extra virgin olive oil
1 onion, finely chopped
45ml/3 tbsp pine nuts
1 sachet of saffron powder, dissolved in 15ml/1 tbsp warm water
15–30ml/1–2 tbsp raisins, to taste
30ml/2 tbsp sun-dried tomato paste
4 bottled or canned anchovies in olive oil, drained and chopped, plus extra anchovies to serve (optional)
salt and ground black pepper
freshly grated Pecorino cheese, to serve

1 Cook the cauliflower sprigs in a large pan of salted boiling water for about 3 minutes. Add the broccoli and boil for a further 2 minutes, then remove the vegetables from the pan with a large slotted spoon and set aside. Add the pasta to the vegetable cooking water and bring back to the boil. Cook the pasta according to the packet instructions until *al dente*.

2 Heat the olive oil in a large skillet or pan, add the finely chopped onion and cook over a low to medium heat, stirring frequently, for 2–3 minutes, until golden. Add the pine nuts, broccoli, cauliflower, saffron water, raisins, sun-dried tomato paste and a couple of ladlefuls of the pasta cooking water until the mixture has the consistency of a sauce. Finally, add plenty of pepper.

3 Stir well, cook for 1–2 minutes, then add the chopped anchovies. Drain the pasta and transfer it into the vegetable mixture. Toss well and season to taste. Serve immediately in four warmed bowls, sprinkled with freshly grated Pecorino. If you like, add one or two whole anchovies to each serving.

Nutritional information per portion: Energy 422kcal/1784kJ; Protein 15.4g; Carbohydrate 73.5g, of which sugars 8.4g; Fat 9.4g, of which saturates 1.1g; Cholesterol 0mg; Calcium 64mg; Fibre 5.2g; Sodium 38mg.

Pipe with **ricotta, saffron** and **spinach**

Tossing pasta in ricotta is popular in Sicily and Sardinia. For best results, use fresh white ricotta.

SERVES 4–6

1 small pinch of saffron threads
300g/11oz/2$^{3}/_{4}$ cups dried pipe
300–350g/11–12oz fresh spinach, stalks removed
nutmeg
250g/9oz/generous 1 cup ricotta cheese
salt and ground black pepper
freshly grated Pecorino cheese, to serve

1 Soak the saffron threads in 60ml/4 tbsp warm water. Cook the pasta in a large pan of salted boiling water according to the packet instructions.

2 Meanwhile, wash the spinach and put the leaves in a pan with only the water clinging to the leaves. Season with freshly grated nutmeg, salt and pepper to taste.

3 Cover the pan and cook over a medium to high heat for about 5 minutes, shaking the pan occasionally, until the spinach is wilted and tender. Transfer into a colander, press to extract as much liquid as possible, then roughly chop it.

4 Put the ricotta in a large bowl. Strain in the saffron water. Add the spinach, mix well, add a ladleful or two of the pasta cooking water to loosen the mixture and season.

5 Drain the pasta, reserving some of the water. Add the pasta to the ricotta mixture and toss well, adding a little of the water if needed. Serve, sprinkled with Pecorino.

Nutritional information per portion: Energy 258kcal/1089kJ; Protein 11.2g; Carbohydrate 39.2g, of which sugars 3.7g; Fat 7.3g, of which saturates 3.9g; Cholesterol 18mg; Calcium 98mg; Fibre 2.5g; Sodium 72mg.

Tagliarini with **white truffle**

The Italian white truffle is one of the rarest and therefore most expensive of truffles.

SERVES 4

350g/12oz fresh tagliarini
75g/3oz/6 tbsp unsalted (sweet) butter, diced
60ml/4 tbsp freshly grated Parmesan cheese
nutmeg
1 small white truffle, about 25–40g/1–1$^{1}/_{2}$oz
salt and ground black pepper

1 Cook the pasta in a large pan of salted boiling water according to the instructions on the packet.

2 Drain the cooked pasta thoroughly and transfer it into a warmed large bowl. Add the butter, Parmesan, nutmeg and a little salt and pepper to taste. Toss well until the pasta is coated in melted butter.

3 Divide the pasta equally among four warmed bowls and shave paper-thin slivers of the white truffle on top.

COOK'S TIP

White Italian truffles can be bought during September and October from specialist food stores and delicatessens. They are expensive, however, and there are other ways of getting the flavour. Some Italian delicatessens sell 'truffle cheese', which has shavings of truffle in it, and can be used instead of the Parmesan and truffle in this recipe. Another alternative is to toss hot pasta in truffle oil and serve it with freshly grated Parmesan.

Nutritional information per portion: Energy 507kcal/2130kJ; Protein 16.5g; Carbohydrate 65g, of which sugars 3g; Fat 21.9g, of which saturates 13g; Cholesterol 55mg; Calcium 205mg; Fibre 2.6g; Sodium 280mg.

Conchiglie from Pisa

Nothing could be more simple than hot pasta tossed with fresh ripe tomatoes, ricotta and sweet basil. Serve it on hot summer days – it is surprisingly cool and refreshing.

SERVES 4–6

350g/12oz/3 cups dried conchiglie
130g/4½oz/generous ½ cup ricotta cheese
6 ripe Italian plum tomatoes, diced
2 garlic cloves, crushed
1 handful fresh basil leaves, shredded, plus extra whole basil leaves to garnish
60ml/4 tbsp extra virgin olive oil
salt and ground black pepper

1 Cook the pasta in a pan of salted boiling water, according to the instructions on the packet.

2 Meanwhile, put the ricotta in a large bowl and mash with a fork. Add the tomatoes, garlic and basil, with salt and pepper to taste, and mix well. Add the olive oil and whisk thoroughly. Taste for seasoning.

3 Drain the cooked pasta, transfer it into the ricotta mixture and toss well to mix. Garnish with basil leaves and serve immediately.

Nutritional information per portion: Energy 322kcal/1358kJ; Protein 9.7g; Carbohydrate 47.6g, of which sugars 5.2g; Fat 11.7g, of which saturates 3.2g; Cholesterol 9mg; Calcium 21mg; Fibre 2.6g; Sodium 9mg.

Spaghetti with **lemon**

If you keep spaghetti and olive oil in the store cupboard and garlic and lemons in the vegetable rack, you can prepare the most delicious meal in minutes.

SERVES 4

350g/12oz dried spaghetti
90ml/6 tbsp extra virgin olive oil
juice of 1 large lemon, plus grated rind to serve
2 garlic cloves, cut into very thin slivers
salt and ground black pepper

1 Cook the pasta in a pan of salted boiling water, according to the instructions on the packet, then drain well and return to the pan.

2 Pour the olive oil and lemon juice over the cooked pasta, sprinkle in the slivers of garlic and add salt and pepper to taste.

3 Toss the pasta over a medium to high heat for 1–2 minutes. Serve immediately in four warmed bowls, with freshly grated lemon rind.

Nutritional information per portion: Energy 448kcal/1886kJ; Protein 10.5g; Carbohydrate 64.9g, of which sugars 3g; Fat 18.1g, of which saturates 2.5g; Cholesterol 0mg; Calcium 22mg; Fibre 2.6g; Sodium 3mg.

Strozzapreti with courgette flowers

This pretty, summery dish is strewn with courgette flowers, but you can make it even if you don't have the flowers. In Italy, bunches of courgette flowers are a common sight on vegetable stalls in summer, and are frequently used for stuffing and cooking.

SERVES 4

50g/2oz/1/4 cup butter
30ml/2 tbsp extra virgin olive oil
1 small onion, thinly sliced
200g/7oz small courgettes (zucchini), cut into thin julienne
1 garlic clove, crushed
10ml/2 tsp finely chopped fresh marjoram
350g/12oz/3 cups dried strozzapreti
1 large handful courgette (zucchini) flowers, thoroughly washed and dried
salt and ground black pepper
thin shavings of Parmesan cheese, to serve

1 Heat the butter and half the olive oil in a medium skillet or pan, add the sliced onion and cook gently, stirring often, for 5 minutes until softened. Add the courgettes and sprinkle with the crushed garlic, chopped marjoram and salt and pepper to taste. Cook for 5–8 minutes until the courgettes have softened but are not coloured, turning them over occasionally.

2 Meanwhile, cook the pasta in a pan of salted boiling water according to the packet instructions.

3 Set aside a few whole courgette flowers for the garnish, then roughly shred the rest and add them to the courgette mixture. Stir to mix, and taste for seasoning.

4 Drain the pasta, transfer it into a warmed large bowl and add the remaining oil. Add the courgette mixture and toss. Top with Parmesan and the reserved flowers.

Nutritional information per portion: Energy 456kcal/1919kJ; Protein 11.7g; Carbohydrate 67g, of which sugars 4.7g; Fat 17.6g, of which saturates 7.5g; Cholesterol 27mg; Calcium 41mg; Fibre 3.2g; Sodium 79mg.

Three-colour tagliatelle

Courgettes and carrots are cut into delicate ribbons so that when they are cooked and tossed with tagliatelle they look like coloured pasta. Serve as a side dish, or sprinkle with freshly grated Parmesan cheese for a light first course or vegetarian main course.

SERVES 4

2 large courgettes (zucchini)
2 large carrots
250g/9oz fresh egg tagliatelle
60ml/4 tbsp extra virgin olive oil
flesh of 2 roasted garlic cloves, plus extra whole roasted garlic cloves, to serve (optional)
salt and ground black pepper

1 With a vegetable peeler, cut the courgettes and carrots into long thin ribbons. Bring a large pan of salted water to the boil, then add the courgette and carrot ribbons. Bring the water back to the boil for 30 seconds, then drain and set aside.

2 Cook the pasta in a large pan of salted boiling water, according to the instructions on the packet.

3 Drain the pasta and return it to the pan. Add the vegetable ribbons, oil, garlic and salt and pepper and toss over a medium to high heat until the pasta and vegetables are well-coated with oil. Serve immediately, with extra roasted garlic, if you like.

Nutritional information per portion: Energy 397kcal/1663kJ; Protein 11.5g; Carbohydrate 52.4g, of which sugars 8.3g; Fat 17.1g, of which saturates 3.3g; Cholesterol 19mg; Calcium 80mg; Fibre 4.8g; Sodium 127mg.

Tagliatelle with fresh mixed herbs

This lovely summer dish is easy to make and ideal for vegetarians.

SERVES 4

30ml/2 tbsp extra virgin olive oil
50g/2oz/$^1/_4$ cup butter
1 shallot, finely chopped
2 garlic cloves, finely chopped
pinch of chilli powder, to taste
400g/14oz fresh egg tagliatelle
3 rosemary sprigs, the leaves stripped from the stalks and chopped
1 small handful fresh flat leaf parsley, finely chopped
5–6 fresh mint leaves, chopped
5–6 fresh sage leaves, chopped
8–10 large fresh basil leaves, chopped
1 bay leaf
120ml/4fl oz/$^1/_2$ cup dry white wine
90–120ml/6–8 tbsp vegetable stock
salt and ground black pepper

1 Heat the oil and half the butter in a skillet or pan. Add the shallot, garlic and chilli powder. Cook gently for 2–3 minutes.

2 Cook the pasta in a pan of salted boiling water according to the packet instructions. Add the herbs and bay leaf to the shallot mixture and stir for 2–3 minutes. Add the wine, increase the heat and boil for 1–2 minutes until reduced. Lower the heat, add the stock and simmer for 1–2 minutes.

3 Drain the pasta and add to the herb mixture. Toss well and discard the bay leaf. Put the remaining butter in a warmed large bowl, add the pasta, toss well and serve.

Nutritional information per portion: Energy 306kcal/1291kJ; Protein 8.3g; Carbohydrate 49.8g, of which sugars 2.6g; Fat 8.2g, of which saturates 4.5g; Cholesterol 18mg; Calcium 37mg; Fibre 2.4g; Sodium 56mg.

Garganelli with spring vegetables

In this fresh-tasting dish, young vegetables both look and taste just perfect with pasta.

SERVES 4

1 bunch asparagus, about 350g/12oz
4 young carrots
1 bunch spring onions (scallions)
130g/4$^1/_2$oz shelled fresh peas
350g/12oz/3 cups dried garganelli
60ml/4 tbsp dry white wine
75g/3oz/6 tbsp unsalted (sweet) butter, diced
a few sprigs of chopped fresh flat leaf parsley, mint and basil
salt and ground black pepper
freshly grated Parmesan cheese, to serve

1 Trim off and discard the woody part of each asparagus stem, then cut off the tips on the diagonal. Cut the stems on the diagonal into 4cm/1$^1/_2$in pieces. Cut the carrots and spring onions on the diagonal into similar pieces.

2 Put the asparagus stems, carrots and peas into a pan of salted boiling water. Bring back to the boil and simmer for 5–8 minutes. Add the asparagus tips for the last 3 minutes.

3 Cook the pasta in salted boiling water according to the packet instructions. Drain the vegetables and return them to the pan. Add the wine, butter and salt and pepper. Toss over a medium to high heat until the wine reduces.

4 Drain the pasta and transfer into a warmed bowl. Add the herbs, vegetables and spring onions and toss. Serve with Parmesan.

Nutritional information per portion: Energy 738kcal/3092kJ; Protein 29.5g; Carbohydrate 74g, of which sugars 5.2g; Fat 38.1g, of which saturates 10.4g; Cholesterol 38mg; Calcium 492mg; Fibre 4.3g; Sodium 416mg.

Pasta salads

Although not traditionally Italian, pasta salads have earned their place in the Italian cook's repertoire. They are extremely versatile in that they can be served as part of an antipasto, as a first course or a main course. Salads can be prepared well in advance, which makes them marvellous party food. They are also a popular choice for picnics, because they are so easy to transport.

Roasted cherry tomato and rocket salad

This is a good side salad to accompany barbecued chicken, steaks or chops. Roasted tomatoes are very juicy, with a powerful, smoky-sweet flavour.

SERVES 4

225g/8oz/2 cups dried chifferini or pipe
450g/1lb ripe baby Italian plum tomatoes, halved lengthways
75ml/5 tbsp extra virgin olive oil
2 garlic cloves, cut into thin slivers
30ml/2 tbsp balsamic vinegar
2 pieces sun-dried tomato in olive oil, drained and chopped
large pinch of sugar, to taste
1 handful rocket (arugula), about 65g/2½oz
salt and ground black pepper

1 Preheat the oven to 190°C/375°F/Gas 5. Meanwhile, cook the pasta in salted boiling water according to the instructions on the packet.

2 Arrange the halved tomatoes cut side up in a roasting pan, drizzle 30ml/2 tbsp of the oil over them and sprinkle with the slivers of garlic and salt and pepper to taste. Roast in the oven for 20 minutes, turning once.

3 Put the remaining oil in a large bowl with the vinegar, sun-dried tomatoes, sugar and a little salt and pepper to taste. Stir well to mix.

4 Drain the pasta, add it to the bowl of dressing and toss to mix. Add the roasted tomatoes and mix gently.

5 Before serving, add the rocket, toss lightly and taste for seasoning. Serve either at room temperature or chilled.

Nutritional information per portion: Energy 344kcal/1444kJ; Protein 8.2g; Carbohydrate 46.2g, of which sugars 6.4g; Fat 15.3g, of which saturates 2.2g; Cholesterol 0mg; Calcium 51mg; Fibre 3.4g; Sodium 37mg.

Chargrilled pepper salad

This is a good side salad to serve with plain grilled or barbecued chicken or fish. The ingredients are simple and few, but the overall flavour is quite intense.

SERVES 4

2 large (bell) peppers (red and green)
250g/9oz/2¹/₄ cups dried fusilli tricolore
1 handful fresh basil leaves
1 handful fresh coriander (cilantro) leaves
1 garlic clove
salt and ground black pepper

FOR THE DRESSING
30ml/2 tbsp bottled pesto
juice of ¹/₂ lemon
60ml/4 tbsp extra virgin olive oil

1 Put the peppers under a hot grill (broiler) and grill for about 10 minutes, turning frequently until charred on all sides. Put the peppers in a plastic bag, seal it and set aside to cool.

2 Meanwhile, cook the pasta in a pan of salted boiling water, according to the instructions on the packet.

3 Whisk all the dressing ingredients together in a large bowl. Drain the cooked pasta well and transfer it into the bowl of dressing. Toss well to mix and set aside to cool.

4 Remove the peppers from the bag and hold them one at a time under cold running water. Peel off the charred skins with your fingers, split the peppers open and pull out the cores. Rub off all the seeds under the running water, then pat the peppers dry on kitchen paper.

5 Chop the peppers and add them to the pasta. Put the basil, coriander and garlic on a board and chop them all together. Add to the pasta and toss to mix, then taste for seasoning and serve.

Nutritional information per portion: Energy 420kcal/1763kJ; Protein 11.1g; Carbohydrate 54g, of which sugars 8.4g; Fat 19.2g, of which saturates 2.9g; Cholesterol 3mg; Calcium 106mg; Fibre 4.7g; Sodium 42mg.

Summer salad

Ripe red tomatoes, mozzarella and olives make a good base for this fresh and tangy salad.

SERVES 4

350g/12oz/3 cups dried penne
3 ripe tomatoes, diced
150g/5oz packet mozzarella di bufala, drained and diced
10 pitted black olives, sliced
10 pitted green olives, sliced
1 spring onion (scallion), thinly sliced on the diagonal
1 handful fresh basil leaves

FOR THE DRESSING

90ml/6 tbsp extra virgin olive oil
15ml/1 tbsp balsamic vinegar or lemon juice
salt and ground black pepper

1 Cook the pasta according to the instructions on the packet. Transfer it into a colander and rinse under cold running water, then shake the colander to remove as much water as possible. Leave the pasta to drain.

2 Make the dressing. Whisk the olive oil and balsamic vinegar or lemon juice in a large bowl with a little salt and pepper to taste.

3 Add the pasta, mozzarella, tomatoes, olives and spring onion to the dressing and toss together well. Taste for seasoning before serving, sprinkled with basil leaves.

VARIATION

Make the salad more substantial by adding other ingredients, such as sliced (bell) peppers, flaked tuna, anchovy fillets or diced ham.

Nutritional information per portion: Energy 635kcal/2658kJ; Protein 18.7g; Carbohydrate 67.3g, of which sugars 5.3g; Fat 34.2g, of which saturates 9.1g; Cholesterol 22mg; Calcium 210mg; Fibre 5.5g; Sodium 1845mg.

Country pasta salad

Colourful, tasty and nutritious, this is the ideal pasta salad for a summer picnic.

SERVES 6

300g/11oz/2¾ cups dried fusilli
150g/5oz green beans, topped and tailed and cut into 5cm/2in lengths
1 potato, about 150g/5oz, diced
200g/7oz baby tomatoes, hulled and halved
2 spring onions (scallions), finely chopped
90g/3½ oz Parmesan cheese, diced or coarsely shaved
6–8 pitted black olives, cut into rings
15–30ml/1–2 tbsp capers, to taste

FOR THE DRESSING

90ml/6 tbsp extra virgin olive oil
15ml/1 tbsp balsamic vinegar
15ml/1 tbsp chopped fresh flat leaf parsley
salt and ground black pepper

1 Cook the pasta according to the packet instructions. Drain it into a colander, rinse under cold running water until cold, then shake to remove as much water as possible. Leave to drain and dry, shaking occasionally.

2 Cook the beans and diced potato in a pan of salted boiling water for 5–6 minutes or until tender. Drain and leave to cool.

3 Make the dressing. Put all the ingredients in a large bowl with salt and pepper to taste and whisk well to mix. Add the baby tomatoes, spring onions, Parmesan, olive rings and capers to the dressing, then the cold pasta, beans and potato. Toss well to mix. Cover and leave to stand for about 30 minutes. Taste for seasoning before serving.

Nutritional information per portion: Energy 381kcal/1600kJ; Protein 13.3g; Carbohydrate 44.4g, of which sugars 3.8g; Fat 18g, of which saturates 5g; Cholesterol 15mg; Calcium 212mg; Fibre 2.9g; Sodium 341mg.

Seafood salad

This is a very special salad which can be served as a first course or main meal. The choice of pasta shape is up to you, but one of the unusual 'designer' shapes would suit it well.

SERVES 4–6

450g/1lb mussels, scrubbed with beards removed
250ml/8fl oz/1 cup dry white wine
2 garlic cloves, roughly chopped
1 handful of fresh flat leaf parsley
175g/6oz/1 cup prepared squid rings
175g/6oz/1½ cups small dried pasta shapes
175g/6oz/1 cup peeled cooked prawns (shrimp)

FOR THE DRESSING
90ml/6 tbsp extra virgin olive oil
juice of 1 lemon
5–10ml/1–2 tsp capers, to taste, roughly chopped
1 garlic clove, crushed
1 small handful fresh flat leaf parsley, finely chopped
salt and ground black pepper

1 Discard any opened mussels or any that do not close when tapped sharply against the work surface.

2 Pour half the wine into a large pan, add the garlic, parsley and mussels. Cover tightly and bring to the boil over a high heat. Cook for 5 minutes, shaking the pan frequently, until the mussels are open.

3 Transfer the mussels and their liquid into a colander over a bowl. Leave to cool. Reserve a few to garnish, then remove the rest from their shells, pouring the liquid from the mussels into the bowl of cooking liquid. Discard any closed mussels.

4 Return the mussel cooking liquid to the pan and add the remaining wine and the squid rings. Bring to the boil, cover and simmer gently, stirring occasionally, for 30 minutes or until the squid is tender. Leave the squid to cool in the cooking liquid.

5 Cook the pasta according to packet instructions. Whisk all the dressing ingredients in a large bowl, adding a little salt and pepper. Drain the pasta well, add to the bowl and toss well. Leave to cool.

6 Drain the cooled squid in a sieve (strainer) and rinse lightly under the cold tap. Add the squid, mussels and prawns to the dressed pasta and toss well. Cover the bowl tightly with clear film (plastic wrap) and chill in the refrigerator for 4 hours. Toss well and adjust the seasoning to taste before serving.

Nutritional information per portion: Energy 231kcal/969kJ; Protein 20.4g; Carbohydrate 9.4g, of which sugars 3.5g; Fat 12.5g, of which saturates 2.6g; Cholesterol 235mg; Calcium 81mg; Fibre 2.6g; Sodium 124mg.

Tuna and corn salad

This is an excellent main course salad for a summer lunch outside.

SERVES 4

175g/6oz/1½ cups dried conchiglie
175g/6oz can tuna in olive oil, drained and flaked
175g/6oz can corn, drained
75g/3oz bottled roasted red (bell) pepper, rinsed, dried and finely chopped
1 handful of fresh basil leaves, chopped
salt and ground black pepper

FOR THE DRESSING
60ml/4 tbsp extra virgin olive oil
15ml/1 tbsp balsamic vinegar
5ml/1 tsp red wine vinegar
5ml/1 tsp Dijon mustard
5–10ml/1–2 tsp honey, to taste

1 Cook the pasta in a pan of salted boiling water according to the packet instructions. Drain and rinse under cold water. Leave until cold and dry, shaking occasionally.

2 Make the dressing. Put the oil in a large bowl, add the two kinds of vinegar and whisk well together until mixed. Add the mustard, honey and salt and pepper to taste and whisk again until thick.

3 Add the pasta to the dressing and toss well to mix, then add the tuna, corn and roasted pepper and toss again. Mix in about half the basil and taste for seasoning. Serve at room temperature or chilled, with the remaining basil sprinkled on top.

Nutritional information per portion: Energy 398kcal/1674kJ; Protein 18.6g; Carbohydrate 47.2g, of which sugars 8.7g; Fat 16.3g, of which saturates 2.4g; Cholesterol 22mg; Calcium 20mg; Fibre 2.2g; Sodium 247mg.

Pink and green salad

Spiked with fresh chilli, this pretty salad makes a delicious light lunch.

SERVES 4

225g/8oz/2 cups dried farfalle
juice of ½ lemon
1 small fresh red chilli, seeded and very finely chopped
60ml/4 tbsp chopped fresh basil
30ml/2 tbsp chopped fresh coriander (cilantro)
60ml/4 tbsp extra virgin olive oil
15ml/1 tbsp mayonnaise
250g/9oz/1½ cups peeled cooked prawns (shrimp)
1 avocado
salt and ground black pepper

1 Cook the pasta in a large pan of salted boiling water according to the packet instructions.

2 Meanwhile, put the lemon juice and chilli in a bowl with half the basil and coriander and season to taste. Whisk well to mix, then whisk in the oil and mayonnaise until thick. Add the prawns and gently stir to coat in the dressing.

3 Drain the pasta into a colander, and rinse under cold running water until cold. Leave to drain and dry, shaking the colander occasionally.

4 Halve, stone (pit) and peel the avocado, then cut the flesh into neat dice. Add to the prawns and dressing with the pasta, toss well to mix and taste for seasoning. Serve immediately, sprinkled with the remaining basil and coriander.

Nutritional information per portion: Energy 420kcal/1761kJ; Protein 19g; Carbohydrate 42.8g, of which sugars 2.6g; Fat 20.3g, of which saturates 3.2g; Cholesterol 125mg; Calcium 112mg; Fibre 3.6g; Sodium 146mg.

Chicken and **broccoli salad**

Gorgonzola makes a tangy dressing that goes well with both chicken and broccoli. Serve for a lunch or evening dish, with crusty Italian bread.

SERVES 4

175g/6oz broccoli florets, divided into small sprigs
225g/8oz/2 cups dried farfalle
2 large cooked chicken breast fillets

FOR THE DRESSING

90g/3½oz Gorgonzola cheese
15ml/1 tbsp white wine vinegar
60ml/4 tbsp extra virgin olive oil
2.5–5ml/½–1 tsp finely chopped fresh sage, plus extra sage sprigs to garnish
salt and ground black pepper

1 Cook the broccoli florets in a large pan of salted boiling water for 3 minutes. Remove with a slotted spoon, rinse under cold running water and leave to dry on kitchen paper.

2 Add the pasta to the broccoli cooking water, bring back to the boil and cook according to the packet instructions. When cooked, drain the pasta into a colander, rinse under cold water until cool, then leave to drain, shaking occasionally.

3 Remove the skin from the cooked chicken breast fillets and cut the meat into bitesize pieces.

4 Make the dressing. Put the Gorgonzola in a large bowl and mash with a fork, then whisk in the wine vinegar followed by the oil and sage and salt and pepper to taste.

5 Add the pasta, chicken and broccoli. Toss well, then season to taste and serve, garnished with sage.

Nutritional information per portion: Energy 472kcal/1977kJ; Protein 25.3g; Carbohydrate 42.5g, of which sugars 2.5g; Fat 23.5g, of which saturates 6.8g; Cholesterol 52mg; Calcium 151mg; Fibre 2.8g; Sodium 310mg.

Pasta salad with **salami** and **olives**

Garlic and herb dressing gives a Mediterranean flavour to a handful of ingredients from the store cupboard and refrigerator, making this an excellent salad for winter.

SERVES 4

225g/8oz/2 cups dried gnocchi or conchiglie
50g/2oz/½ cup pitted black olives, quartered lengthways
75g/3oz thinly sliced salami, any skin removed, diced
½ small red onion, finely chopped
1 large handful fresh basil leaves

FOR THE DRESSING

60ml/4 tbsp extra virgin olive oil
good pinch of sugar, to taste
juice of ½ lemon
5ml/1 tsp Dijon mustard
10ml/2 tsp dried oregano
1 garlic clove, crushed
salt and ground black pepper

1 Cook the pasta in a pan of salted boiling water, according to the packet instructions.

2 Meanwhile, make the dressing for the pasta. Put all the ingredients for the dressing in a large bowl with a little salt and pepper to taste, and whisk well to mix.

3 Drain the pasta thoroughly, add it to the bowl of dressing and toss well to mix. Leave the dressed pasta to cool, stirring occasionally.

4 When the pasta has cooled, add the remaining ingredients and toss well to mix again. Taste for seasoning, then serve immediately.

Nutritional information per portion: Energy 392kcal/1641kJ; Protein 11g; Carbohydrate 43g, of which sugars 2.8g; Fat 20.8g, of which saturates 4.6g; Cholesterol 16mg; Calcium 28mg; Fibre 2.2g; Sodium 621mg.

Pasta basics

The following section covers the many different types of pasta available – both dried and fresh – and all the preparation and cooking equipment you need. There are also clear step-by-step instructions on cooking and serving pasta, and making your own, by hand or with a machine. Finally, there is a handy guide to the oils, herbs, flavourings and cheeses essential for a well-stocked pasta pantry.

Dried pasta

There are many forms of dried pasta. Long, short and flat shapes are the most common, but there are also stuffed shapes, shapes for stuffing and tiny shapes for soups.

LONG PASTA/PASTA LUNGA

Dried long pasta in the form of spaghetti is probably the best-known pasta of all time. Spaghetti is still very widely used, but nowadays there are many other varieties of long pasta that look and taste just as good. Feel free to experiment with sauces, but remember that long pasta is best served with either a thin, clinging sauce or a smooth, thick one. Rich sauces made with olive oil, butter, cream, eggs, finely grated cheese and chopped fresh herbs are good with long pasta. When ingredients such as vegetables, fish and meat are added to a smooth thick sauce, they should be very finely chopped.

Long pasta comes in different lengths and widths, but 30cm/12in is about the average length. You may come across dried pasta that is much longer than this, but think twice before buying it because extra-long pasta can be tricky to cook and eat.

Fine long pasta, such as spaghetti, is often too delicate to be made with egg, so most long shapes are available in plain durum wheat only. The shapes made with egg (all'uovo) are very delicate, and are either packed in nests or compressed as waves.

Always buy dried pasta made from 100 per cent durum wheat. If you decant pasta into storage jars, use up any remaining pasta before adding more from a new packet.

Bavette

Well known in Italy, bavette is narrow and flat, like tagliatelle, only slimmer. Indeed, some Italians use the name bavette to describe tagliatelle.

Bucatini

Sometimes referred to as perciatelli, bucatini looks like spaghetti but is slightly chunkier with hard, hollow strands. This type of pasta is best known in the Roman dish, Bucatini all'Amatriciana, which has a tomato, bacon and pepper sauce.

ABOVE: *Capelli d'angelo*

Capelli d'angelo

The name means 'angel's hair', an evocative description for this very fine pasta. It is typically used in broths and soups. You may find it packed in nests, labelled capelli d'angelo a nidi. These nests are easy to handle and cook – serve one nest per person. Capellini and capel Venere are similar.

Chitarra

Also known as spaghetti alla chitarra, this type of pasta is cut on a special wooden frame strung with wires like guitar strings (*chitarra* is Italian for guitar). It is therefore square-shaped rather than round, but can be used as an alternative to spaghetti.

ABOVE: *Bavette*

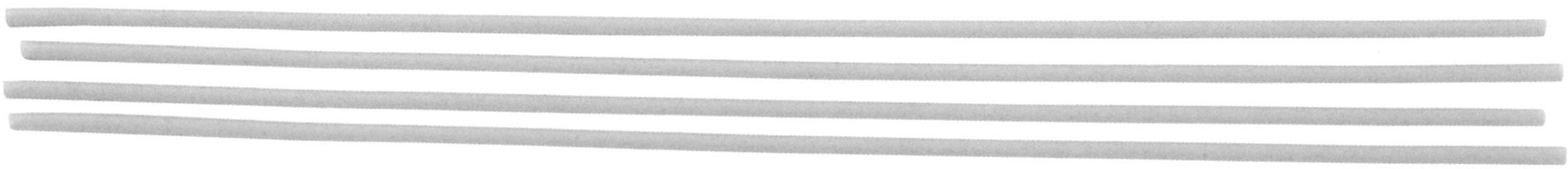

ABOVE: *Bucatini*

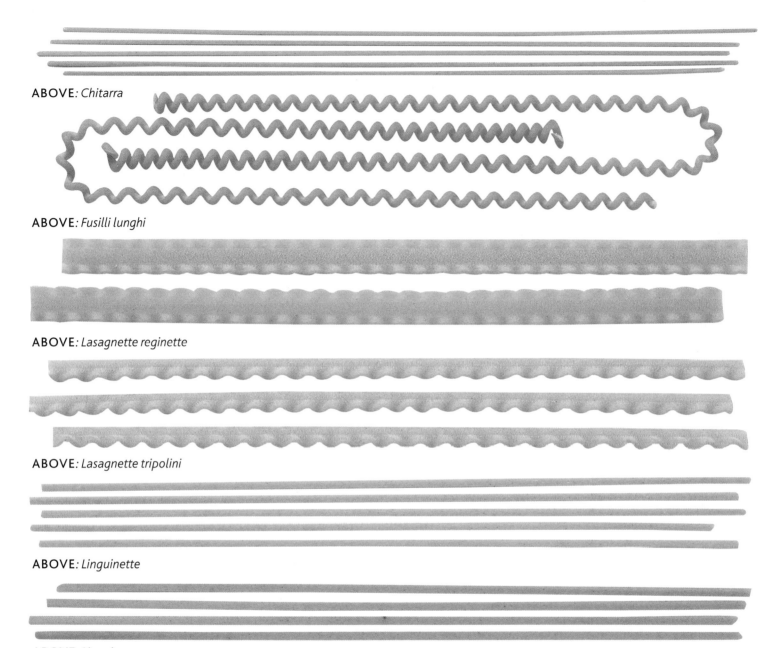

ABOVE: *Chitarra*

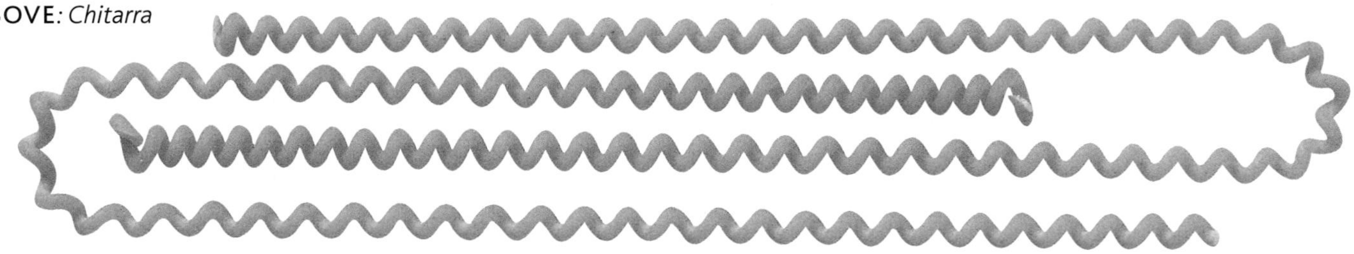

ABOVE: *Fusilli lunghi*

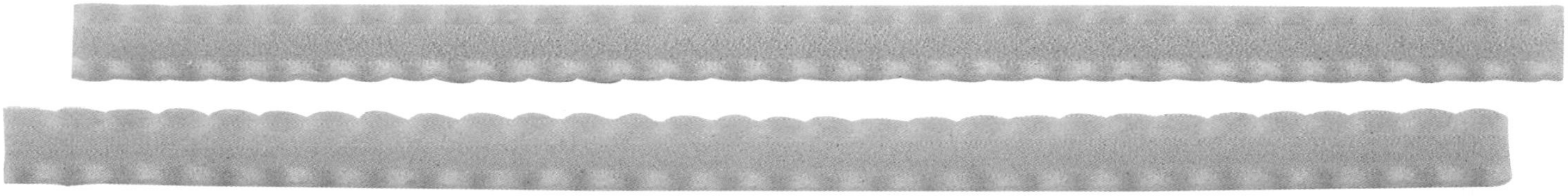

ABOVE: *Lasagnette reginette*

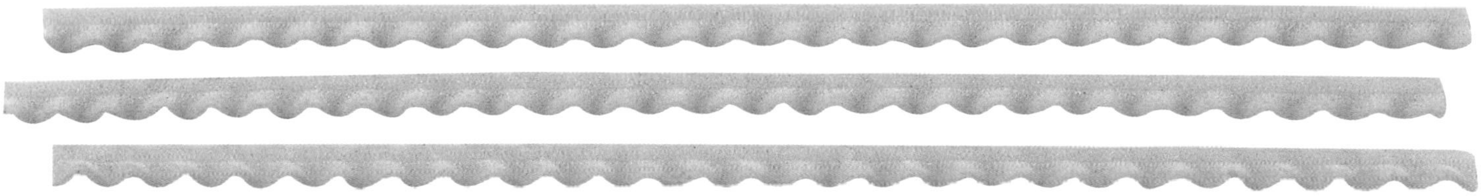

ABOVE: *Lasagnette tripolini*

ABOVE: *Linguinette*

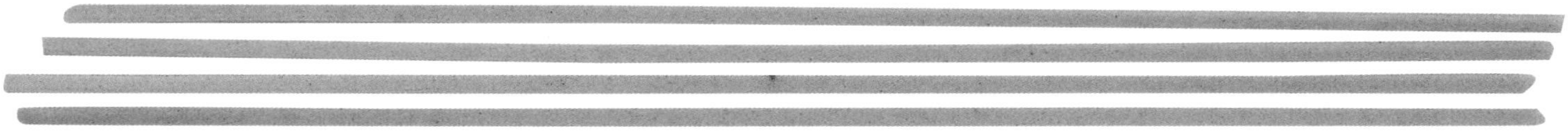

ABOVE: *Linguine*

Fusilli

These long, twisted spaghetti spirals look like stretched corkscrews. You may see this type of pasta labelled fusilli lunghi or fusilli col buco, which distinguishes it from the more widely known short pasta shapes fusilli and eliche. This type of pasta is widely used with tomato based sauces.

Lasagnette

This flat type of pasta resembles tagliatelle, but the noodles are slightly wider. It is a narrower version of the lasagne noodle. There are several types of lasagnette, most of which have frilly edges. Reginette is also similar. You can use lasagnette in baked dishes or in a sauce in place of any ribbon pasta.

Linguine

In Italian the name means 'little tongues' and accurately describes this very thin spaghetti-like pasta that has flattened edges. You may also see narrower versions, such as linguinette and lingue di passera ('sparrows' tongues'). All are good with the simple olive oil-based sauces and smooth tomato sauces.

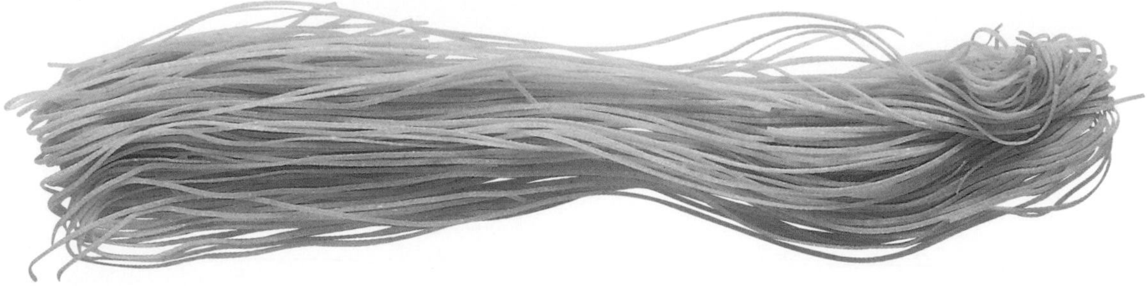

ABOVE AND BELOW: *Maccheroncini*

BELOW: *Spaghetti*

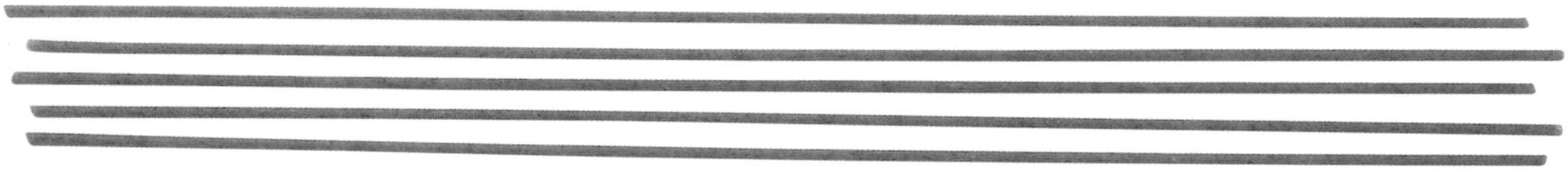

BELOW: *Spaghetti integrali*

Maccheroni

We know a short version of this pasta as macaroni, but in Italy the long thick tubes are widely used for a variety of sauces – in some regions, maccheroni is used as a generic term for pasta. Maccheroni comes in different lengths and thicknesses, with straight or angled ends, in plain, egg and wholewheat varieties. There is even a square-shaped chitarra version, from Abruzzi.

Spaghetti

This familiar pasta takes its name from the word *spago*, which means 'string'. Spaghetti literally means 'little strings'. It originated from Naples, but is now also produced in other parts of Italy. It varies in length and width depending on the region. Numerous varieties are available, including: wholewheat (integrali), spinach (spinaci) and chilli (peperoncini).

Tagliatelle

The most common form of ribbon noodles, tagliatelle derives its name from the Italian verb *tagliare* meaning 'to cut'. The noodles are usually about 8mm–1cm/$\frac{1}{3}$–$\frac{1}{2}$in wide, but there are finer versions called tagliatellina, tagliarini, tagliolini and tagliolini fini. It is traditionally made both with and without egg and with spinach (verdi).

All types of tagliatelle are sold in nests, which conveniently unravel during cooking when given a good stir. Paglia e fieno, which literally means straw and hay, is a mixture consisting of half plain egg and half spinach egg pasta, packed together in bundles. The noodles are quite thin, either tagliarni or tagliolini. Both paglia e fieno and tagliatelle are popular as they go well with most sauces, though strictly speaking, tagliatelle should not be served with a fish sauce.

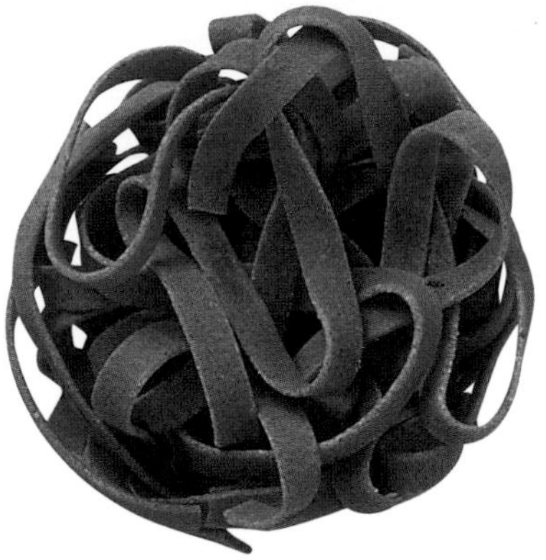

ABOVE: *Tagliatelle verdi*

BELOW: *Tagliatelle*

BELOW: *Vermicelli*

BELOW: *Ziti*

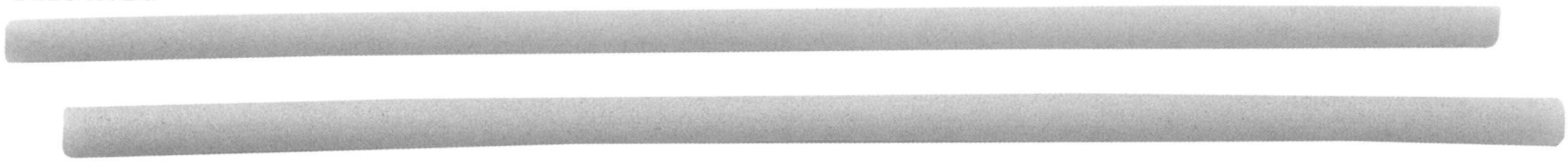

Vermicelli

This sounds appealing, but the name means little worms, which is rather unfortunate. It describes a very fine form of spaghetti – the original Neapolitan name for spaghetti was vermicelli, and southern Italians still sometimes refer to spaghetti as vermicelli, which can be confusing. This type of pasta comes in plain and egg (all'uovo) varieties and is very versatile, going especially well with most light sauces, especially the light, fresh tomato and seafood sauces for which Naples is famous. There is an even finer version called vermicellini.

Ziti

This pasta takes its name from the word zita, meaning 'fiancée'. In the old days it was traditional in southern Italy to serve ziti at wedding feasts and on other special occasions. Ziti is very long, thick and hollow, and the custom is to break it into the length required when you cook it. Because of their size, the tubes go well with chunky sauces; they are also sometimes broken into short lengths and baked in a timballo, which is a cup-shaped mould. The pasta is used to line the mould, which is then filled with a savoury mixture such as mushrooms, ham or chicken livers combined with a sauce and topped with cheese. Zitoni are fatter than ziti; mezza zita are thinner.

Some regional types of long dried pasta

Fettuccine comes from Lazio, and is used in classic Roman pasta dishes, such as *Fettuccine all'Alfredo*. The three most common types are plain durum wheat, with egg (all'uovo) and with spinach (verdi). Like tagliatelle but narrower (about 5mm/¼in wide), fettucine can be used interchangeably with tagliatelle. Fettuccelle is similar, but is straight rather than coiled.

Frappe comes from Emilia-Romagna. The 2.5–4cm/1–1½in wide noodles are flat, with wavy edges, about halfway in size between tagliatelle and lasagne. Made with egg and very delicate, the noodles are packed by a machine that presses them into waves.

Pappardelle are broad ribbon noodles (2–2.5cm/¾–1in wide), with wavy edges. They come from Tuscany, where they are still made fresh with egg every day, but dried versions are now becoming more widely available, many of them with only one wavy edge or straight edges. They are good with heavy meat and game sauces.

Trenette are noodles from Liguria, where they are traditionally served with pesto sauce. The Genoese dish, *Trenette alla Genovese*, combines trenette with pesto, potatoes and beans. The noodles are about 3mm/⅛in wide, and are made with egg. They resemble bavette and linguine, which can be substituted for them if you find trenette difficult to find.

RIGHT: *Fettuccine al nero*

SHORT PASTA/PASTA CORTA

Short types of pasta are easier to cook and eat than long types. They also go well with many different sauces, and in most cases, with any shape you fancy.

Short pasta is divided into two main groups. The largest group, pasta secca, is factory-made, using durum wheat flour and water. Pasta all'uovo, made with the addition of eggs, is a brighter yellow than pasta secca and has more nutritional value. Pasta all'uovo goes especially well with the rich creamy and meaty sauces. It cooks slightly more quickly than plain durum wheat pasta and is less likely to become overcooked and soggy.

For many years, tomato (pomodoro) and spinach (verdi) were the only varieties available, but today there seems to be no end to the number of different colour and flavour combinations, ranging from garlic, chillies and herbs to beetroot (beet), salmon, mushroom, squid ink and even chocolate. Wholewheat pasta, called pasta integrale, is made from durum wheat and other cereals. It is higher in fibre than plain durum wheat pasta and takes longer to cook. It has a chewy texture and nutty flavour.

Benfatti

The word *benfatti* means 'well made' and originally describes the little offcuts of pasta left over from other shapes, such as tagliatelle. They proved so popular that they are now made and marketed as a shape in their own right. Benfatti are available plain and with egg, and are good in salads and soups.

ABOVE: *Eliche all'uovo*

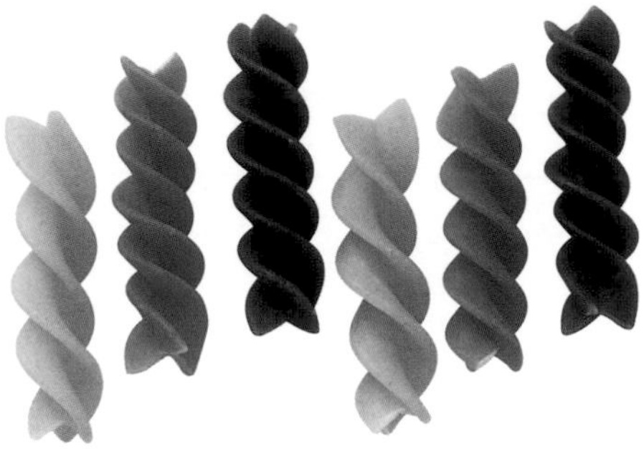

ABOVE: *Eliche tricolori*

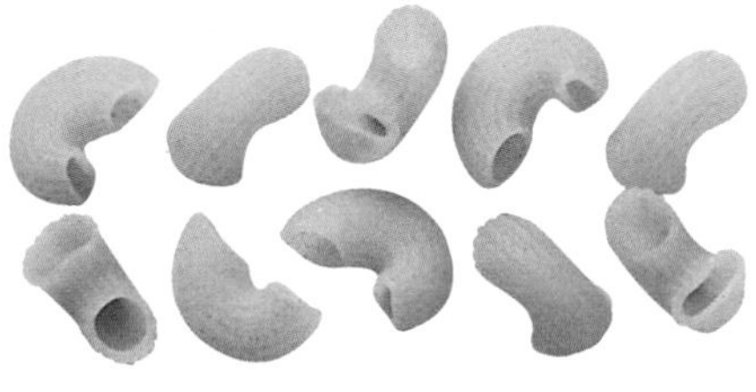

ABOVE: *Chifferini rigatini*

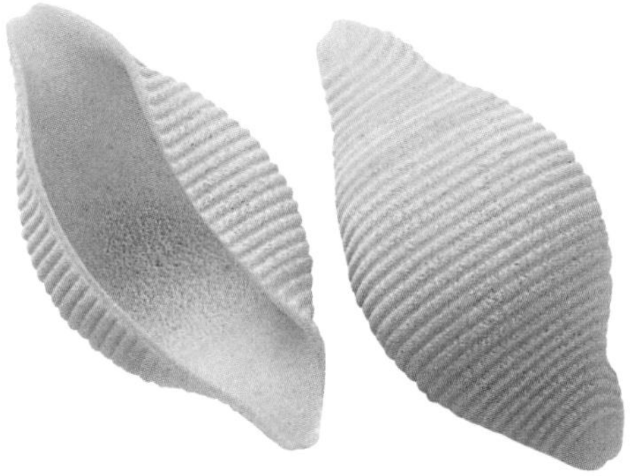

ABOVE: *Conchigliette rigati*

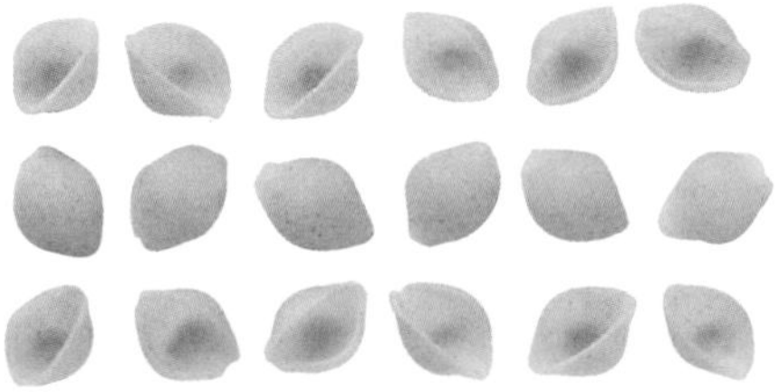

ABOVE: *Conchigliette rigate*

Chifferini

Also called chifferi, chifferoni and chifferotti, these are small curved tubes, like short maccheroni that has been bent. Some versions are ridged (rigatini). The holes in the middle fill with sauce, making them an excellent shape for all types of sauces and soups.

Conchiglie

As the name suggests, these shapes resemble small conch shells. Sometimes they are ridged, in which case they are called conchiglie rigate. They are extremely popular and are widely available in different colours and flavours. Sizes vary too, from tiny conchigliette for soups to conchiglione, which are jumbo shells for stuffing.

Eliche

The name comes from the Italian word for screws or propellers, which are what these shapes look like. They are often mis-labelled as fusilli, which are similar. Eliche are short lengths of pasta, each twisted into a spiral, like the thread of a screw. They are available in different thicknesses, colours and flavours, and are good with tomato-based sauces.

Farfalle

The word means 'butterflies', but these shapes are also described as bow-ties. They have crinkled edges, and are sometimes ridged. They are available in a wide variety of colours and flavours. Farfalle can be served with any sauce, but are particularly good with cream and tomato sauces.

ABOVE: *Farfalle*

ABOVE: *Farfalle verde*

ABOVE: *Lumache rigate*

ABOVE: *Farfalle salmonseppia*

ABOVE: *Farfalle tricolore*

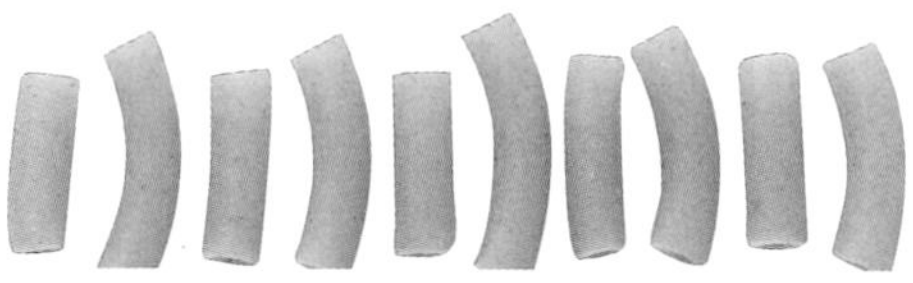

ABOVE: *Maccheroni*

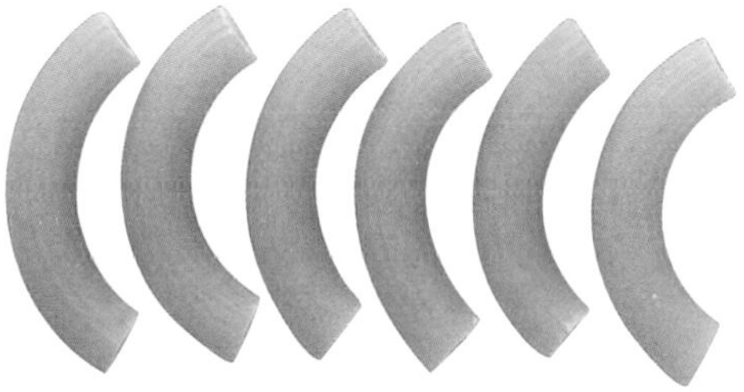

ABOVE: *Maccheroncelli*

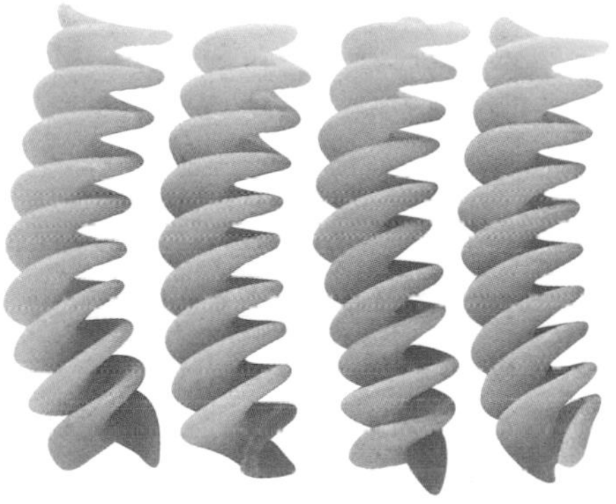

ABOVE: *Fusilli*

ABOVE: *Fusilli con spinaci*

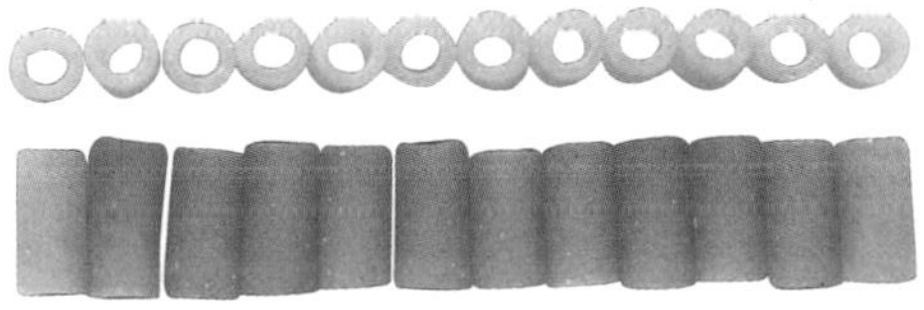

ABOVE: *Tubetti*

Fusilli

These spirals of thin pasta look like tight coils or springs and are formed by winding fresh dough around a thin rod. The spiral opens out, rather than remaining solid as it does in the case of eliche, for which fusilli are often mistaken. Check when buying, because most packages of fusilli are in fact eliche. Genuine fusilli is likely to be plain, neither made with egg nor coloured. The shape of fusilli goes especially well with thin sauces.

Lumache

Snail shells were the inspiration for this attractively shaped pasta. Unlike conchiglie, they are not shaped like conch shells, but resemble a larger version of pipe, because they are fashioned out of hollow pasta. Lumache are excellent for trapping sauces due to their shape. The most common type available is lumache rigate (ridged), and there is also a large version called lumaconi. Gomiti is another type of pasta which has a similar conch shell shape.

Maccheroni

When cooks in the south of Italy speak of maccheroni, they usually mean long pasta, but in the north of the country they prefer it short. It is the short type that is generally exported as macaroni or 'elbow macaroni', although some brands are straighter than others. Being hollow, it is good for both sauces and baked dishes. Plain and egg versions are available, and there are various sizes, including a thin, quick-cooking variety. Tubetti is the miniature version that is often used in soups.

ABOVE: *Penne lisce*

ABOVE: *Penne rigate con soinaci*

ABOVE: *Mezze penne tricolori*

ABOVE: *Pennoni*

Penne

Like maccheroni, penne are hollow tubes, but their ends are cut diagonally, so they are pointed like quills (*penne* means 'feather' or 'quill pen'). In the popularity stakes, they seem to have taken over from maccheroni, possibly because of their more interesting shape. They go well with virtually every sauce and are particularly good with chunky sauces as their sturdiness means they hold their weight well. Penne lisce are smooth; penne rigate are ridged. Other less common varieties include the small and thin type, called pennette, the even thinner types, pennini and penne mezzanine, the short and stubby variety, mezze penne or 'half penne', and the larger type, called pennoni. Penne made with egg and flavoured penne are very common.

Pipe

These shapes look like a cross between conchiglie and lumache. They are curved and hollow (the name means 'pipes') and more often than not ridged (pipe rigate). As short pasta shapes go, they are quite small. They are excellent for catching sauce and make an interesting change from other hollow varieties. Plain and wholewheat types are available, and there is also a smaller version called pipette.

Rotelle

These are cartwheel shapes. There is a ridged variety, rotelle rigate, and sometimes this shape goes under other names such as ruote, ruote di carro and trulli. Although not a classic Italian shape, the spokes of the wheels are very good for holding chunky sauces. Children like them and supermarkets sell a variety of colours and flavours.

Rigatoni

From the maccheroni family, these are ridged, hollow, chunky-looking shapes. They are very popular because they are sturdy enough to hold chunky sauces and they come in many flavours. There is a short version called mezzi rigatoni and a straight, stubby version called millerighe. The texture of rigatoni always seems slightly chewier than that of other short pasta. Similar in shape but slightly narrower are elicoidali, which have curved ridges (their name means 'helixes').

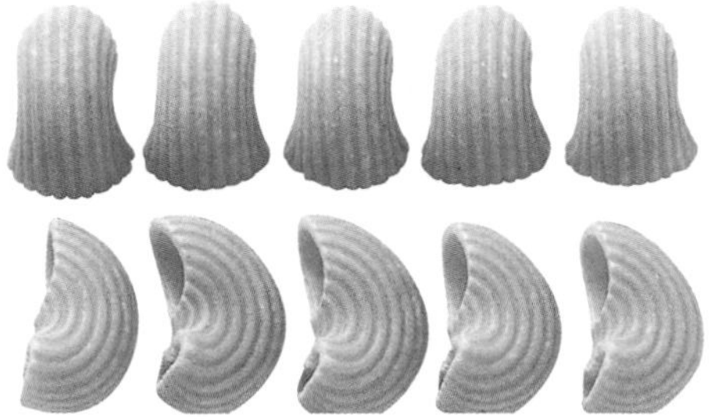

ABOVE: *Pipe rigate*

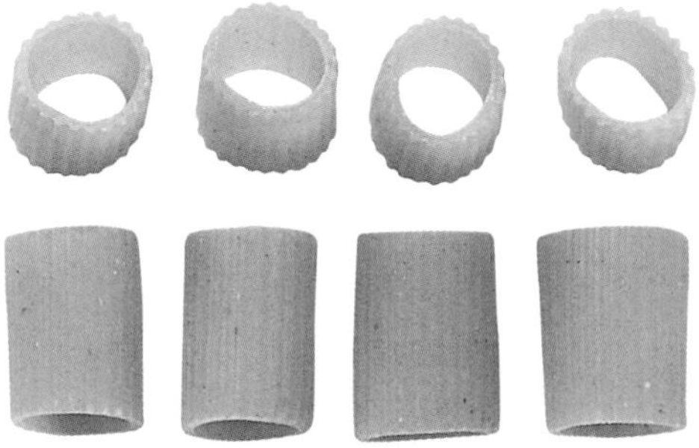

ABOVE: *Mezzi rigatoni*

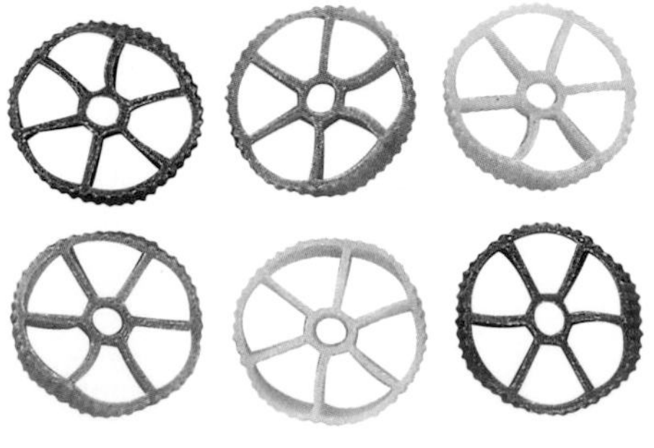

ABOVE: *Rotelle tricolore*

Some regional types of short dried pasta

Garganelli are tubular egg pasta shapes that resemble penne, but look more like scrolls than quills.

Gnocchi sardi, from Sardinia, are named after the gnocchi potato dumplings, but are smaller, like little razor shells. Gnocchetti sardi are smaller still, and are mostly used for soups. Malloreddus is another Sardinian name for gnocchi. These chewy shapes are often flavoured with saffron, and served with traditional meat and vegetable sauces.

ABOVE: *Gnochetti sardi*

ABOVE: *Orecchiette*

ABOVE: *Pizzocheri a nidi*

ABOVE: *Short-cut pizzocheri*

ABOVE: *Garganelli all'uovo*

ABOVE: *Strozzapreti*

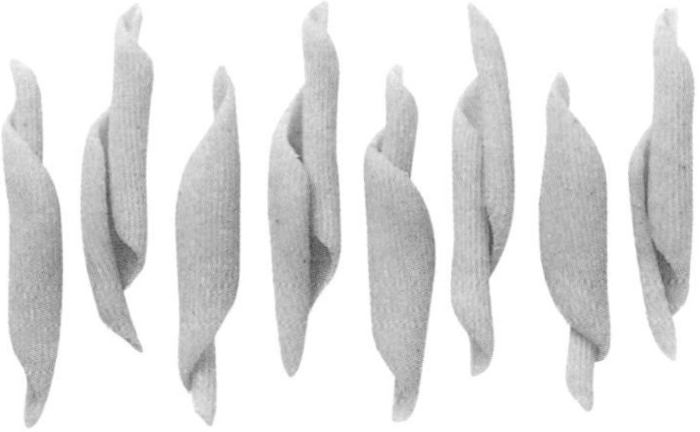

ABOVE: *Trofie*

ABOVE: *Garganelli paglia e fieno*

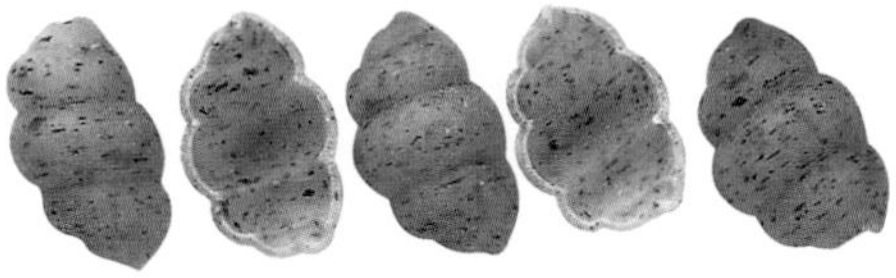

ABOVE: *Gnocchi sardi integrali*

ABOVE: *Gnocchi sardi*

Orecchiette, or 'little ears', are made with durum wheat and are best served with traditional sauces, especially those made with broccoli.

Pizzoccheri are buckwheat noodles from Valtellina in Lombardy. They are thin and flat and usually sold in nests (a nidi) like fettuccine, but are about half the length. Their nutty flavour goes well with cabbage, potatoes and cheese in the baked dish of the same name.

Strozzapreti literally means 'priest stranglers' a name derived from the story of a priest who liked them so much he ate too many – and nearly choked to death. In fact, strozzapreti consist of two pieces of pasta twisted or 'strangled' together. Other similar twisted shapes are caserecce, fileia and gemelli. The Genoese trofie, although not twisted, are similar, and can be substituted for strozzapreti.

Trofie are from the Ligurian port of Genoa, where they are traditionally served with pesto sauce. They are rolls of solid pasta with pointed ends, quite small and dainty. Once homemade only, they are now available dried in some Italian delicatessens, sometimes open along one side rather than solid. They are well worth buying if you want to make an authentic Genoese Trofie al Pesto.

FLAT PASTA

There is really only one broad, flat pasta used for baking in the oven (*al forno*), and that is lasagne.

Plain lasagne

Made from durum wheat and water, plain lasagne comes in three different colours – yellow (plain), green (verdi) and brown or wholewheat (integrali) – and a variety of shapes.

Regular plain lasagne needs to be pre-cooked before being layered or rolled. The usual method is to boil about four sheets at a time in a large pan for about 8 minutes until *al dente*, then carefully remove each sheet with a large slotted spoon and/or tongs and lay it flat on a damp cloth to drain. The cooking time in the oven is usually about 30 minutes.

Lasagnette are long, narrow strips of flat pasta, crimped on one or two sides. They are used in the same way as lasagne, layered with sauces, then topped with grated cheese and baked in the oven. Festonelle are small squares of lasagnette, which are also used in baked dishes. Pantacce are tiny diagonal pieces cut from lasagnette. They are similar to the hand-cut quadrucci and can be used in either baked dishes or soups, but are more often added to soups.

Lasagne all'uovo

Made with durum wheat, water and egg, lasagne all'uovo is a brighter yellow than plain lasagne, and richer in flavour and nutrients. It also comes in different shapes and sizes, and is available as plain egg (lasagne all'uovo) and egg and spinach (lasagne verdi all'uovo).

Easy-cook lasagne

This type of lasagne is layered in the baking dish straight from the packet. Baking time is at least 40 minutes. Use a runnier than usual sauce because this type of lasagne absorbs liquid during baking.

BELOW*: Lasagne*

BELOW*: Lasagne*

BELOW*: Lasagne verdi all'uovo*

BELOW*: Lasagnette*

BELOW*: Festonelle*

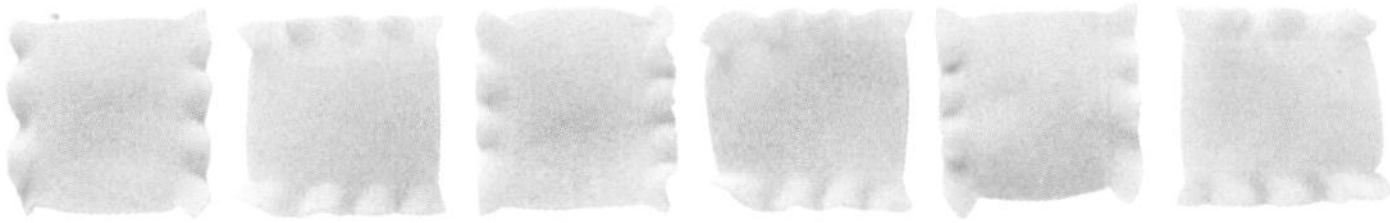

DRIED STUFFED PASTA/ PASTA RIPIENA

The most common dried stuffed pasta shapes are tortellini (little pies), also known as anolini. Some Italian delicatessens also sell dried cappelletti (little hats), which are more likely to be sold fresh than dried, as are ravioli and agnolotti.

Dried tortellini are generally available with meat (alla carne) or cheese (ai formaggi) fillings. The pasta is made with egg and may be plain and yellow in colour, green if flavoured with spinach, or red if flavoured with tomato.

All types of tortellini need to be cooked for at least 15 minutes. For a soup, only a handful of the filled shapes are needed. Tortellini are also good boiled, then drained and tossed in melted butter and herbs or a cream, tomato or meat sauce, and served with grated Parmesan.

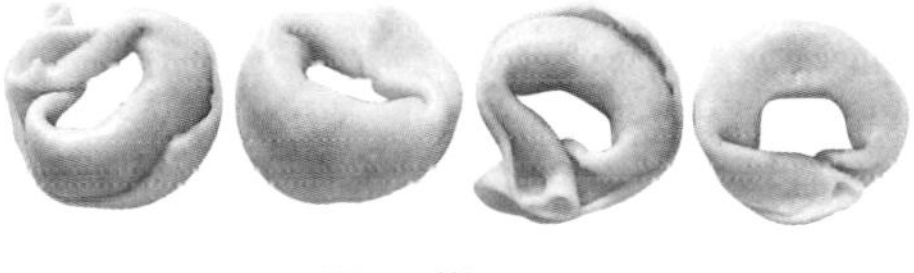

ABOVE: *Tortellini all'uovo*

ABOVE: *Tortellini verdi*

ABOVE: *Ravioli all'uovo*

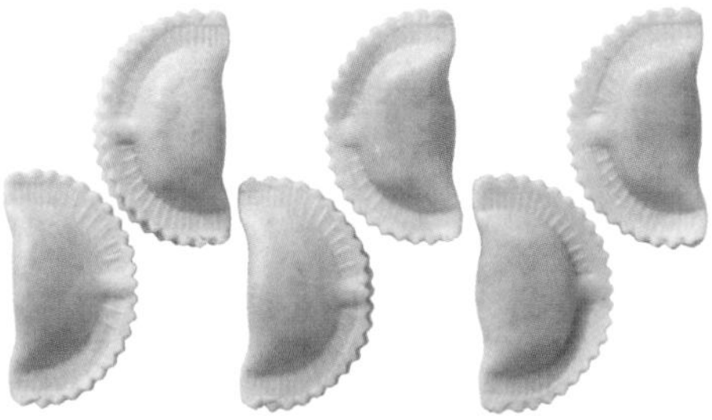

ABOVE: *Agnolotti all'uovo*

Dried pasta for stuffing

Large pasta shapes are made commercially for stuffing and baking in the oven. Fillings vary, from meat and poultry to spinach, mushrooms and cheese, and the pasta can be baked in either a béchamel or a tomato sauce. Keep the filling moist and the sauce runny to ensure that the finished dish will not be dry. They do not need to be boiled before being stuffed.

Cannelloni

These large pasta tubes are about 10cm/4in long. Plain, spinach and wholewheat versions are available. In Italy, cannelloni is traditionally made from fresh sheets of lasagne rolled around a filling, but the ready-made dried tubes are more convenient.

Conchiglie

Sometimes also called conchiglioni, these jumbo conch shells are available in plain, spinach and tomato flavours, both smooth and ridged.

Lumaconi

These are like conchiglie, but are elbow-shaped with an opening at either end. The most common types are plain and ridged, but you may find different colours in specialist delicatessens. Similar shapes include chioccioloni, gorzettoni, manicotti and tuffolini.

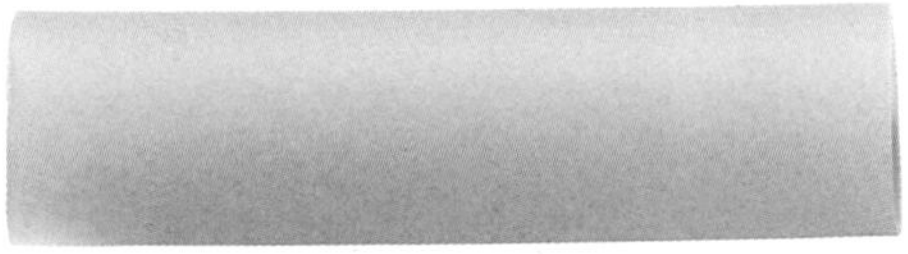

ABOVE: *Cannelloni*

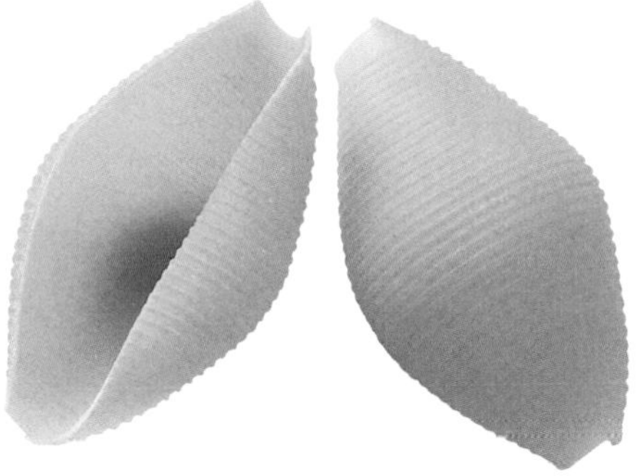

ABOVE: *Conchiglie*

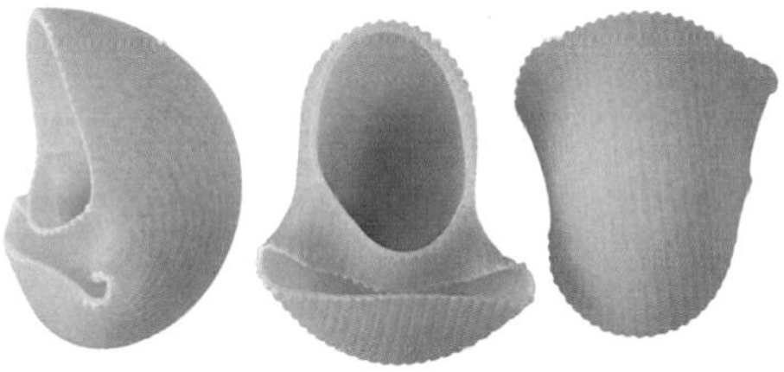

ABOVE: *Lumaconi*

Dried Pasta for Soup/pastina

Pastina are mostly made from plain durum wheat, and sometimes with egg, carrot or spinach. In Italy, they are always served in broths and clear soups.

The smallest and plainest pasta per minestre (pasta for soups) are like tiny grains. Some look like rice and are in fact called risi or risoni; others are more like barley and are called orzi. Coralline, grattini and occhi are three more very popular tiny shapes.

Another category of pasta per minestre consists of slightly larger shapes, more like miniature versions of types of short pasta. The smaller varieties are for use in clear broths; the larger ones are more often used in thicker soups, such as minestrone.

Fresh pasta

In Italy there has long been a tradition for buying fresh pasta, and now the custom has caught on in other countries too. The creative talent is running wild and the choice of different shapes, flavours and fillings is continually increasing – by popular demand.

The quality of fresh pasta is excellent, especially with the loose kinds sold in Italian delicatessens. Pre-packaged brands are clearly not as 'just-made' and silky-textured as the pasta made daily in an Italian delicatessen, but are quite good nevertheless. Flavours vary, but the usual ingredients are spinach, tomato, chestnut, mushroom, beetroot (beet) juice, saffron, herbs, garlic, chillies and squid ink.

Buy freshly made pasta on the day you need it or keep it in its wrapping and use it within 1–2 days of purchase (or according to the packet instructions). If you buy fresh pasta loose from an Italian delicatessen, ask the shopkeeper for advice on storage. Fresh pasta is made with egg, which shortens its storage time but increases the nutritional value and flavour, and gives the plain varieties a lovely sunshine yellow colour.

Fresh pasta takes far less time to cook than dried pasta, but the cooking technique is generally the same. Most plain shapes will be *al dente* in 2–4 minutes, while stuffed shapes take 5–7 minutes, but always ask advice in the shop where it is made (or check the label).

The same rules apply for matching sauces to shapes as with dried pasta: – long shapes with smooth sauces; short shapes with chunky sauces.

LONG AND FLAT SHAPES

These were the first forms of fresh pasta to be available commercially, and were generally made in the local Italian delicatessen. The choice used to be between plain egg tagliatelle and fettuccine, but now you can also buy fresh fettuccelle (interchangeable with fettuccine), spaghetti, spaghettini, capelli d'angelo, lasagne, linguine and pappardelle.

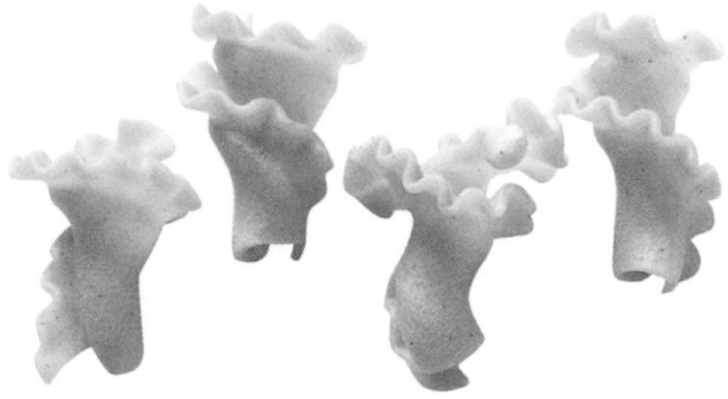

ABOVE*: Ballerine*

SHORT SHAPES

Supermarkets and other large outlets sell fresh short shapes, but the range is limited. Italian delicatessens sometimes sell a few simple home-made shapes. However, as many short shapes need special machines for cutting and shaping, the range is limited. Making them by hand would be too time-consuming to be commercially viable.

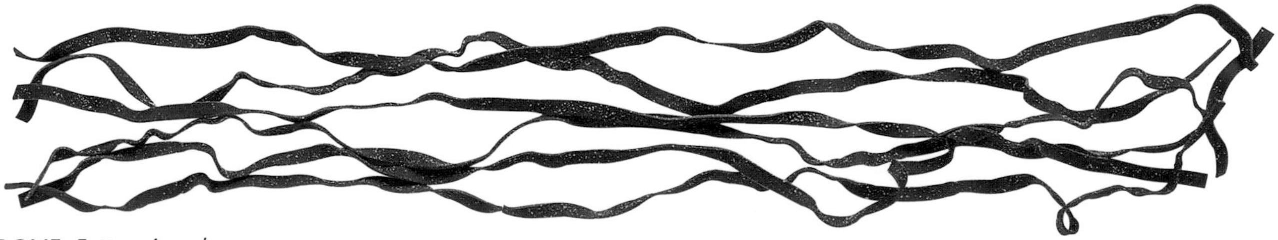

ABOVE*: Fettuccine al nero*

ABOVE*: Pappardelle*

Short shapes tend to stick together, so in supermarkets they are kept in plastic bags in the chilled cabinets; these packs are useful in that they can be stored in the freezer. In some small shops, excess moisture is removed by briefly fan-drying the shapes straight after they are made. These are then described as semi-dried and must be sold within 24–48 hours.

Shapes vary widely, depending on whether they come from large manufacturers or individual shops. Conchiglie, fusilli and penne are easy to find, while other shapes, such as garganelli and ballerine, are less widely available.

TRADITIONAL STUFFED SHAPES

Until recent years, the only stuffed fresh pasta shapes available were the classic ones traditionally associated with specific regions of Italy. Ravioli was the best-known shape, followed by tortellini. These regional specialities are still popular, but nowadays the traditional shapes and fillings often vary, whether they are made by a large-scale manufacturer or a single cook working at a local market. Individual interpretations of the basic shapes, a wide variety of fresh seasonal ingredients for the fillings and eye-catching colour combinations for both the pasta and the fillings have led to seemingly endless variations. Some are more successful than others, so experiment to find which stuffed shapes you like best. After ravioli and tortellini, the most popular and widely available traditional shapes, are agnolotti, cappelletti and pansotti.

BELOW: *Semi-dried tomato-flavoured cappelletti stuffed with sun-dried tomato filling*

ABOVE: *Large rectangular ravioli stuffed with Roquefort cheese*

ABOVE: *(Left to right) Plain ravioli stuffed with asparagus fillling, squid ink-flavoured ravioli stuffed with a herb filling and saffron-flavoured ravioli stuffed with smoked salmon and mascarpone cheese*

OTHER STUFFED PASTA SHAPES

Creative cooks have started a trend for making shapes that are not based on regional traditions, so check out your local Italian delicatessen or supermarket for the latest shapes to arrive – you will find new ones appearing all the time. Two very popular pasta shapes are caramelle and sacchetti. Caramelle means 'caramel' and this pasta takes its name and appearance from the shape of caramels or toffees with their wrappings twisted at both ends. They are often stuffed with ricotta. Sacchetti are like little purses or moneybags with scrunched tops, with cheese or meat fillings. Sacchettini are a tiny version, most often served in soups but also good with smooth, creamy sauces.

BELOW: *Sacchetti filled with a spinach and ricotta filling and tied with thin strips of spring onion*

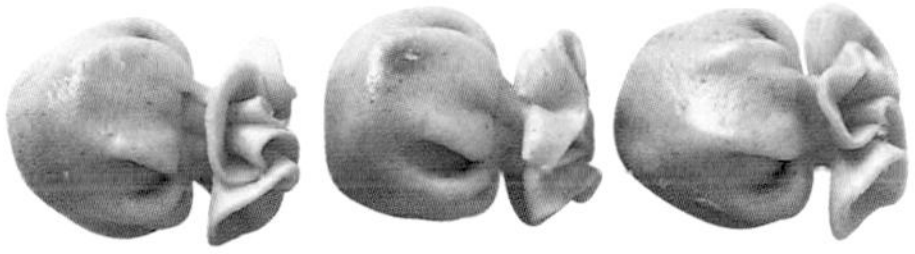

ABOVE: *Sacchettini*

BELOW: *Sweet-shaped caramelle all'uovo stuffed with spinach and ricotta cheese*

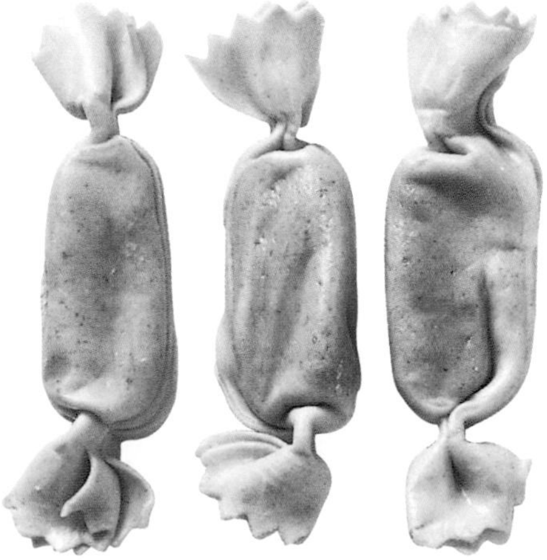

Designer pasta

Relative newcomers to the market are pasta shapes that bear little or no resemblance to the traditional or regional Italian varieties. Many of these are made outside Italy, while those made in Italy are often for export only.

ABOVE: *Five-coloured chioccioloni*

ABOVE: *Spinach, plain and tomato conchiglie*

ABOVE: *Seven-colour orecchiette*

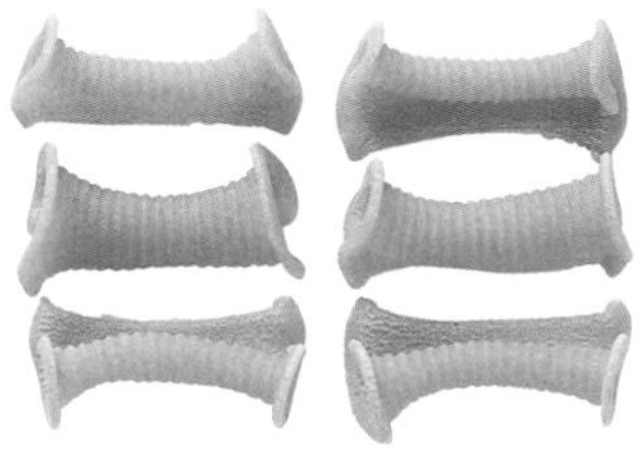

ABOVE: *Rochetti rigati*

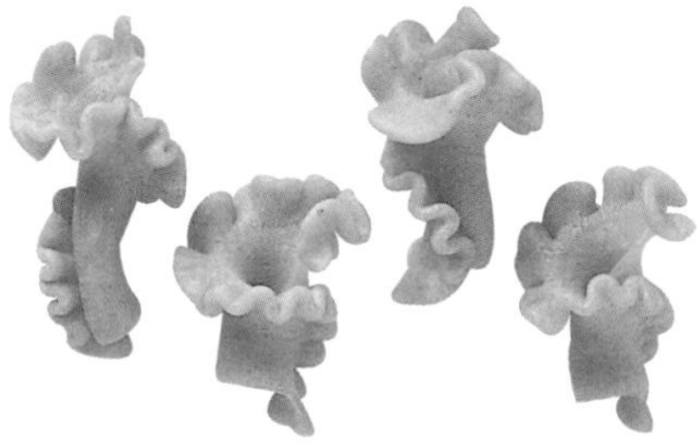

ABOVE: *Gigli del gargano*

ABOVE: *Fiorelli tricolori*

LONG SHAPES AND NOODLES

Spaghetti and tagliatelle are often flavoured and coloured. These shapes are either dramatically long or coiled in nests (a nidi). You can even buy a cross between the two – spagliatelle. Flavours include spinach, tomato, mushroom, beetroot (beet), saffron, smoked salmon chilli, garlic, black squid ink (nero di seppia), herbs and seeds. From Venice hails arlecchino (harlequin), a mixture of black (squid ink), green (spinach and herbs), red (tomato and beetroot) and blue (blueberry and blue Curaçao liqueur). From Umbria comes strangozzi, a thin noodle, available in plain, spinach, basil and tomato varieties. It is sometimes sold in a long, thick plait, which is best broken before cooking.

ABOVE: *Porcini-flavoured bavette*

ABOVE: *Multi-coloured arlecchino*

SHORT SHAPES

The most inventive and unusual designer shapes are short. Because short pasta is the easiest to eat, and therefore most popular, competition in the pasta industry has thrived on the 'design' of different short shapes since the 19th century. Among these are the frilly ballerine, gigli del gargano and spaccatella, all of which trap sauces quite well but somehow give a strange sensation in the mouth. Shapes such as banane, coralli rigati, creste di gallo, radiatori and riccioli are perhaps too gimmicky for their own good. So too are the mixed bags of highly coloured pasta shapes, such as seven-colour orecchiette (little ears) and five-colour chioccioloni (snails), which includes chocolate-flavoured pasta along with the more run-of-the-mill plain, tomato, squid ink and wild mushroom (porcini) varieties.

Equipment

Pasta demands little in the way of specialist equipment. There are a few items that will make cooking and serving easier, however, and if you eat pasta frequently you will find them a wise investment.

BELOW: *Skillet and pan*

GENERAL COOKING EQUIPMENT

You may already have some of these basic items in your kitchen.

Pasta cooking pot

Made of stainless steel, this pan has straight sides with two short handles and an inner draining basket, which also has two handles. Different sizes are available, so choose the one that suits your needs best. One that comfortably holds at least 3 litres/5 pints water is adequate to cook for 2–3 people; for 6–8 servings, you will need a 5 litre/8 pint pan.

RIGHT: *Pasta cooking pot*

Skillet

A skillet was originally a cooking pot that stood on three or four legs in the hearth. Nowadays, the term is used on both sides of the Atlantic to describe a wide, deep pan with a long handle and a lid. This is perfect for making sauces. Look for one that is at least 23cm/9in in diameter and 5–7.5cm/2–3in deep.

Pasta measurer

Spaghetti is difficult to weigh on the scales or measure by hand. This wooden gadget has four or five holes, each of which holds enough pasta for a given number of people.

Long-handled fork

This is useful for stirring pasta during cooking to help keep the pasta from sticking together. Wooden pasta rakes or hooks look like flat wooden spoons with prongs on one side are also available. The pasta does not slip off when lifted.

ABOVE: *Pasta measurer*

BELOW: *Long-handled fork*

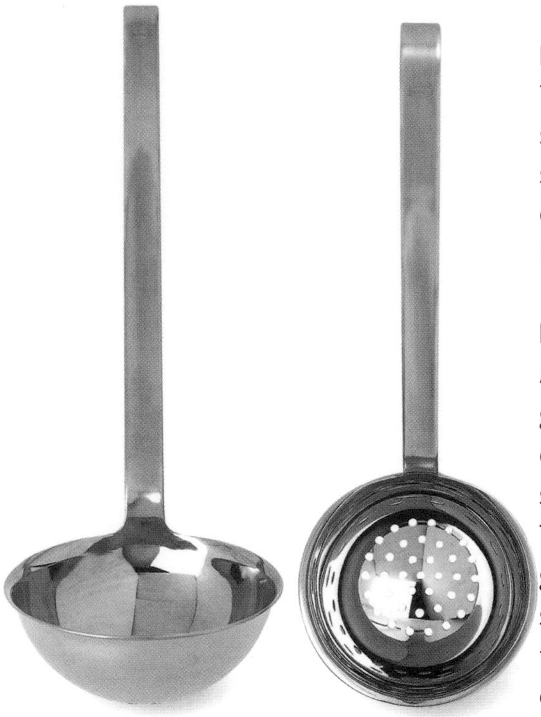

ABOVE*: Ladle and perforated ladle*

BELOW*: Tongs*

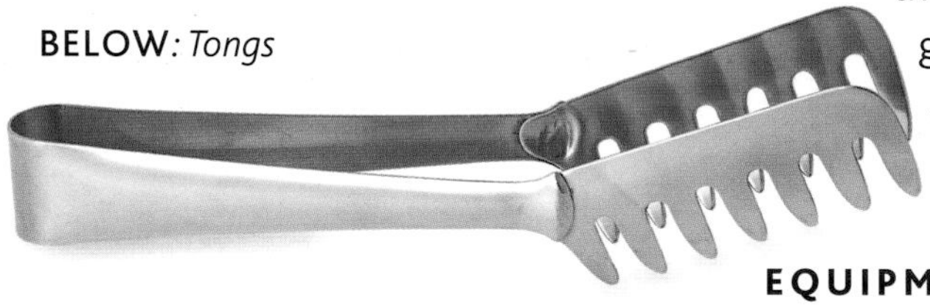

Tongs
A good pair of tongs is essential for picking spaghetti and long noodles out of hot water. Sturdy stainless steel tongs are the best, preferably with long handles for safety.

Scoop or draining spoon
A large, deep perforated, slotted or mesh spoon – ideally, stainless steel – is perfect for lifting short pasta shapes out of boiling water.

Ladle
A deep-bowled ladle – ideally, stainless steel – is most effective for spooning sauce over pasta and for serving soups.

Parmesan knife
This short, stubby little knife with a shaped handle and a small and sturdy, double-sided blade is quite effective for scraping shavings of Parmesan cheese from a block.

Parmesan graters
A simple stainless steel box grater will grate Parmesan and other hard cheeses. It is also possible to buy a small grater especially for Parmesan. This consists of a single rectangular grating plate that is designed specifically for grating hard cheese finely, and has a small handle, which can be grasped firmly. Mechanical Parmesan mills are also good, as are small, hand-cranked rotary graters, and there are special Parmesan graters available with a box and a lid so that the cheese can be stored after grating.

EQUIPMENT FOR MAKING PASTA AT HOME
You can make pasta at home with nothing more sophisticated than a set of scales, some measuring spoons, a work surface and an ordinary rolling pin. That said, a few special items make the job easier.

Tapered rolling pin
The traditional pin used in Italy for rolling out pasta dough is very long – it measures almost 80cm/32in in length. It is about 4cm/1½in wide in the centre and tapers almost to a point at either end. This type of rolling pin is very easy to use and is well worth buying if you enjoy making pasta by hand and don't intend to buy a special machine. A conventional, straight rolling pin can be used instead, but try to get one that is quite slim – no more than 5cm/2in in diameter.

Mechanical pasta machine
The same type of hand-cranked pasta machine has been used in Italian kitchens for many, many years. It has stood the test of time well, because it is still manufactured and used today, with very little modification. Made of stainless steel, it has rollers to press out the dough as thinly as possible and cutters for creating different shapes. The standard cutters usually

BELOW*: Parmesan graters*

RIGHT: *Pasta machine*

BELOW: *Pasta wheel*

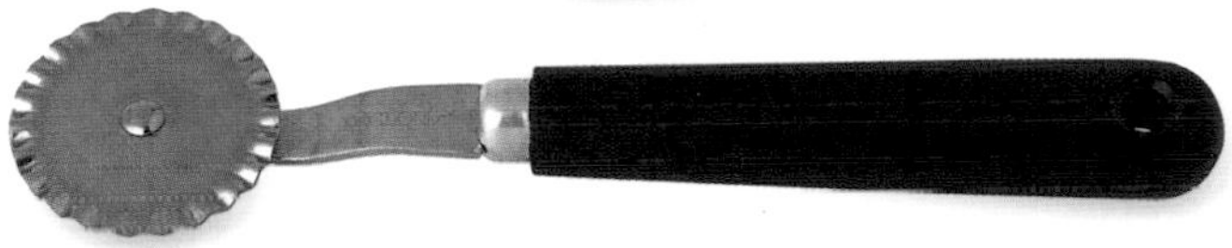

allow you to make tagliatelle and tagliarini, but you can get attachments and accessories for other shapes, including pappardelle, ravioli and cannelloni. The machine is clamped to the edge of a work surface or table and worked by turning the handle. If you make pasta often, it is a very good buy, because it is cheap, fun to use and makes excellent pasta in a very short time.

Pasta wheel

This is a useful gadget for cutting lasagne and noodles such as tagliatelle when you don't have a pasta machine. The wheel can be straight or fluted, and there are some types that will cut several lengths of noodle at a time. You can use a sharp knife instead, but a pasta wheel is easier and gives a much neater finish. With a pasta wheel, the pasta edges are less likely to be torn or dragged out of shape.

Ravioli cutter

This is virtually the same as a fluted pastry (cookie) cutter except that it has a wooden handle and can be square or round. If you want to make square ravioli and cappelletti, you can use a pasta wheel instead of this cutter, so it isn't a vital piece of equipment. For round ravioli, tortellini and anolini you can use a pastry cutter if you have one. The most useful sizes are 5cm/2in and 7.5cm/3in.

Ravioli tray

You can buy a special metal tray for making your own ravioli. A sheet of rolled-out pasta dough is laid over the tray, then pressed into the indentations using your fingertips. The filling is then spooned into the indentations and another sheet of dough is then placed on top. The ravioli squares are cut out by rolling a rolling pin over the serrated top. This is good for making very small ravioli, which are difficult, fiddly and can be extremely time consuming to make individually. Sometimes, the tray is sold as a set with its own small rolling pin included, or it may come as an accessory for a pasta machine.

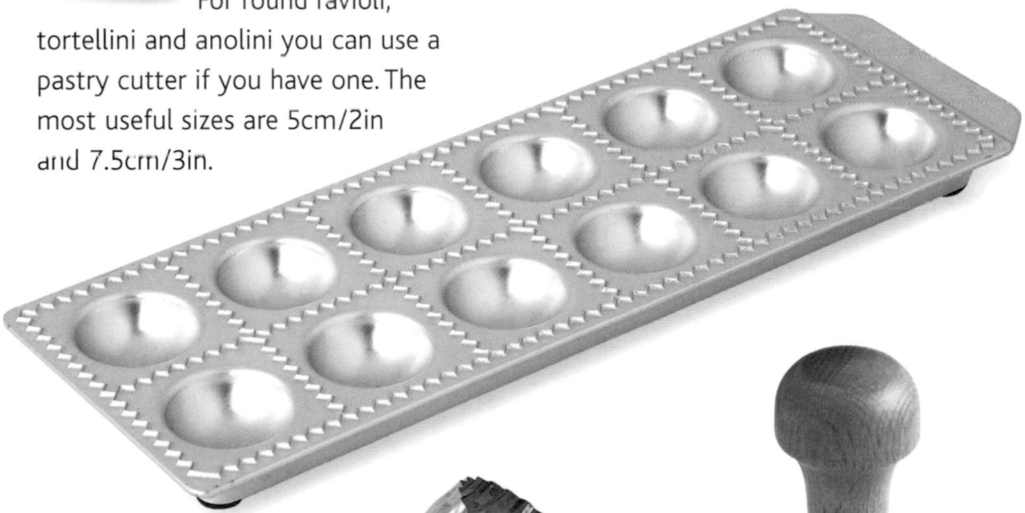

ABOVE: *Ravioli tray*

RIGHT: *Fluted and plain pastry cutters*

FAR RIGHT: *Ravioli cutter*

How to cook and serve pasta

It is easy to cook pasta properly, but without care and attention it is equally easy to cook it badly. So, it's always best to observe a few simple guidelines

Synchronize sauce and pasta

Before starting to cook either sauce or pasta, read the recipe carefully to find out which needs to be cooked for the longest time. The sauce can often be made ahead of time and reheated. It is quite unusual for the timing of a sauce to be crucial, but pasta is almost like a hot soufflé – it waits for no one. Fresh pasta often needs only a few minutes. So, have the sauce ready and waiting before the pasta hits the water.

Use a big pan

There needs to be plenty of room for the pasta to move around in the large amount of water it requires, so a big pan is essential. The best type of pan is a tall, lightweight, straight-sided, stainless steel pasta cooking pot with its own in-built draining pan. Both outer and inner pans have two handles each, which ensure ease and safety. If you cook pasta a lot, it is well worth investing in one of these special pans; otherwise use the largest pan you have for cooking the pasta and a large stainless steel colander, preferably one with feet for stability, for draining it.

Use a large quantity of water

The recommended amount is 5 litres/8 pints water for every 450g/1lb pasta. If you are cooking less pasta than this, use at least 3 litres/5 pints water. If there is not enough water, the pasta will stick together and the pan will become overcrowded. This will result in unpleasant, gummy-textured pasta.

Get the water boiling

Before adding the pasta, the water should be at a fast rolling boil. The quickest way to do this is to boil water in the kettle, then pour it into the pasta pan, which should be set over a high heat. You may need as much as 2–3 kettlefuls, so keep the water in the pan simmering, covered by the lid, while you boil the kettle again.

Add enough salt

Pasta cooked without salt is more or less tasteless, and with insufficient salt it is hardly any better. The recommended amount is 22.5–30ml/$1\frac{1}{2}$–2 tbsp salt for every 450g/1lb pasta. Cooking salt is perfectly fine. Add the salt when the water is boiling, just before you add the pasta. As the salt is added, the water will bubble furiously. This is your cue to add the pasta.

Add in the pasta all at once

Try to get all the pasta into the boiling water at the same time so that it will cook evenly and be ready at the same time. The quickest and easiest way is literally to shake it out of the packet or the bowl of the scales, covering the surface of the water.

Return the water quickly to the boil

Once the pasta is submerged in the water, give it a brisk stir with a long-handled fork or spoon and then cover the pan tightly with the lid – this will help to bring the water back to the boil as quickly as possible. Once the water is boiling, lift off the lid, turn down the heat slightly and let the water simmer over a medium to high heat for the required cooking time.

Stir the pasta frequently during cooking

To prevent the pasta from sticking together, stir it frequently during cooking so that it is kept constantly on the move. Use a long-handled wooden fork or spoon so that you can stir right down to the bottom of the pan.

Drain carefully and thoroughly

If you have a pasta pot with an inner drainer, carefully lift the draining pan up and out of the boiling water. Shake the draining pan vigorously and stir the pasta well so that any water trapped in pasta shapes can drain out as quickly as possible. It is also a good idea to reserve a few ladlefuls of the cooking water from the pasta pan, just in case the pasta needs a little extra moistening when it is tossed with the sauce before serving.

ACCURATE TIMING IS ESSENTIAL FOR COOKING PASTA

Start timing the pasta from the moment the water returns to the boil after adding the pasta. Always go by the time given on the packet or, in the case of fresh home-made pasta, by the time given in the recipe. For the greatest accuracy, use a kitchen timer with a bell or buzzer because even half a minute of overcooking can ruin pasta, especially if it is freshly made. Dried egg pasta is more difficult to spoil, so if you are new to pasta cooking and nervous about getting it right, start with this type.

For fresh pasta

As a general guide, thin fresh noodles will take only 2 3 minutes, thicker fresh noodles and pasta shapes 3–4 minutes, and stuffed fresh pasta 5–7 minutes.

For dried pasta

The cooking time for dried pasta will vary from 8–20 minutes depending on the type and the manufacturer. Always check the time on the label.

When is the pasta cooked?

The Italian term *al dente* is used to describe pasta that is cooked to perfection. Literally translated this means 'to the tooth', meaning that it should be firm to the bite, which is how Italians like their pasta, and therefore how it should be served. Dried pasta, which is made from durum wheat, is always served *al dente*, whereas fresh pasta is made from a softer wheat and so is never as firm as dried, but it should still have some resistance to it. Overcooked pasta is limp and unpalatable and an Italian cook would not serve it.

To check that the pasta is ready, test it frequently towards the end of the recommended cooking time by lifting out a piece with tongs, a pasta scoop or a slotted spoon and biting into it. When you are satisfied that it is done to your liking, it is time to stop the cooking.

At-a-glance quantities

Amounts of pasta given here are intended only as a guide to the number of people they will serve. If you are cooking fresh pasta, you may need a little more than if you are using dried, but the difference is really negligible. What is more significant is whether you are serving a light or substantial sauce with the pasta.

For an Italian-style first course (primo piatto) for 4–6 people, or a main course for 2–3 people:
3 litres/5 pints water
15ml/1 tbsp salt
250–350g/9–12oz fresh
 or dried pasta

For a first course for 6–8 people, or a main course for 4–6 people:
5 litres/8 pints water
22.5–30ml/1½–2 tbsp salt
300–450g/11oz–1lb fresh
 or dried pasta

Cooking fresh pasta

1 For freshly made pasta that has been drying on a dish towel, gather the cloth up around the pasta in a loose cylindrical shape and hold it firmly at both ends.

2 Hold the towel over the water, then let go of the end nearest to the water so that the pasta shoots in.

Cooking long dried pasta

1 When cooking spaghetti, you need to coil the pasta into the water as it softens. Take a handful of the pasta at a time and dip it in the boiling water so that it touches the bottom of the pan.

2 As the spaghetti strands soften, coil them round using a wooden spoon or fork until they are all completely submerged.

Cooking stuffed pasta

1 Stuffed shapes require more gentle handling or they may break open and release their filling into the water. Try to stir them gently throughout cooking.

2 The best method of draining stuffed shapes after cooking is to lift them carefully out of the water with a large pasta scoop or slotted spoon.

Combining pasta and sauce

Recipes vary in the way they combine sauce and pasta. Most recipes add the sauce to the pasta, but with some it is the other way around. When adding the sauce to the drained pasta, the most important thing is to have a warmed bowl ready – the larger the better, to allow the sauce and pasta to be tossed together easily.

1 After draining, immediately transfer the pasta into the warmed bowl, pour over the sauce and quickly toss the two together.

2 If the pasta is not moist enough, add a little of the pasta cooking water. Some recipes call for extra butter or oil to be added at this stage, others have grated Parmesan or Pecorino cheese tossed with the pasta and sauce.

3 Use two large spoons or forks for tossing, or a large spoon and a fork. Lift the pasta and swirl it around, making sure you have scooped it up from the bottom of the bowl. The idea is to coat every piece of pasta evenly in sauce, so keep tossing until you are satisfied that this is done.

4 Occasionally, recipes call for the pasta to be returned to the cooking pan, to be combined with oil or butter and seasonings and tossed over heat until coated. A sauce may be added at this stage too, but care should always be taken not to cook the pasta too much in the first place; otherwise, it may overcook when it is reheated.

How to make pasta

Home-made pasta has a wonderfully light, almost silky texture – quite different from the fresh pasta that you buy pre-packaged in shops. If you use egg in the mixture, the dough is easy to make, either by hand or machine. Kneading, rolling and cutting do require some patience and practice.

PASTA WITH EGGS

The best place to make, knead and roll out pasta dough is on a wooden kitchen table, the larger the better. The surface should be warm, so marble is not suitable.

INGREDIENTS

300g/11oz/2³/4 cups flour
3 eggs
5ml/1 tsp salt

1 Mound the flour on a clean work surface and make a large, deep well in the centre with your hands. Keep the sides of the well quite high so that when the eggs are added they will not run out of the well.

2 Crack the eggs into the well, then add the salt. With a table knife or fork, mix the eggs and salt together, then gradually start incorporating the flour from the sides of the well. Try not to break the sides of the well or the runny mixture will escape.

3 When the egg mixture is no longer liquid, dip your fingers in the flour and work the ingredients together to form a rough, sticky dough. Scrape up any that sticks to the work surface with a knife, then scrape this off the knife with your fingers. If the dough is too dry, add a few drops of cold water; if it is too moist, sprinkle a little flour over it.

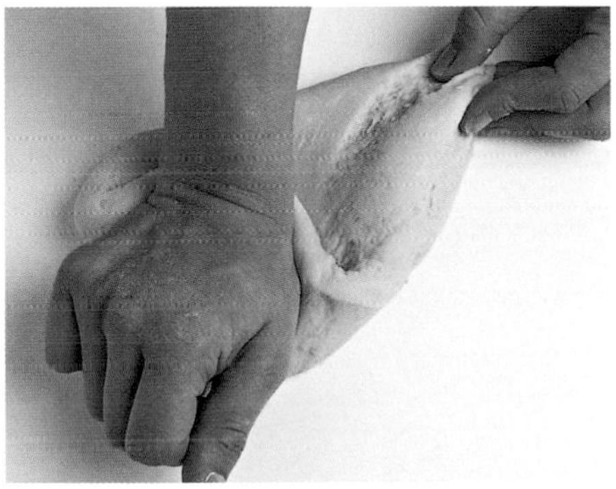

4 Press into a rough ball and knead it as you would bread. Push it away from you with the heel of your hand, then fold the end back on itself so that it faces towards you. Push it out again. Continue folding the dough back a little further each time and pushing it out until you have folded it back all the way towards you and all the dough has been kneaded.

5 Give the dough a quarter turn anti-clockwise, then continue kneading, folding and turning for 5 minutes if you intend using a pasta machine, or for 10 minutes if you will be rolling it out by hand. The dough should be very smooth and elastic. If you are going to roll it out and cut it by hand, thorough kneading is essential.

6 Wrap the dough in clear film (plastic wrap) and leave to rest for 15–20 minutes at room temperature. It will then be ready to roll out.

Ingredients for Pasta with Eggs

Only three inexpensive ingredients are used for making pasta with eggs: flour, eggs and salt. Ultimate success depends as much on their quality as on the technique used for making the dough. Some cooks add olive oil to the mixture, especially in Tuscany, but it is by no means essential. It gives the pasta a softer texture and a slightly different flavour, and some say it helps make the dough easier to work with, especially if you don't have a pasta machine. For a 3-egg quantity of dough, use 15ml/1 tbsp olive oil and add it with the eggs.

The best flour is called Farina Bianca 00 or Tipo 00, available from Italian delicatessens. With ordinary plain (all-purpose) flour, the dough is difficult to knead and roll, especially by hand. If you can't get 00 flour, use a strong plain white bread flour.

Very fresh eggs are essential, and the deeper the yellow of the yolks the better the colour of the pasta. Use fresh eggs at room temperature. Take out eggs stored in the refrigerator 1 hour before use. Salt is important for flavour.

Making pasta dough in a food processor

If you have a food processor, you can save a little time and effort by using it for making pasta dough. It will not knead the dough adequately, however, so you may find it just as quick and easy to make it by hand, especially if you take into account the washing and drying of the bowl and blade. The ingredients are the same as when making pasta by hand.

1 Put the flour and salt in the bowl of a food processor fitted with the metal blade.

2 Add one whole egg and then pulse-blend until the ingredients are mixed.

3 Turn the food processor on to full speed and add the remaining whole eggs through the feeder tube. Keep enough to form a dough.

4 Turn the dough out on to a clean work surface. Knead as when making pasta by hand, then wrap in clear film (plastic wrap) and leave to rest at room temperature for 15–20 minutes.

MAKING PASTA SHAPES BY HAND

Once you have made your pasta dough and let it rest, it is ready to be rolled out and cut into various shapes. If you don't have a pasta machine, the following steps show how to do it by hand. The technique is quite hard work and the pasta may not be quite as thin as that made in a machine, but it is equally good nevertheless. If you enjoy making your own pasta and think you would like to make it regularly, it is well worth buying a mechanical pasta machine to save you both time and effort, and for better results.

1 Unwrap the ball of dough and cut it in half. Roll and cut one half at a time, keeping the other half wrapped in clear film (plastic wrap) as before.

2 Sprinkle a very large, clean work surface lightly with flour. Put the unwrapped dough on the surface, sprinkle it with a little flour and flatten it with the heel of your hand. Turn the dough over and repeat the process to form the dough into a 13cm/5in disc.

3 Using a lightly floured rolling pin, start to roll the dough out. Always roll the dough away from you, stretching it outwards from the centre and moving the dough round a quarter turn after each rolling. If the dough gets sticky, sprinkle the rolling pin, dough and work surface lightly with flour.

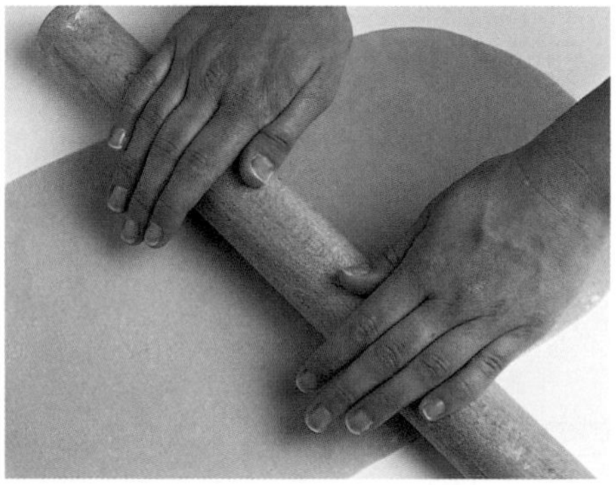

4 Continue rolling, turning and stretching the dough until it is a large oval, as thin as you can possibly get it. Ideally it should be about 3mm/⅛in thick. Try to get it even all over or the shapes will not cook in the same length of time. Don't worry if the edges are not neat; this is not important.

Cutting ribbon noodles

1 Before you begin, have ready plenty of clean dish towels lightly dusted with flour; you will need to spread the shapes out on them after cutting. Dust the sheet of pasta (called la sfoglia in Italian) lightly with flour. Starting from one long edge, roll up the sheet into a loose cylinder.

2 With a large sharp knife, cut cleanly across the pasta roll. Cut at 1cm/½in intervals for tagliatelle, slightly narrower (about 5mm/¼in) for fettuccine, and as narrow as you can possibly get for tagliarini or capelli d'angelo. Take care not to drag the knife or the edges of the ribbons will be ragged.

3 With floured fingers, unravel the rolls on the work surface, then toss the noodles lightly together on the floured dish towels, sprinkling them with more flour.

4 Repeat the rolling and cutting with the remaining pasta. Leave the strips to dry on the dish towels for at least 15 minutes before cooking, tossing them from time to time and sprinkling them with a little flour if they become sticky.

Cutting pappardelle

1 Using a fluted pasta wheel, cut the pasta sheet into long strips about 2–2.5cm/¾–1in wide. Try to keep the strips the same width or they will not cook evenly.

2 Spread the pappardelle strips out in a single layer on floured dish towels and sprinkle them with a little more flour. Then leave the pappardelle to dry on the towels for at least 15 minutes before you start cooking.

Cutting lasagne and cannelloni

1 With a large sharp knife, cut the pasta sheets into 15–18 x 7.5–10cm/6–7 x 3–4in rectangles or whatever size best fits your baking dish.

2 Spread the rectangles out in a single layer on floured dish towels, sprinkle them with more flour and leave to dry for at least 15 minutes before you start cooking. The rectangles can be used for both lasagne and cannelloni.

Cutting quadrucci (for soups)

1 Stack two pasta sheets, one on top of the other, with a light sprinkling of flour in between. With a large sharp knife, cut the pasta diagonally into 4cm/1½in wide strips, then cut across the strips in the opposite direction to make 4cm/1½in squares.

2 Spread the squares out on floured dish towels and sprinkle with more flour. Leave to dry for at least 15 minutes before cooking.

Cutting maltagliati (for soups)

1 Dust one pasta sheet lightly with flour. Starting from one long edge, roll the sheet up into a cylinder. Lightly flatten the cylinder, then, with a sharp knife, slice off the corners at one end, making two diagonal cuts to form two sides of a triangle. Cut straight across to complete the triangle. Repeat all the way along the cylinder, then unfold the maltagliati.

2 Spread out the maltagliati on floured dish towels. Sprinkle the shapes with a little more flour and leave them to dry for at least 15 minutes before cooking.

Cook's tip
Don't throw away the trimmings when making pasta shapes, such as lasagne and tagliatelle. Cut them into small pieces and pop into soups at the last minute. Also, maltagliati means 'badly cut', so don't worry if the pasta is misshapen – it is meant to be. Quadrucci and maltagliati can also be cut from fresh lasagne rectangles, but this will take slightly longer.

MAKING SHORT SHAPES

Most short pasta shapes are best left to the professionals as they take so long to make or require special equipment. Garganelli and farfalle are exceptions.

Garganelli

1 Cut the pasta sheets into 5cm/2in squares. Lay butter paddle ridges horizontally on the work surface, with the ridges facing towards you. Angle the square so that it is diamond-shaped and place it over the ridges. Put a pencil diagonally across the corner of the square that is closest to you.

2 Roll the square around the pencil, pressing down hard to imprint the ridges on the pasta.

3 Stand the pencil upright on the work surface and tap the end so that the tube of pasta slides off.

4 Spread the garganelli out in a single layer on floured dish towels, sprinkle with more flour and leave them to dry for at least 15 minutes before cooking.

Farfalle

1 With a fluted pasta wheel, cut the pasta sheets into rectangles measuring 4 x 2.5cm/1½ x 1in. Pinch the long sides of each rectangle between your index finger and thumb and squeeze hard to make a bow-tie shape. If the pasta will not hold the shape, moisten your fingers with water and try again.

2 Spread the farfalle out in a single layer on floured dish towels, sprinkle them with a little more flour and leave to dry for at least 15 minutes before cooking.

MAKING PASTA SHAPES USING A MACHINE

Rolling the dough

A machine makes light work of rolling pasta dough, as well as thinner, even dough. For noodles, it is invaluable.

1 Clamp the machine securely to your work surface and insert the handle in the roller slot. Set the rollers at their widest setting and sprinkle them lightly with flour. Unwrap the ball of pasta and cut it into quarters. Work with one quarter at a time, wrapping the other three pieces of pasta dough in clear film (plastic wrap).

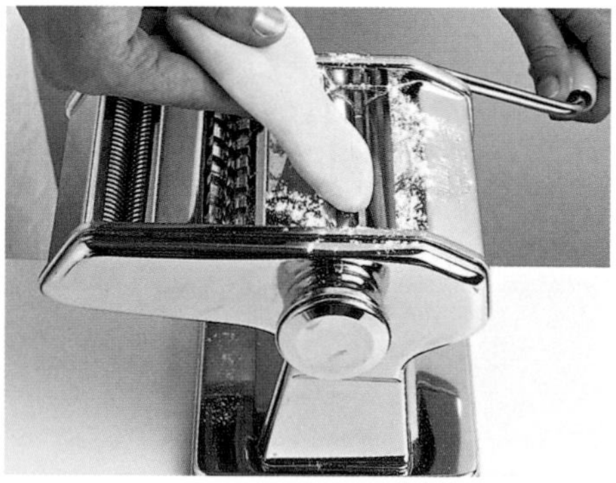

2 Flatten the quarter of dough with lightly floured hands and make it into a rough rectangle, just a little narrower in width than the rollers of the machine. Feed this through the rollers.

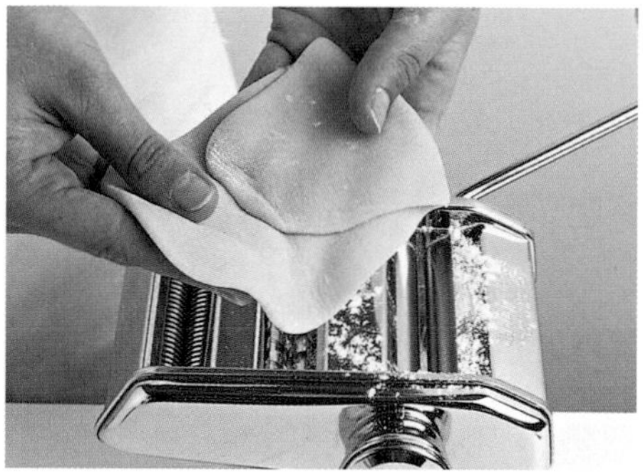

3 Fold the dough into thirds, then feed it lengthways through the rollers. Repeat the folding and rolling five times.

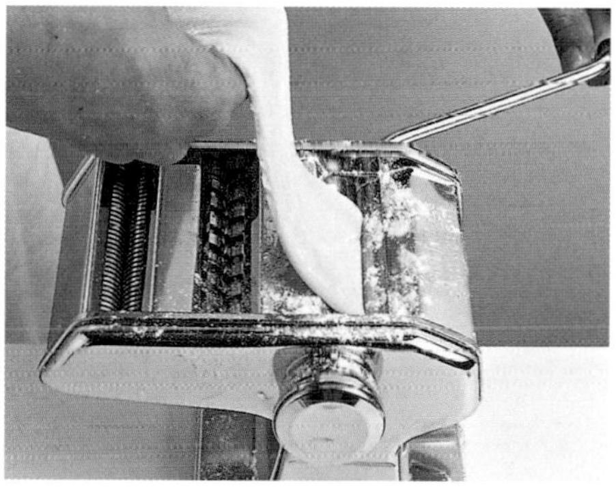

4 Turn the roller setting one notch. Sprinkle the pasta lightly with flour and feed it through the rollers again, only this time unfolded.

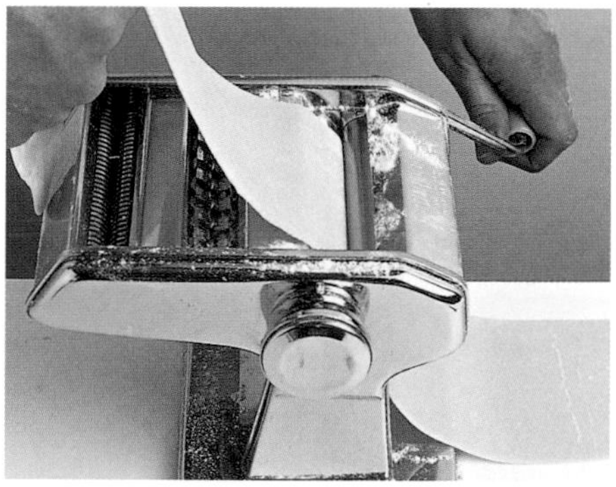

5 Turn the roller setting another notch and repeat the rolling, then continue in this way without folding the dough until you get to the last setting, turning the roller setting another notch after each rolling and sprinkling it lightly with flour if it becomes sticky. The dough will get longer and thinner with every rolling until it reaches 90–100cm/36–40in in length. Once the dough has been rolled, it is ready for cutting into the required shape.

Cook's tips

- About halfway through the rolling process, you may find that the pasta strip becomes too unwieldy and difficult to handle because it is so long. If this happens, cut the strip in half or into thirds and work with one piece at a time. Remember, however, to return the notch on the roller to the setting where you left off when you start with the next piece of dough.
- You may find that the dough is thin enough on the penultimate setting, in which case you can stop there. This will definitely be the case if you are going to make tonnarelli or spaghetti alla chitarra.
- Keep sprinkling the pasta dough lightly with flour if it becomes sticky, and always keep the rollers lightly floured to prevent the pasta sticking to the machine.
- Keep the trimmings and leftover pieces of pasta dough, as they can easily be re-rolled and more shapes cut from them.
- Once they are dry, noodles and pasta shapes can safely be stored in a paper bag for 3–4 days, or in the refrigerator in plastic bags for up to 1 month.

Cutting tagliatelle and fettuccine

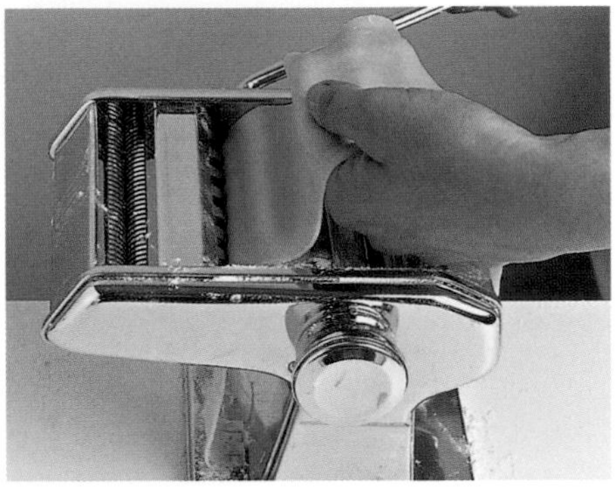

1 Insert the handle in the slot for the widest cutters and sprinkle them lightly with flour. Cut the pasta strip to about 30cm/12in long, sprinkle it lightly with flour and feed it through.

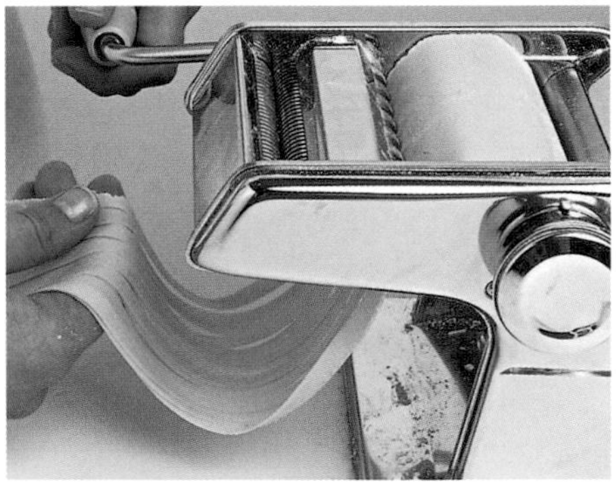

2 Continue turning the handle steadily, guiding the strands with your free hand.

3 Toss the noodles in flour and spread them out on a floured dish towel to dry. Roll and cut the remaining dough.

Cutting lasagne and cannelloni

1 Using a sharp knife, cut the rolled lasagne or cannelloni strip into 15–18 x 7.5–10cm/6–7 x 3–4in rectangles, or whatever size best fits your baking dish.

2 Spread out the cut lasagne or cannelloni rectangles in a single layer on floured dish towels and sprinkle with flour.

Cutting tonnarelli and spaghetti alla chitarra

1 Stop rolling the pasta strip after the last but two or last but one setting. Insert the handle in the slot for the narrowest cutters and feed the pasta through the machine.

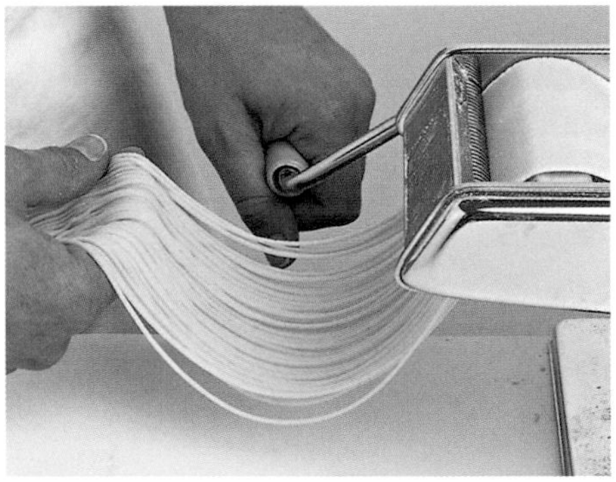

2 Turn the handle and guide the long strands with your other hand. Toss the pasta in flour and spread out on floured dish towels to dry.

Cook's tip

When you are making spaghetti alla chitarra, the thickness and width of the pasta should be equal to ensure that the noodles come out square. You may need to experiment with this shape a few times until you get it just the right thickness.

Variations

To make a variation on the above, such as tagliarini or spaghettini, simply insert the pasta machine handle in the slot for the narrowest cutters and proceed to cut as for tonnarelli and spaghetti alla chitarra. Sprinkle with flour and leave to dry on a dish towel in the same way.

Making ravioli

1 Using a large sharp knife, cut the rolled pasta strip into two 45–50cm/ 18–20in lengths, if this has not been done already.

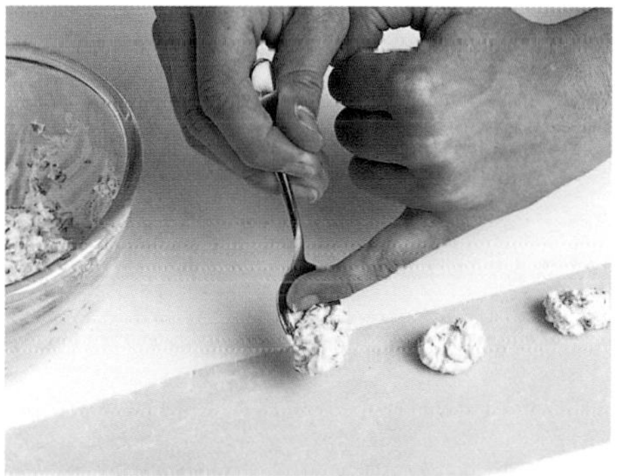

2 Using a teaspoon, put 10–12 little mounds of your chosen filling along one side of one of the pasta strips, spacing them evenly.

3 Using a pastry brush, carefully brush a little water on to the pasta strip around each mound of filling.

4 Fold the plain side of the pasta strip over the filling.

5 Starting from the folded edge of the past strip, press down gently, with your fingertips around each mound, to push the air out at the unfolded edge. Sprinkle lightly with flour.

6 With a fluted pasta wheel, cut along each long side of the pasta strip. Then very carefully position it in between each mound to cut small square shapes.

7 Put the ravioli on floured dish towels, sprinkle lightly with more flour and leave to dry. Repeat the process with the remaining dough. For a 3-egg dough, you should get 80–96 ravioli, more if you re-roll the trimmings.

Fillings for stuffed pasta

These vary from one or two simple ingredients to special traditional recipes. The ingredients are mixed together and often bound with beaten egg, Seasoning is added to taste.

Simple ideas:

• Spinach, Parmesan, ricotta and nutmeg.

• Crab, mascarpone, lemon, parsley and chillies.

• Taleggio cheese and fresh marjoram.

Regional specialities:

• Minced (ground) pork and turkey with fresh herbs, ricotta and Parmesan.

• Fresh herbs, ricotta, Parmesan and garlic.

• Puréed cooked pumpkin, prosciutto, mozzarella and parsley.

Cook's tip

Ravioli made this way are not perfectly square. For a more precise finish, use a ravioli tray.

Making agnolotti

1 Using a sharp knife, cut the rolled strip of pasta dough by hand into two 45–50cm/18–20in lengths, if this has not been done already.

2 Using a teaspoon, put 8–10 little mounds of your chosen filling along one side of one of the pasta strips, spacing them evenly.

3 Using a pastry brush, carefully brush a little water on to the pasta strip around each mound of filling.

4 Fold the plain side of the pasta strip over the filling.

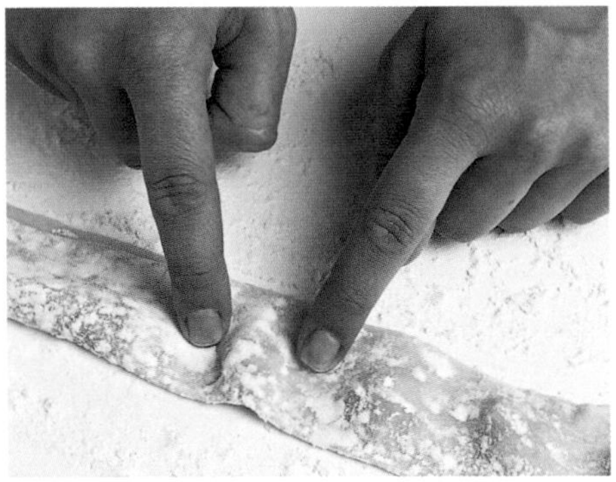

5 Starting from the folded edge of the pasta strip, press down gently, with your fingertips around each mound, to push out the air out at the unfolded edge. Sprinkle lightly with flour.

6 Using only half of a 5cm/2in fluted round ravioli or pastry (cookie) cutter, very carefully cut around each mound of filling to make a half-moon shape.

7 If you like, press the cut edges of the agnolotti with the tines of a fork to give a decorative effect.

8 Put the agnolotti on floured dish towels, sprinkle lightly with more flour and leave to dry while repeating the process with the remaining dough. For a 3-egg dough, you should get 64–80 agnolotti, more if you re-roll the trimmings.

Cook's tips

- When cutting out the agnolotti, make sure that the folded edge is the straight edge.
- Don't re-roll the trimmings after cutting each pasta strip, but wait until you have done them all. If there is no filling left for the rolled pasta trimmings, you can use them to make noodles or small shapes for soup.

Making tortellini/ tortelloni

1 Using a sharp knife, cut the strip of pasta dough into two 45–50cm/ 18–20in lengths.

2 To make tortellini: with a 5cm/2in fluted ravioli or pastry (cookie) cutter, cut out 8–10 discs from one pasta strip. For tortelloni, use a 6cm/2½in cutter.

3 Using a teaspoon and a fingertip, put a little mound of your chosen filling in the centre of each disc.

4 Holding each disc gently but firmly in place with two fingertips, brush a little water around the edge of each one, taking care to avoid the filling in the centre.

5 Very carefully fold each disc in half over the filling in the centre so that the top and bottom edges do not quite meet. Press gently with your fingertip to seal.

6 Wrap the half-moon shape around an index finger and pinch the ends together to seal.

7 Put the tortellini or tortelloni on floured dish towels, sprinkle with flour and leave to dry while repeating the process with the remaining dough. For a 3-egg dough, you should get 64–80 tortellini, more if you re-roll the trimmings.

Making pansotti and cappelletti/cappellacci

Pansotti are made from 5cm/2in squares of pasta that are folded in half over the filling to form little triangles. Moisten the edges of the triangles with a brush and press gently with your fingertips to seal in the filling.

Cappelletti and cappellacci are made in the same way as tortellini, using squares of pasta rather than discs. The edges are turned up so they look like little hats.

MAKING FLAVOURED AND COLOURED PASTA

There are many different ingredients you can use to change the flavour and colour of pasta, by hand or machine, although you will get a more even colour with a machine. The following flavourings are the most successful, and the amounts of ingredients given are for a 3-egg quantity of pasta all'uovo (pasta dough with eggs). With porcini, tomato, spinach and squid ink, the dough will be stickier than usual, so add more flour during kneading, rolling and cutting.

ABOVE: *Porcini*

ABOVE: *Tomato*

ABOVE: *Spinach*

ABOVE: *Squid ink*

ABOVE: *Herb*

ABOVE: *Saffron*

Black pepper

Put 30ml/2 tbsp black peppercorns or mixed peppercorns in a mortar and crush them coarsely with a pestle. Add to the eggs in the well before you start to incorporate the flour.

ABOVE: *Black pepper*

ABOVE: *Chilli*

Chilli

Add 5–10ml/1–2 tsp crushed dried red chillies to the eggs in the well before you add the flour.

Porcini

Soak 15g/½oz porcini (dried wild mushrooms) in 175ml/6fl oz/¾ cup warm water. Drain, squeeze to remove water, dry on kitchen paper, chop finely and add to the eggs in the well before adding the flour. Try adding the porcini soaking water to the water for boiling the pasta to intensify the flavour.

Tomato

Add 30ml/2 tbsp tomato purée (paste) to the eggs in the well before you add the flour.

Spinach

Wash 150g/5oz fresh spinach leaves and place in a large pan with only the water clinging to the leaves. Add a pinch of salt, cover and cook over a medium heat for 8 minutes or until the spinach is tender. Drain, leave for a few minutes to cool, squeeze hard to remove water, dry on kitchen paper, then finely chop. Add to the eggs in the well before you add the flour.

Squid ink

Add two 4g sachets of squid ink to the eggs in the well before you add the flour.

Herb

Wash and dry three small handfuls of fresh herbs, such as basil, flat leaf parsley, sage or thyme. Finely chop and add to the eggs in the well before adding the flour.

Saffron

Sift three or four sachets of saffron powder with the flour before starting to make the pasta dough.

MAKING STRIPED PASTA

You can use different colours to make striped dough that can be cut into rectangles for lasagne and cannelloni. It is quite fiddly, and the rolling out is best done with a pasta machine.

Plain or saffron yellow and spinach doughs look very good together, and another excellent combination is plain or saffron yellow dough contrasted with dough coloured with tomato or squid ink. To make pasta tricolore (three-coloured pasta), mix stripes of tomato dough, squid ink or spinach dough and plain dough. Some creative chefs make check and tartan patterns with coloured pasta, but this is very time-consuming for the home cook.

1 Roll out two different coloured pieces of dough on a pasta machine, keeping them separate and taking them up to and including the last setting but two.

2 With a fluted pasta wheel, cut one strip of each colour lengthways into three or four narrower strips. Then select three strips of one colour and two of the other, setting the rest aside for the next batch of striped pasta.

3 The aim is to join the past strips together, using water as a glue. Brush one long edge of one pasta strip with a little water, then join a different coloured strip to it, placing it over the moistened edge, and pressing firmly to seal the join. Repeat this process, alternating the pasta colours, until you have a length of pasta resembling a scarf, with three stripes of one colour and two of the other.

4 Sprinkle the pasta liberally with flour, lift it very carefully and put it through the pasta machine, which should be on the last but one setting.

5 Cut the dough into rectangles or squares for cannelloni or lasagne and spread these out in a single layer on floured dish towels. Sprinkle them with flour and leave to dry for at least 15 minutes before cooking.

Cook's tips

- When cutting flavoured tagliatelle or tagliarini on a pasta machine, sprinkle the cutters liberally with flour before putting the dough through. The noodles tend to stick together as they come through the machine, so you may need to separate them gently with floured hands before putting them on dish towels and tossing them in more flour.
- When cooking flavoured pasta, start testing it earlier than usual. The ingredients added for some flavours make the pasta more moist and soft than usual, and this means that it cooks a little more quickly.
- You can use striped pasta for making ravioli: keep the strips fairly narrow and make sure that they are well sealed, otherwise the ravioli may split open during cooking.

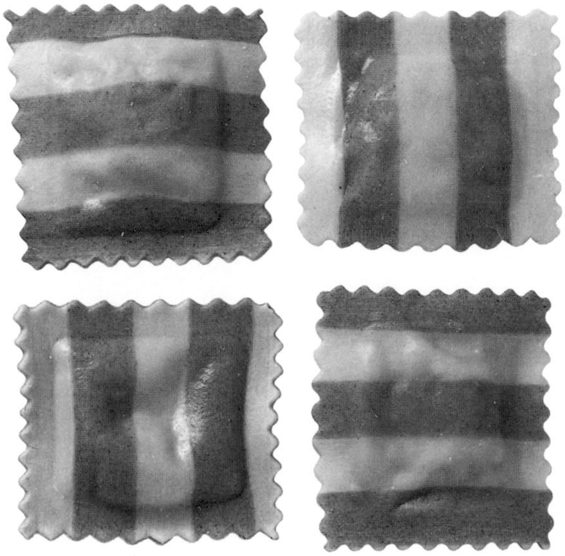

The pasta pantry

Certain ingredients crop up time and time again in sauces for pasta. Some can be kept in the pantry or store cupboard, while fresh ones must either be bought just before use, or kept in the refrigerator.

FRESH HERBS AND LEAVES

Basil/Basilico

Basil is used in large quantities for pesto, with tomatoes and in tomato sauces. Tear, shred and add at the last moment. Fine chopping and long cooking spoil the flavour.

Bay/Alloro/lauro

Both fresh and dried bay leaves are used all over Italy for flavouring soups, broths and long-cooking sauces, especially those made with meat, poultry and game. Remove the leaves before serving.

RIGHT: *Basil*

RIGHT: *Bay*

LEFT: *Marjoram*

RIGHT: *Oregano*

Marjoram and Oregano/ Maggiorana e Origano

Marjoram is sweet and delicate, while oregano, a wild variety of marjoram, is pungent and should be used sparingly. Both are used in sauces for pasta and oregano is sprinkled over pizza. Chop both finely.

Mint/Mentuccia

Although not usually associated with Italian cooking, mint is often used in Roman dishes, in central Italy and as far south as Calabria. Mentuccia is a particular kind of wild mint with small leaves grown in Rome; nepitella is another. Fresh mint is used in pasta soups and, very occasionally, in pasta sauces.

Parsley/Prezzemolo

Flat leaf (continental or Italian) parsley looks similar to coriander (cilantro) and has a stronger flavour than curly parsley. It is used frequently in pasta sauces, often roughly chopped and fried in olive oil with onion and garlic at the start of sauce-making.

Radicchio/Radicchio

A member of the chicory family, radicchio di Verona is small and round with very tightly furled leaves. Radicchio di Treviso is streaked creamy white and red, with long, loose tapering leaves. Both have a bitter flavour, best used in small quantities in pasta sauces. Add shredded leaves at the last moment to preserve their colour.

Rocket (Arugula)/Rucola

Add peppery hot rucola to pasta sauces at the last minute or strew it liberally over pasta dishes just before serving. Bunches of large-leaved rucola from the greengrocer are best; the small packets sold in supermarkets are expensive and lack flavour. Use as soon as possible after purchase, especially in warm weather.

RIGHT: *Flat leaf parsley*

RIGHT: *Rosemary*

Rosemary/Rosmarino
Use this fragrant and pungent herb sparingly in meat and tomato sauces, either very finely chopped or on the sprig, which is removed before serving.

Sage/Salvia
Roman cooks sizzle fresh sage in butter to create a classic sauce for ravioli. Fresh sage leaves are also used with meat, sausage, poultry and game sauces, either finely shredded or chopped or as whole leaves, which are removed before serving. Fresh sage is preferred to dried sage, which is occasionally used in winter sauces that are cooked for a long time.

Thyme/Timo
This aromatic and distinctively flavoured Mediterranean herb is used both fresh and dried. It goes well with tomato-based sauces and with meat and poultry, and mixes well with rosemary and bay.

SPICES AND SALT

Chilli/Peperoncino
Small red chillies are frequently used in pasta sauces, most famously the hot and spicy Penne all'Arrabbiata from Rome, which depends on chilli for its flavour. Usually, however, chillies are added more sparingly. Crushed dried red chillies or chilli flakes are very handy when a recipe requires just a pinch or two.

Cinnamon/Cannella
Ground cinnamon is used in stuffings for pasta, both with meat and cheese. It gives a fragrant aroma and subtle sweetness, and is always used sparingly.

Nutmeg/Noce moscata
Whole nutmeg is grated fresh when needed. It is used for flavouring béchamel sauce (la beschiamella) and often in combination with spinach and ricotta cheese. In Emilia-Romagna, it is used for flavouring meat sauces and stuffings for pasta.

Pepper/Pepe
Freshly grind black peppercorns in a pepper mill as and when needed, in cooking and at the table. If coarsely crushed peppercorns are required, use a mortar and pestle.

RIGHT: *Fresh chillies*

ABOVE: *Saffron*

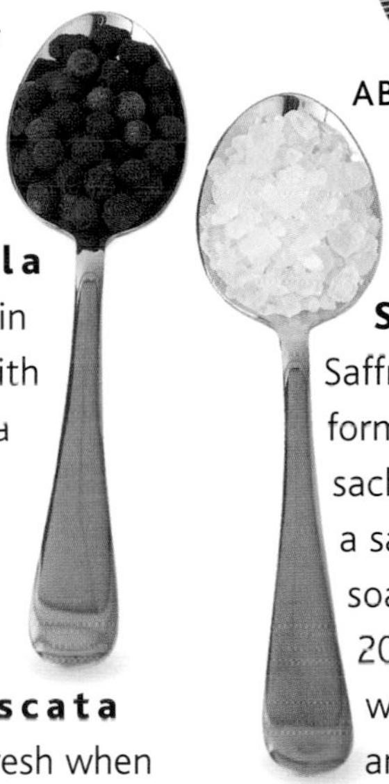

LEFT: *Peppercorns and sea salt*

Saffron/Zafferano
Saffron comes in two different forms. Saffron threads are sold in sachets and can be sprinkled into a sauce. More often, they are soaked in warm water for 20–30 minutes, the strained water then used for colouring and flavouring. More convenient, less expensive (and some say inferior), saffron powder is sold in sachets and can be sprinkled directly into sauces.

Salt/Sale
Coarse sea salt and rock salt are ground in a salt mill and used both as a seasoning in cooking and at the table. It is essential that salt is added to the water when boiling pasta to give it flavour, but for this you can use refined cooking salt rather than the more expensive sea or rock salt. Just about every pasta sauce will have salt as a seasoning, except perhaps those containing salty anchovies or bottarga (air-dried mullet or tuna roe).

OILS AND VINEGARS

Olive oil/Olio d'oliva

Extra virgin olive oil is the best and most expensive olive oil. Use it for salads, for sprinkling over warm food or for tossing with pasta in dishes.

Tuscan oil is reputedly among the best of the extra virgin olive oils, although some cooks prefer more delicate oils from Umbria, Veneto or Liguria. Oils from the South are stronger and more intensely flavoured.

For cooking and heating, use the less expensive virgin olive oil. With pasta sauces, base ingredients – onion, garlic, celery, etc – fried in oil with a good flavour will have a strong base flavour (soffritto) that permeates the other ingredients during the cooking.

LEFT: *Virgin olive oil (left), extra virgin olive oil (centre) and balsamic vinegar (right)*

Vinegar/Aceto

Although occasionally added to a pasta sauce, wine vinegar is usually used in salad dressings. Flavour wise, red and white vinegars are interchangeable, though the colour of the salad ingredients may dictate which you use.

Dark and syrupy, balsamic vinegar (aceto balsamico) from Modena in Emilia-Romagna is aged in wooden casks for many years – the best varieties for 40–50 years. Labelled tradizionale di Modena, it is only used a drop at a time, usually at the moment of serving on fish, meat, salads and even strawberries. For flavouring a pasta sauce or salad, use the cheaper balsamic vinegar, which has been aged for 5–10 years.

FLAVOURINGS

Capers/Capperi

Capers add piquancy to sauces and are sold in various ways. The best are the large, salted variety sold in small jars in Italian delicatessens. Check before you buy that the salt is white and has not discoloured at all. Yellow salt means that they are well past their best. Before use, soak salted capers in several changes of water for 10–15 minutes, drain, rinse in fresh water and dry.

ABOVE: *Salted capers*

ABOVE: *Capers bottled in brine*

Tiny, strong-flavoured capers are also available in small bottles of brine or vinegar. Rinse well before use, chop very finely and use sparingly.

Olives/Olive

Both black and green olives are used in making sauces and salads, although black olives are preferred. The best type

BELOW: *Olives*

for pasta sauces are the small, shiny, very black gaeta olives from Liguria. Use plain olives only for cooking and flavoured olives for antipasto.

Pancetta

Pancetta is the cured belly of pork and has a spicy, sweet flavour and aroma. Unsmoked pancetta – pancetta arrotolata or pancetta coppata – is sold in a roll at Italian delicatessens. Pancetta affumicata is smoked and comes in rashers. Pancetta stesa is long and flat. Smoked pancetta, cut into strips or diced, is the base for ragù and many other pasta sauces, most famously carbonara.

Pine nuts/Pinoli

Best known for their inclusion in pesto, these small, creamy white nuts have an unusual waxy texture and resinous flavour. They also add a welcome crunchy bite to salads.

ABOVE: *Pancetta*

BELOW: *Pine nuts*

ABOVE: *Anchovies in brine (left) and salt*

BELOW: *Bottarga*

FISH AND SHELLFISH

Anchovies/Acciughe

The best anchovies are the salted ones packed in large cans, available from Italian delicatessens, which must be rinsed, skinned and filleted before use. If you can't get salted anchovies, try anchovy fillets bottled in olive oil rather than those canned in vegetable oil.

Bottarga

This is the salted and air-dried roe of mullet or tuna. The best is the mullet, bottarga di muggine, a great delicacy in Sardinia, Sicily and the Veneto, where it is grated over pasta or very thinly sliced as an antipasto with lemon juice and olive oil. It is available in delicatessens. Tuna bottarga, which comes in a thick, dark block, is grated over pasta in small quantities and keeps well in the refrigerator. Texture and flavour wise, ready-grated bottarga in small jars really does not compare.

RIGHT: *Fresh clams (left) and canned clams*

Clams/Vongole

Small vongole cook quickly and have a tender texture and sweet flavour, which make them ideal for pasta sauces. Don't buy the large ones. Frozen or bottled shell clams in natural juices – not vinegar – are good substitutes.

Squid ink/Nero di seppia

Handy 4g sachets of squid ink are available from fishmongers and Italian delicatessens. Two sachets are enough to colour a 3-egg quantity of pasta all'uovo.

Tuna/Tonno

For pasta sauces, use only best-quality canned tuna in olive oil, not vegetable oil, water or brine.

LEFT: *Dried chargrilled aubergines (eggplant)*

VEGETABLES

Aubergines (eggplants)/ Melanzane

Fresh aubergines are a main ingredient in many pasta sauces. Dried aubergines are not used as a substitute for fresh, but are added to fresh vegetables for their earthy flavour and meaty texture.

Garlic/Aglio

Garlic is used in many pasta sauces. The best Italian garlic is pink or purple tinged, with plump juicy cloves. Buy garlic little and often so that it neither sprouts green shoots nor becomes papery and dry.

BELOW: *Garlic*

BELOW: *Dried porcini mushrooms*

Porcini mushrooms/ Funghi porcini

Dried porcini (boletus edulis) are invaluable for their intense, musky aroma and flavour. Italians use them all year round. Don't buy cheap porcini, but look for packets containing large, pale-coloured pieces.

Peppers/Peperoni

Sun-dried red (bell) peppers add a piquant flavour and a meaty bite to sauces. Roasted peppers can be bought loose or in jars, in oil or brine.

Tomatoes/Pomodori

In summer, fresh Italian plum tomatoes are wonderful for sauce making, but there are other excellent tomato products to use at other times. Canned peeled plum tomatoes (pomodori pelati) come whole and chopped. Only use top-quality Italian brands, especially those with San Marzano on the label.

Plain chopped tomatoes save time but are slightly more expensive. Those labelled polpa di pomodoro are more likely to be very finely chopped or even crushed. Filetti di pomodoro, the nearest thing to home-bottled tomatoes, are sold in jars at good Italian delicatessens.

ABOVE: *Bottled roasted pepppers*

ABOVE: *Chopped canned plum tomatoes*

Crushed tomatoes, in bottles and jars, range from the smooth passata (bottled strained tomatoes) to the chunky polpa and sugocasa.

Sun-dried tomatoes (pomodori secchi) are sold as dry pieces and in oil. The dry pieces have a chewier texture, while those in oil have the best flavour.

Sweet and mild, sun-dried tomato paste is a thick mixture of sun-dried tomatoes and olive oil. Use it on its own as a quick sauce for pasta or add it by the spoonful to tomato sauces.

Tomato purée (paste) or concentrate (concentrato di pomodoro) is a very strong, thick paste made commercially from tomatoes, salt and citric acid. You can buy it in tubes, jars or cans. Only use it in small quantities or it may make a dish too acidic.

CHEESE AND CREAM

Fontina

A nutty, sweet mountain cheese from the Val d'Aosta in the north-west of Italy, fontina is used in baked pasta dishes, such as lasagne.

Gorgonzola

This blue-veined table cheese from Lombardy is also good in sauces and stuffed pasta. Gorgonzola piccante is the very strong version, while dolcelatte is milder and sweeter.

Mascarpone

This smooth, tangy, full-fat cream cheese is often used in pasta sauces instead of cream.

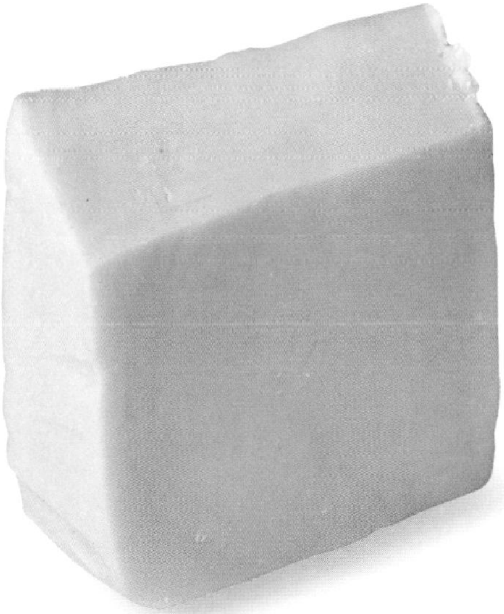

ABOVE: *Fontina*

ABOVE: *Gorgonzola*

ABOVE: *Mozzarella*

Mozzarella

This soft white cheese is used in both salads and pasta sauces. It melts quickly in hot sauces to serve with pasta but must not be overcooked or it may become stringly. Buy only the type that is swimming in whey in little bags. The whey should be drained off and discarded before the cheese is used. Mozzarella di bufala has the best texture and flavour.

Parmesan

Grated Parmesan is commonly used for sprinkling over pasta at the table. It is also tossed with pasta after draining or added to sauces at the end of cooking. Genuine Parmigiano Reggiano has its name stamped on the rind and must be aged for a minimum of two years. A cheaper option is Grana Padano. Never buy either ready grated.

Pecorino

This salty, hard sheep's milk cheese is called Pecorino Romano if it comes from Lazio, and Pecorino Sardo if it is Sardinian. Like Parmesan, it is used for grating into strong, spicy southern Italian and Sardinian sauces.

Ricotta

This soft white cheese is used in fillings for stuffed and baked pasta dishes and for tossing with fresh raw vegetables for uncooked sauces. Low in fat and bland, it goes well with herbs and garlic. Fresh ricotta does not keep well, so only buy it if it is snowy white in colour. Ricotta salata, a hard, salted version of ricotta cut from the block, is used for grating or crumbling over soups and pasta.

Cream/Panna da cucina

For creamy pasta sauces, Italians use a type of cream called panna da cucina (cream for cooking), which comes in tubs of 100ml/$3\frac{1}{2}$fl oz/ scant $\frac{1}{2}$ cup, which is enough to make a pasta sauce to serve four people. Panna da cucina is a good long-life product for the store cupboard. It is available in Italian markets.

ABOVE: *Pecorino (left) and Parmigiano Reggiano*

Index